920

As I Remember

As I Remember

by

Edgar J. Goodspeed

HARPER & BROTHERS, PUBLISHERS, NEW YORK

To the Memory of

ELFLEDA

the heroine of the story

CONTENTS

As I Remember

ONE

I Fall in Love with My Parents

ON THE night Alexander the Great was born, the temple of Artemis in Ephesus was burned to the ground, and in the very month of my birth, the city of Chicago was reduced to ashes. I am sure the reader will not draw any hasty inferences from this fact, struck though he must be by the coincidence. I certainly have never ventured to do so.

The value of this historical allusion here is simply that it will break to the reader the news, if it may be called news, that I was born in October, 1871, the month of the Great Fire.

But not in Chicago. In the (then) next largest city in Illinois, Quincy, on the Mississippi, which I like to regard as the literary axis of the continent. For just across the river was born the dean of American letters, Mark Twain.

In Quincy my father, Thomas Wakefield Goodspeed, was pastor of the Vermont Street Baptist Church. He was about thirty, and my mother about twenty-eight. I am well aware that I should here, following the current fashion in autobiography, introduce a moving chapter entitled "I Accuse My Parents," telling how mean and selfish they were, and how abused and thwarted and frustrated I was as a child. But that would be sheer fiction. On the contrary, they were without doubt the most generous, patient, understanding, long-suffering and altogether amiable young couple you can imagine. All their relatives thought so too, and turned to them for help in every emergency. The family burdens were generally thrust upon their willing shoulders from youth to old age. I should like to dilate upon this, but my feelings would overcome me. In short, my brother Charles and I fell in love with our parents, and as far as he was concerned, he never fell in love again. His mother remained the idol of his affections as long as she lived.

At the time of my arrival, Father was giving up his Quincy pastorate to go to the aid of his eldest brother Edgar, as his associate in the pastorate of the Second Baptist Church of Chicago. Uncle Edgar was hardly forty years old, but his health was breaking. My father was devoted to his brother and was only too glad to go to his relief. The Second Church was essentially a people's church, but it included some of the leading figures of the Chicago of that day. Foremost among them was E. Nelson Blake, afterward president of the Chicago Board of Trade. It is said that one day in later years when S. F. Smith, the author of "America," was noticed in the Visitors' Gallery of the Board, a member (I have no doubt it was Mr. Blake) went up to the gallery and brought him down onto the floor, and then led the assembled brokers in singing Dr. Smith's great hymn. Certainly that action was just like Mr. Blake. Mr. Blake's daughter Mabel became the wife of Herman H. Kohlsaat, one of the rising young men of the church and of the city; he became the publisher and editor of the *Times-Herald* and then of the *Record-Herald*, and a journalist of national renown. Their daughter married Potter Palmer, Jr. Sometimes at church socials my uncle and Mr. Blake would entertain the company by reciting scenes from Shakespeare, denouncing or applauding each other with right good will, as the poet directed. Years later, Mr. Blake said to me of those days,

"Your uncle was a prince of pastors!"

Mr. Blake's generous support enabled my father a few years later to get the Baptist Theological Seminary in Chicago on its feet financially, and later still he made the most important local gift to the fund for founding the University, becoming the first President of the Board of Trustees. Blake Hall at the University perpetuates his memory there.

Another great Chicagoan in the church was Deacon Samuel Hoard. He was a pillar in the spiritual life of the church, while in the city he was appointed Postmaster of Chicago by President Abraham Lincoln.

But I must not be betrayed into giving an account of all the leaders of that extraordinary church, which under my uncle's ministry had in ten years grown from a membership of three hundred to thirteen hundred, and to a foremost place in the denomination. Let me only speak of Aunt Lizzie Aiken, the church missionary. She was a woman of extraordinary spiritual gifts; one might say her conversation was wholly religious, so real was her religious life. At a first meeting her way of talking might seem something put on; it seemed so to my uncle the first time he met her. But he came to know her better. She had been an army nurse in the Civil War, and she made a great contribution to the work of the church in the growing city. Mrs. Galusha Anderson afterward wrote her biography.

Forty-nine Aberdeen Street was the first home that I remember. It was a pleasant enough shady street, as I remember it, and the house was a medium-sized wooden one, adjoining the garden and small orchard of Mr. Coan. I think he must have been the partner of my uncle Charles Ten Broeke, in what had been until the Great Fire the most prosperous carriage manufacturing business in the city, and probably in the west. Certainly they made very fine carriages. But the Fire had burned them out; my father, a very vigorous, athletic young man, had worked hard with many others the night of the Fire dragging the carriages out of the factory, in a vain effort to save them.

Across the street was Mr. Schuettler's barn, a sizable brick structure, which gave Charles and me much pleasure when, at the first approach of winter, the Schuettlers' sleighs and cutters were carefully lowered from the second floor door to the ground, in readiness for the sleighing season. An old book on early Chicago—John Drury's *Old Chicago Houses*— recently informed me that Mr. Schuettler's place occupied a whole block, and his grounds, lawns, gardens and so forth were the most extensive in the city. He was the great wagon manufacturer of the period, and in my boyhood one seldom saw wagons made by anyone else in northern Illinois. The whole district is now a desert, devoted to storage and factories.

Mr. Frederick T. Haskell used to tell a story of early Chicago relating to a conversation between Mr. Clem Studebaker and my uncle. Mr. Haskell said that Mr. Studebaker had heard that Uncle Charles had said that Mr. Studebaker could not make a wagon that was worth a darn, and Mr. Studebaker taxed him with having made this objectionable remark; Mr. Studebaker was becoming the leading wagon manufacturer of his time, having succeeded to Mr. Schuettler's position in that industry. Mr. Haskell described my uncle as a very handsome and well-dressed man, as indeed he was, and as quite outshining Mr. Studebaker in these respects. My uncle laughed heartily, but stoutly denied having made the remark.

"What I said was," he explained, "that you couldn't make a carriage that was worth a darn."

As my uncle knew all about carriage-making, this restored peace. Edward Ely, famous Chicago tailor of the nineteenth century, once told me that Uncle Charles was his first customer when he opened his shop in Chicago in 1853.

My mother had brought me to Chicago as soon after my arrival as seemed possible, so that I never really saw my birthplace, Quincy, Illinois, until half a century later. But my father and mother always retained happy memories of their five years there, and some very pleasant people who had become friends of theirs in Quincy called upon us now and then through the years that followed.

My father and mother had met in Chicago when he was the minister of the North Baptist Church, in 1866, and she was the organist. She was studying in Dearborn Seminary (where its founder, Zwinglius Grover, was still active) and staying first with her sister Libbie (Mrs. James Duffy), and then with her brother Charles Ten Broeke and his wife. My uncle had left his rural home, near Vergennes, Vermont, at an early age, to seek his fortune in the west, and was doing remarkably well, and he and Libbie thought a lively and gifted girl like my mother ought to see the world. She naturally went to the nearest Baptist church, and her musical gifts raised her at once to the position of organist.

Uncle Edgar had greatly influenced Father in many ways. Father followed him to the University of Rochester for his later studies; he had already graduated at the University of Chicago, in 1862, but he took a second college degree at

Rochester, in 1863, and went through the Seminary there, graduating in 1866.

It was in my childhood that Chicago was still raising its level in the down-town district, or the Loop as we now call it, a matter of seven feet, so that as we walked along, suddenly we would descend twelve or fifteen wooden steps and walk a few yards along that lowel level, then go up as many wooden steps to a frontage that had already been raised. I do not know how long this state of things lasted, but I learned to walk in Chicago, and so I must have experienced it in the middle seventies. George M. Pullman began his career as an engineer in this period, raising old buildings to the required new level. I also remember well going to Field and Leiter's store with my mother when I was hardly tall enough to see what lay on the counter. Another vivid childhood memory is being taken to the doctor in a baby carriage I had outgrown. But I had had an attack of infantile paralysis as we then called it, and had to be wheeled to the doctor for some kind of electrical treatments which proved wholly successful. A somewhat twisted smile was the only marked trace of the ailment that stayed with me. I have met other men of my own age who had the same disease about that time in Chicago; there must have been quite an epidemic of it, probably in a rather mild form.

Of my ancestors I learned gradually, as children do. While Mrs. Goodspeed had no difficulty in tracing her ancestry on her father's side back to Francis Eaton and the heroic *Mayflower* company who came to Plymouth in 1620, the more cautious Goodspeeds did not impinge upon these shores until 1639. In that year Roger Goodspeed took up his abode at Barnstable on Cape Cod. My distant cousin Charles E. Goodspeed, the famous Boston bookseller, has found that

Roger came of yeoman stock, and was from Oxfordshire. I find it very touching that his old father, in his will, left the sum of ten shillings (I believe it was) to Roger, in case he ever came back to England from the New World. He did not want his son to return penniless and not have a shilling he could call his own. Of course, a shilling then was more valuable than it is today, or has been in our memory. But Roger did not return.

My grandfather Stephen Goodspeed was born in 1810, in Caldwell, New York, near the head of Lake George. While Stephen was still a child, about 1815, his father Jason set out alone for the Holland Purchase, three hundred miles away, in the western part of the state, and was never heard of again. It was a perilous journey for a man traveling alone, for the country was for the most part wild and unsettled. His disappearance left the children wholly dependent upon their mother, but she did not long survive her husband, dying in the same year. Her maiden name was Isabella Millard. Her father, Stephen Millard, had come into the wilds of northern New York from Rhode Island, and was a public-spirited miller, in the town of Queensbury, a few miles west of Glens Falls. This Millard connection suggests that the Goodspeeds may be related to that Millard Fillmore, the thirteenth President of the United States, whose people came from New England into New York, and whose parents had settled about 1800 in the Oswego valley at Locke. His mother's maiden name was Phoebe Millard, and it seems not unlikely that Phoebe and Isabella Millard were related and that Jason Goodspeed was moved by the establishment of the Fillmores in western New York to seek his fortune there near them.

Grandfather Goodspeed's older brother James was brought

up by his Goodspeed grandparents, but Grandfather found a home with his mother's people, the Millards, and they brought him up. I do not know that the brothers ever met again, though both lived to be very old, Grandfather could remember seeing the soldiers returning from the War of 1812, for they wickedly stole his grandmother's geese from the yard before his eyes.

Grandfather married a girl named Jane Johnson, who was a member of the Baptist church, and who brought up her five sons so religiously that two of them became ministers. They regarded her with the utmost reverence and affection, as a being from another world. Another son died in youth, and the other two became publishers, one in New York and one in Chicago. Uncle Edgar thus found himself fully equipped with publishers by nature, if we may say so. In fact I think it was these energetic uncles who urged him into publishing his books on the Great Fire and the life of Christ. It gave me great satisfaction seventy years later on looking for my author's card in the New York Public Library to find that I had none. My books were listed on my uncle's card! Somehow this made me strangely happy. I would not have it otherwise. I felt that I had carried on.

Grandfather Goodspeed was not at all an educated man. He was a blacksmith and a foundryman, but he helped his sons who wanted to go to college, as the eldest and the youngest did.

My grandfather James Ten Broeke, on the other hand, was a London boy destined by his father for the British Navy. His people had come over some generations earlier from Holland to establish the family business in London. As far as I can learn they were tea merchants; his father James

Ten Broeke, head of the family, belonged to the Royal Exchange, as his daughter's tombstone in Panton, Vermont, records. In a panic incident to the Napoleonic Wars he is said to have lost ten thousand pounds, practically overnight. This has always been an impressive family legend. One member of the family, Uncle Anthony, went into the army, and lost his life in the Indian Mutiny of 1857. My grandfather was born in 1800, but was thought old enough to be a midshipman in the navy about 1814, when he found himself in Quebec concerned with the exchange of prisoners. My mother's eldest sister remembered that Grandfather Ten Broeke in his midshipman days had been rowed about by a crew of—I believe it was eight—tars. This impressed her, as it did me, as being considerable state, especially for a boy of fourteen.

My grandfather was a sensitive boy, and the British Navy in his day was notoriously a hell upon earth. Perhaps he was none too good a sailor, too. At any rate, he left his ship, honorably I am sure, and decided, I must suppose, never to cross the sea again. Friends he made in Montreal generously offered to adopt him, and to send him to college, but he preferred to find his own way in the world. He was well educated for his years, being especially proficient in penmanship and spelling. At any rate, he soon made his way down into New England, became interested in religion, joined the Baptist church, and became a preacher of the gospel. In Panton, Vermont, where he was teaching school, he fell in love with Mollie Tappan, the Squire's daughter, and they were married. He built a farmhouse of the native stone, and later kept a boarding school in it. I have met men who had studied with him, and remembered him well. I once asked my mother what kind of a looking man he was, and she laughed and said, "Go look in the looking glass!" But how much she meant by this I do not know.

The old house with a splendid view of Lake Champlain and the Adirondacks beyond is now occupied by his great-grandson, William Kent, a member of the Senate of the State of Vermont, while Mrs. Kent is a member of its House of Representatives. My grandfather's faith in his adopted country was such that he afterward persuaded two of his sisters to follow him to Vermont, where they spent the rest of their days. A memorial window commemorates him in the little village church of which he was the pastor and in which some twelve years after his death my mother was married. It has always interested me that she was a seventh child.

My grandfather certainly built himself into the new American society with which he cast his lot, for he worked diligently through his short life as farmer, preacher and teacher in rural Vermont. I still have among my books Grandfather's copy of *The Complete Works of Andrew Fuller,* famous English Baptist preacher of the turn of the century, upon whom Yale and Princeton both conferred the Doctor of Divinity. The works had just been published in Boston, in 1833, and my grandfather autographed his copies as of January 1, 1834. A copy of *Matthew Henry's Commentaries,* written a century earlier, and a stand-by of the older preachers, was also in my grandfather's library, but has not come down to me. He was, however, a preacher of scholarly tastes and interests, and his eldest daughter remembered that when in 1848 Layard's first success in excavating the Assyrian mounds was reported in *Nineveh and Its Remains,* he was greatly interested and forecast a great future for such researches.

We left Chicago for the suburb of Morgan Park in 1876, when I was five, as Father had taken a position with the Baptist Union Theological Seminary, which had been moved there. He hoped to raise its debt in a single year! He was led to do this in part by his devotion to Dr. George W. Northrup, the President of the Seminary, under whom he had studied at Rochester Seminary a dozen years before, and these two men worked together most harmoniously and effectively for many years after. It was Dr. Northrup who used to say to his young men, "Hold your plan of life loosely!"

i.e. allow for changes god may bring. Be flexible in the faith.

TWO

A Suburb in the Eighties

OUR house in Morgan Park was a large new wooden house, of two stories, with a big attic. There was a small barn for the cow, and a chicken house, where for some years we raised our own chickens. We had a croquet lawn, on which I spent a great deal of time, a flower garden, and a perfectly fabulous vegetable garden, besides abundant cherries, currants and raspberries. This garden was kept up chiefly by my vigorous old grandfather who made his home with us for the last thirty years of his long life and seemed to enjoy the active role of a small farmer. A ten-acre lot between the barn and Western Avenue was rented and enclosed for a cow pasture.

There were no houses anywhere near us; we seemed to have the prairie all around us. This may have been hard for the old folks of the household, but for us boys it seemed to make the world our playground. In the spring the hayfields were full of wild flowers, and in them the meadow larks and even an occasional prairie chicken nested. We roamed the fields summer and winter with the keenest enjoyment.

Our household included my father's parents, and my mother's mother and eldest sister Jane, twenty years my mother's senior. All four of these old people ended their

days under my father's roof. Somehow they were happier
and more welcome with Thomas and Ellen than their other
children were able to make them. But our house was just as
attractive to the younger relatives of my generation, and it
was often full of my cousins, mostly girls, from both sides
of the family. My uncle and aunt soon came to occupy the
nearest house, which might be described as a block west of
us, and another uncle later came to the growing little village.
But he had no children to contribute to our juvenile society.
My grandmothers, both confined to their rooms and mostly
to their beds, were wonderful old ladies, and greatly beloved
by their children and grandchildren.

Seventy years ago Morgan Park was to the naked eye an
ambitious real estate venture that had not clicked. On the
"hill" or island of high land that can still be distinguished
running from Blue Island several miles north, gracefully
curving drives with romantic names—Rinaldo, Genevra, and
others drawn from the poet Tasso, I believe—had been cleverly laid out and planted with rows of elms and maples, to
give shade to generations to come. But there were no sidewalks, pavements, street lamps, sewers, or gas or water pipes.

The sparse population consisted of a few genuine farmers,
of a very superior kind, and a number of down-town busi-
nessmen who took the 8:04 on the Rock Island every morning
down to business. The leading institutions of the village, as
it presently came to be, were the Chicago Female College,
headed by Dr. Gilbert Thayer, the Morgan Park Military
Academy, headed by Captain E. N. K. Talcott, and the Baptist Union Theological Seminary, under Dr. Northrup, with
such professors as Dr. Eri B. Hulbert, General T. J. Morgan,
of Civil War fame, and a young man of twenty-two named
William R. Harper who came to Morgan Park in 1879 as

instructor in Hebrew. In Henry Justin Smith, Harry Atwood, Harry W. Thayer, and Judge William M. Northrup, my brother Charles and I found lifelong friends.

Life in general and Christmas in particular centered around the church, a fine wooden Gothic building with a comfortable mortgage. On Sundays it was filled with neighbors, the farmers of whatever denomination turning out to hear my father one Sunday and a young theological student from Evanston named Frank Bristol the next. Mr. Bristol married a very attractive Morgan Park girl named Nellie Frisbie in 1878; he became a bishop, though not immediately. The whole line of pews along the east side was filled every Sunday with the girls from the Ladies' College, or fem sem, as we familiarly called it, while the west side pews were filled with the military boys, known to us village boys as the milmils. Both schools marched to church in procession; I don't mean together. My mother played the little organ and trained the quartette, which used to practice Saturday evenings at our house.

Christmas was a great occasion in the community, centering in an evening affair at the church, under the auspices of the Sunday School. There was a huge tree loaded with popcorn, red berries and lighted candles (there were no fire ordinances out there to cramp our style), and candy and oranges for all of us children, for which we walked up to the platform in turn. Captain Talcott, who had a strong baritone voice and led the singing in Sunday School, was usually master of ceremonies. I remember once he called my mother before the Christmas throng and presented her with a gold watch, then a great rarity, on behalf of the community, in recognition of her musical services, a remarkable civic gesture for those days.

At home it was always Christmas trees too, and Christmas dinners with turkey and mince pie. But we boys used to get our presents when we woke up Christmas morning, so that we had the benefit of them all Christmas Day. Ice skates were favorite gifts with us, for the prairies would thaw and then freeze again, so that you could skate on and on for miles over the thinly flooded fields, a winter paradise for boyhood. Then there was the Morgan Avenue hill down which we coasted. It was a gay scene of a winter afternoon, when the coasting was good, and a lively center of village youths and maidens. There were no motors to make us afraid, for even telephones and electric lights were still unknown to us. All we had to look out for was the afternoon trains on the Rock Island, which crossed our slide at its further end. In fact, we generally aimed for, or at least hoped to reach, the "tracks." Snow at least as I remember it was always abundant, and it had plenty of chance, for our houses were mostly a few hundred yards apart, with wide snow fields (in summer hay fields) between.

Among my personal treasures were a scroll saw and a very small printing press, for rainy days, as well as a miniature steam engine, a tiny steamboat, and a magic lantern. And when the roadside ditches were full of water, Will Northrup and we would dam one up, and set up a miniature water wheel of our own make which gave us great satisfaction.

Of course, we never dreamed of driving down town in those days. The only people who did were the farmers who raised principally hay, and their big hay wagons could often be seen moving slowly north on Western Avenue toward the city, the southern limits of which were then some eight miles away.

Winters were cold, with only coal or wood stoves, and later

furnaces, to warm us. But our days really had all the interest of country life, for a small boy. Many years later, golfing over some of that same prairie, I picked up a feather that carried me back to those boyhood days, and I thought:

> Tramping the fields in the summer weather,
> Finding a yellow-gray meadow-lark's feather
> Made me a boy again,
> Tramping the fields in the summer weather,
> Finding a yellow-gray meadow-lark's feather,
> Not forty years old, but ten.

The other center of village life beside the church was the store and post office, a two-story wooden building on Morgan Avenue, under the hill, and opposite the suburban station of the Rock Island railway. The village store provided our groceries and a limited supply of meat. My grandfather obligingly went down to it every morning, and also got the mail, and usually the morning *Tribune*. But as we kept a cow, and had a garden, and kept chickens, we were not wholly dependent upon Mr. Washburn, or later Mr. Husted, the genial storekeepers.

Over the store was a large hall, where occasional church or village socials known as strawberry festivals, oyster suppers, and the like were held. Occasionally political meetings were held in the hall. At one of these my father spoke so effectively for the candidates that the Republican local committee asked him to speak for it during the campaign at one hundred dollars a night. As this was equivalent to five hundred dollars in our modern currency, it must have tempted him but he declined. He was and remained all his life a winning and acceptable speaker. When he was eighty he ordered a new Tuxedo from his tailor because the University was having him speak at so many alumni dinners.

My grandfather was as vigorous as my grandmothers were enfeebled, and taught us boys to use the ax and saw and hammer, as well as how to whittle correctly. I must confess, however, with some confusion, that we never learned from him the care of the cow, or sought to invade that part of his province. Something seemed to warn us that those were accomplishments we could not afford. But we did a little gardening, picked berries, mowed the lawn and looked after the furnace, when we acquired one, or the kerosene lamps which were our only illuminants.

Grandfather was not a reader; I do not know that he ever read a book, except the Bible. He was full of stories, however, of his boyhood and young manhood as a blacksmith and amateur strong man at county fairs and the like. He had been a great wrestler in his younger days, amateur, of course, and was very fond of what he called "wrastling." In my bookishness, I always regarded this as a solecism in Grandfather's diction, but long after his death I acquired a first printing of King James, and observed that while Jacob "wrestled" with the angel, Rachel "wrastled" with her sister Leah, with mighty "wrastlings." I thus came to see that Grandfather's English was just as good as mine, but I was in the line controlled by Samuel Johnson and his famous dictionary of 1755, which told Englishmen what was right and what was wrong. He had preferred "wrestling," but the other form, which was just as literate, had come down by oral transmission to my grandfather's less bookish circle. I really felt as though I owed him an apology for the injustice I had tacitly done his culture.

Aunt Jane not only helped my mother about the house in all sorts of ways, but began the education of my brother and myself. She had been a teacher in her father's farmhouse school in Panton, Vermont, where he took both boarding and day pupils, and she put before us his own beautifully written copies affirming that Honesty was the Best Policy, and so on. So our education began at home. Evenings in the back parlor my father generally read aloud to us; I remember while I was still playing on the floor hearing his fine voice delivering the siege of Londonderry, in Macaulay's *History of England*. My aunt's praiseworthy efforts to make us children what we now call Spencerian penmen were less successful than her drills in spelling, a field in which we did rather better, even though there were no crossword puzzles to develop our vocabularies. As for those dear old grandmothers of ours, one a shut-in upstairs, the other a shut-in downstairs, they made it their business, especially on Sunday afternoons, to make us boys and girls learn by heart all the Psalms they could, and when I still recite them to myself in the night watches, I remember their efforts with gratitude.

As we grew older we got to singing together about the piano evenings, with Mother playing, and leading, and sometimes at our urging singing us old songs of other days, like "Don't be Sorrowful, Darling," which I still think a very moving song. Mother had always been phenomenally proficient at the piano; in her girlhood, she had heard a band at Vergennes play a piece that was new to her, and when she got home to Panton, she electrified her family (she was the youngest) by sitting down at the piano and playing it through, supplying the harmony. This was one of the pieces we used to ask her for. "The Battle of Prague" was also a great piano piece in Mother's family, but she could play anything. She had been carefully taught from her childhood and had finally studied in the Dearborn Seminary with a piano teacher who could claim to have been a student of Liszt. That was supposed to be the highest of qualifications.

Many years after, when my mother died, her Morgan Park doctor recalled in the village papers an incident of those years which I cannot write without tears. The small children of one of the seminary students had come down with scarlet fever, a scourge much more dreaded then than now. Mother immediately sent us boys off to my aunt's house not far away and took the stricken family in until the childern had recovered. Nothing could have been more characteristic of my mother.

The bringing of the Seminary to Morgan Park produced a mild influx of new residents, even more than the establishment of the C.F.C. and the M.P.M.A. had done, and quickened the church life of the community. We all went to the one church which was now organized as a Baptist church. The voters soon organized a village with Father as president. A one-room public school was opened down below the hill, and Charles and I attended it. The population now became mildly stratified, the people on the hill being the more bookish, or professional, than those under it. The finest places were along the brow of the hill or out along Prospect Avenue under the hill.

At the school we met a variety of children, all very decent and civilized, however. I rashly mixed in a little roughhouse one day (I was seven years old), somewhat injuring a young colleague. But my amiable mother, on learning that I had "killed" a fellow student, promptly sought out my victim with cotton and candy, and all was well. Next morning our delightful teacher, Miss Libbie Myrick, felt it necessary to

inform the school that Percy Myrick (her brother) and Edgar
Goodspeed were "the rowdies of the school," a verdict which
was greeted with a roar of laughter by the whole room. Of
course, I regarded this as a verdict of not guilty. In fact, Miss
Myrick herself could hardly repress a smile. But she had done
her duty by an incident she felt she could not fairly overlook.
Such was my first academic degree.

On January 1, 1879, Dr. William R. Harper, a young man
of twenty-two, came from Denison University at Granville,
Ohio, to the Seminary in Morgan Park as instructor in
Hebrew, and this event was destined to have a profound
effect upon the lives of all of us. He was that kind of man.
He was, to begin with, a most genial, kindly and capable
young man. I remember so well walking up the street with
him one day in my childhood, on some chance encounter,
and his playful banter. He was laughing teasingly at my
stockinged legs—I was in knickerbockers—which seemed to
amuse him very much. He was very carefully dressed in a
cutaway coat, and carried a cane. I am not sure whether he
usually wore a tall hat then as he always did a few years later
in New Haven.

At a Denison alumni meeting many years ago, an old
neighbor of Dr. Harper's in his Granville days told this story.
The Doctor was barely twenty-one when President E. Benjamin Andrews made him principal of the Preparatory Department, and one hot morning that summer he had dragged
his study table outdoors under a tree on the lawn and was
hard at work. This greatly amused our friend who was passing
by, and he stopped to remonstrate with him.

"Why, Doctor," he protested, "don't you know it's too hot
to work today?"

To which the indefatigable young student replied,

"I consider my time worth a dollar an hour!"

Of course, this appeared mere nonsense to his sensible neighbor for in those days an able-bodied workman in Ohio was getting a dollar a day. Well, he made his time worth a dollar an hour, didn't he?

My cousin George Goodspeed came to Morgan Park soon after, in the spring of 1881, and entered the Seminary, where he and Dr. Harper became great friends; in fact, George was to the end of his life his most intimate friend. George had graduated from Brown in 1880, and had entered Rochester Theological Seminary, where his father and my father had been graduated in 1856 and 1866 respectively. But his father's death at Columbia, South Carolina, in the spring of 1881 brought him back to Chicago and to our house, and Father and Mother invited him to live with us while he continued his theological course. In return he was to tutor us boys two or three hours a day. He also introduced the strange game of lawn tennis among us. He was a wonderful student, having divided graduation honors at Brown with his great friend W. H. P. Faunce, who afterward became president of Brown.

So we boys began Latin. Dr. Harper, young as he was, saw the value of the inductive method in learning languages; that was his way of teaching Hebrew and he was already beginning his inductive textbooks. George, at his suggestion, wrote out the opening lines of Caesar's *Gallic War* with the English word-for-word below and this became our textbook. For three years we studied at home and our familiar association with the village children ceased. But we made friends with other young folks like the Thayers, Talcotts, and Northrups, Dr. Morgan's boy Fred, and Dr. Smith's son Harry, afterward the managing editor of the Chicago *Daily News*.

As for the inductive method of learning Latin, I got hold of the other end of the stick ten years later when I came home from Yale to teach the Morgan Park young people Latin by the same method in the Owen Academy.

George brought his father's large library with him, and in many ways he interested me very much. At Brown, Professor Diman, in history, had influenced him most. He was full of college songs and stories, and fascinated me by his tales. One song he taught me had to do with a policeman who sang, "A policeman's lot is not a happy one, happy one!" Imagine my surprise many years later to hear that very song in *The Pirates of Penzance,* and to learn that that operetta was first performed in America on December 31, 1879. George must have heard it in 1880, in the winter or spring of his senior year, and passed it on to me the year following. I had no idea we were so up to date.

Another of the benefits brought me by my cousin George was a song book of one of the Ivy League institutions, the joyous lyrics of which I was soon rapidly storing my mind with. There was, of course, nothing wrong with this book but it certainly possessed no great cultural value and Mother soon felt that my mind would be better off without it. Anyway it disappeared. It was the only book I remember that was withheld from me by my parents! Still, one must read something and somebody sent Aunt Jane a beautiful copy of Wordsworth's *Intimations of Immortality.* With the indiscriminateness of childhood I picked it up and began memorizing it at a great rate. Nobody suggested it, nor even thought of it, but I was soon able to repeat the whole poem, to my own great satisfaction. Could there be a greater contrast?

It must have been about 1880 that my beautiful cousin

unpretentious

chased it from the United States in 1839, following the exodus of the Indians." Mr. Morgan's own house, built of stone, is said to have stood about half a mile north of what is now Ninety-fifth Street.

In John Morgan's day what is now Morgan Park was known as North Blue Island. Thomas Morgan found many deer and foxes in his large tract and hunted them with his hounds. In 1869 John sold much of his father's tract to the Blue Island Land and Building Company, a real estate promoting organization with which George C. Walker was identified, and they laid out the roads, planted the shade trees, and named the new venture Morgan Park. Among the first things they did was to attract to the place the military academy and the women's college, for which they built or helped to build buildings, and then the Baptist Union Theological Seminary, of which my father was Secretary. They must have hoped to create out on the far South Side another Evanston, as it were. We may remember that it was Mr. Walker's father, Charles Walker, who on hearing Judge Stephen A. Douglas speak of his wish to give a site of ten acres for a university in Chicago in 1856, had accepted it on behalf of the Baptists of the city, and thus brought about the founding of the Old University of Chicago. The son was to have a considerable part in the building of the new one.

A third old house was that of Mr. Charles Iglehart, at the corner of Morgan Avenue and Western, being for a long time the western limit of the village. Mr. Iglehart was a Maryland tobacco planter who had come to the Ridge in 1856, and built his house in 1857, enlarging it some time early in the seventies. It seemed to be a modest farmhouse, with a very large and elegant drawing-room front later added to it. Certainly when I first saw it in 1876 it stood complete as it is today. He was a fine old farmer, who could often be seen on his white saddle horse going about among his hay-fields. He talked very sociably and agreeably to us boys. He had two sons and also three daughters, who were all splendid women. The second, Miss Nellie, studied art and used to form summer classes of us neighborhood children in draw-ing, which we much enjoyed. But I remember her best as the worshiped teacher of the big infant class I first went to at the village church, a tall, beautiful, gracious, gifted young lady.

When Mr. Iglehart died years later, his old white horse, saddled as he had used it, was led after the hearse in the funeral procession out Morgan Avenue to Mount Green-wood, in the good old historic fashion. Oh, we had our mo-ments of imagination in those old days.

There is a legend that some ravine or other along the beau-tifully wooded ridge where Charles and I used to get our hickory nuts in the fall was once known as Horse Thief Hollow, but in my boyhood days in Morgan Park, well-acquainted as I was with Mr. Iglehart and Mr. Washburn, and thirsty for romance, I never heard of it. I am sorry I cannot confirm this quaint bit of the legendry of my peace-ful boyhood home. But this is, of course, nothing against it; all my associates were at the opposite end of the moral scale. Perhaps the keepers of the secret thought it wise not to con-fide in me.

THREE

Footings in the Church

THE church, and especially the Baptist Church, has always been a second home to me, and not unnaturally, for my earliest recollections include going to Mrs. Nutting's great infant class, in the Second Baptist Church, in Chicago, where my uncle Edgar and my father were the pastors. We Goodspeeds have always remembered with pride that under their leadership that church became the largest white Baptist church in the world, with more than thirteen hundred members. Of course, at that time Mr. Spurgeon's great work in London had not yet begun, and the present day of churches twice that size was undreamed of.

I possess my uncle's ministerial journal and read in it that in the month of my birth he had as guest preachers at his Sunday evening service Washington Gladden and Dwight L. Moody. His church had originated in a division in the First Baptist Church over abolition, those who favored it withdrawing to form the Second. The church building stood at the corner of LaSalle and Washington Streets facing the city hall square in the heart of what is now the Loop. This old brick building was taken down and rebuilt for the Second Church at the corner of Morgan and Monroe Streets, in what was then a popular residence section just west of the river.

The seating capacity of twelve hundred proved unequal to my uncle's Sunday evening congregations, and in a few years it was enlarged to eighteen hundred, as Uncle Edgar's Sunday evening audience was one of the largest in the city.

Lloyd Lewis has made a study of the reaction of northern preachers to Lincoln's murder as reflected in their sermons the Sunday after and he reports that Uncle Edgar was one of the few who expressly warned their people not to be stampeded by it into an attitude of bitterness and retaliation —which nevertheless became the public state of mind and led to the evils of the Reconstruction period. Nor was there anything narrow or sectarian about my uncle's message; "he used to say that he would cross Chicago on his knees to make a man a Christian, but he would not lift a finger to make him a Baptist." We talk about being modern, but this was eighty years ago. No wonder people streamed into his church.

But we moved into the southern suburbs, and there, as my Morgan Park chapter has told, we were even more closely identified with the church. My brother became a member of it when he was nine, I think, and I when eleven or twelve, with Father the minister and Mother the organist and director of the quartette. Mother also organized the girls of the congregation and Sunday School into a missionary society which met regularly at our house. (Even as I write, the Morgan Park church is preparing a pageant in celebration of its seventy-fifth anniversary, and I am being asked for some material as to my mother's very active part in its beginnings.) Grandfather was one of the deacons, and we boys felt identified with the church in the fullest sense of the word. And this sense of really belonging to the church we never lost.

As boys, our social life was mostly in the church. I don't remember when I began to teach in Sunday School, but I know I did my first teaching there, and kept it up for some thirty years, latterly helped by my wife's social gifts, for she made the class an active social group, enrolling more than ninety young people, most of them about her own age. When I add that once in my boyhood when the church lost its janitor, my brother Charles and I undertook his duties for a time, you will see the range of my church connections. In later years, of course, I became a deacon, then chairman of the board of deacons, master of ceremonies at the annual dinner, and of course chairman of various committees, but never of the Finance Committee, which was always held by my father or my brother. My mother's great church activity was ably taken over by my wife when she joined our clan; in Hyde Park, I remember, she was one of the very few women who held the presidency of the Women's Society for three years.

Her own inheritance was a deeply religious one, too. She was descended from the Thomas Olney who shared with Roger Williams in the founding of Providence, Rhode Island, and in defining our great basic American principle of the separation of Church and State. On her father's side she was descended from Francis Eaton and the Puritans of Plymouth Rock. And while she and I did not exactly meet in church, we came very near it for it was after a dinner meeting and program of the Baptist Social Union of Chicago that Dean Shailer Mathews introduced me to Miss Elfleda Bond, and while he escorted Mrs. Bond to her carriage, I followed with Miss Bond.

My college, Denison University, was a denominational college in the heart of Ohio where the day began for all of us with college chapel. At Sunday School we found great satisfaction in the informal classes taught by our Greek professor, Richard S. Colwell, and our Latin professor, Charles Chandler, both very intelligent and stimulating men. My brother Charles found himself in senior year President of the College Y.M.C.A., and never lost his deep interest in the "Y." He was active in the formation of the Hyde Park Department of the great Chicago Association, and later became a member of the Board of the Chicago Association, where for thirty years he was its recording secretary. Indeed he wrote and published the biography of one of its distinguished general secretaries, Loring Wilbur Messer.

Among the pleasantest memories of my childhood are the times when the Seminary commencement in May would bring alumni and other guests to Morgan Park, and the Seminary men of course opened their houses to entertain them. Then all the able-bodied members of our family would camp out in the great attic, which accommodated us all with reasonable privacy for the week of the Commencement doings. It had not dawned upon me, as I grew up in a theological seminary, that I would spend my active life in one, and its enveloping University. But so it was, and the friendship of those Seminary professors had great significance for me. Dr. Eri B. Hulbert in particular, whom we knew so well from camping out with him and his family, became the Dean of the Divinity School of the new University when it opened in 1892, and was for a long time my dean.

I must make especial mention of Dr. James R. Boise, the professor of New Testament and Biblical Greek, if only because later I became in a sense his successor. He was a small, aged man, with a wig, who wore a shawl in winter weather, after the old American fashion. When I began

Greek as a boy I remember one morning at church he looked up the text in his Greek Testament as was his wont and then leaned over the back of our pew and handed it to me so that I might read it too. This friendly gesture may be described as my introduction to New Testament Greek. I remember his kindliness to me as a child; he used to offer me foreign stamps for my very small collection. And later when Charles and I needed some Greek coaching, he let us put our sentences on the blackboard and corrected them for us—a very marked condescension for an old professor of the old school. As a young instructor at Brown University, it is said Mr. Boise was asked by the great President, Francis Wayland, whether he could teach young men to pronounce Greek as the ancient Greeks did. He said that he could not, that nobody in this country could; it was understood only in the German universities. "Then go to Germany and learn to do it!" said the vigorous President. Mr. Boise went to Tuebingen and became one of the first Americans to take a Ph.D. in Germany, and one of the pioneers in introducing the continental, instead of the "English," pronunciation of Greek in this country. He later became professor of Greek in the University of Michigan, but came to the old University of Chicago when its attitude toward women students seemed to him more liberal than Michigan's then was. Michigan first opened its doors to women in 1870. Dr. Boise had two daughters, both very able women, whom he wished to educate, so the school's position mattered to him.

Dr. Thomas J. Morgan was another seminary professor of distinction. He had been a brigadier general in the Civil War, and later was very active in normal school education at Providence, Rhode Island, and at Potsdam, New York.

Not only the church but the seminary laid its hands upon

me from the first. It was young Dr. Harper, whom I knew
from my childhood, who created the unescapable impression,
in a way he had, that I was going to study Hebrew with him
and become a professor! I think my cousin George when he
was tutoring us boys must have suggested to Dr. Harper that
I had a linguistic bent; at any rate, by the time I was a junior
in college it was understood that when I got through I was
to go to Yale to study with Dr. Harper, which of course I did.

Dr. Harper remained with the Seminary at Morgan Park
only five years, and then was called to Yale as professor of
Semitic languages. But in those few years he had developed
his inductive Hebrew textbooks, his correspondence courses
in Hebrew, and his series of summer schools of Hebrew
which awakened a large section of the country to summer
schooling, correspondence study and Hebrew study as nothing had ever done before. These summer school courses were
later extended to include New Testament study and New
Testament Greek, as well as the other Semitic languages
beside Hebrew. They convinced American educators of the
value of summer study, and later led President Harper in
1894 to introduce a full-fledged summer quarter at Chicago,
which has had wide influence. In fact, the absurdity of shut-
ting up buildings, museums, laboratories and libraries for
three or four months in the summer has become apparent to
most institutions of learning, especially as for so many busy
people, particularly teachers, the summer is the only time
they have for further study. It is interesting to note that it
was from a desire to make the Bible better known in America
that this great movement for summer study started.

In college at Granville the evening sermon-lectures by the
Baptist pastor, Dr. C. J. Baldwin, made a very definite con-

tribution to our interest in English literature and to our enjoyment of it. He enriched his discourses with quotations from the English poets and did us all a real and recognized service, and many a famous passage from the Victorians still brings Dr. Baldwin again before me. This enjoyment of literature was especially important as our college was then without any adequate interpreter of English literature.

In New Haven my cousins and I attended the Calvary Baptist Church near the University and heard the very able preaching of Dr. Edwin M. Poteat. He was admirably seconded by Mrs. Poteat, the daughter of Dr. A. J. Gordon of Boston, one of the leading Baptist figures in the north. She was a very charming and capable woman, and had a great influence over all the young people of the parish. I took a Sunday afternoon class in an outlying mission of the church, conducted by one of my fellow students in the Divinity School. At the University we occasionally heard one or another of the visiting preachers at the University Church at Battell Chapel; in particular I remember hearing Phillips Brooks, whom I heard again the following July in his own pulpit in Trinity Church, Boston, a memorable experience.

When the University of Chicago opened in 1892, there was soon organized at President Harper's suggestion the Christian Union, an informal organization of faculty and students, the chief expression of which was a Sunday evening service in the so-called Chapel which occupied the whole first-floor north end of Cobb Lecture Hall. I cannot remember how it came about, but I found myself in the unenviable position of Secretary of this body, and charged with the task of finding speakers for these Sunday evening meetings. There were no funds to remunerate them, but we managed to have a very interesting and distinguished series of speakers from the faculty and the city, and arranging for them certainly increased my acquaintance.

How well I remember calling on Mrs. Palmer—Alice Freeman Palmer, Dean of Women, the former President of Wellesley, the wife of George Herbert Palmer of Harvard —to ask her to take a Sunday evening. Very tactfully she soon elicited the fact that my father was Secretary of the Board of Trustees, and she replied, in her indescribably winning way, "Oh, then you're one of *us!*"—a remark which did much to put a bashful and not very experienced young man at his ease, you may be sure. The chimes in Mitchell Tower beautifully commemorate the presence in the University those first years of this gifted and gracious woman.

Dr. Ernest Stires, the eloquent young rector of Grace Church, was another whom I had the temerity and satisfaction of bringing to our small Sunday evening audience. He had just come to Chicago, and was later to become rector of St. Stephen's in New York, and then Bishop of Long Island. But most of our speakers that year were naturally from the University faculty.

When in 1893 we moved from Morgan Park to Hyde Park to be near the new University, we all joined the Hyde Park Baptist Church and to its leadership my father at once made a vigorous contribution. He came to head its finance campaigns, especially in raising the funds for its new building on Woodlawn Avenue, and was for many years chairman of its finance committee. Later my brother Charles took this responsibility over. There we enjoyed for many years the valued ministry of Dr. John L. Jackson. Father was chairman of the committee that found Dr. Charles W. Gilkey and brought him to the church for his distinguished ministerial service which led to his becoming the Dean of the University's Rockefeller Chapel. His assistant, Dr. Norris L. Tibbetts was also very close to us, later going to a similar post in the Riverside Church in New York.

The architect of our Woodlawn Avenue church was none other than James Gamble Rogers, but his magnificent first design was too costly for our resources, and he selected a less expensive Romanesque. I have seemed to recognize the superb tower he first offered us in the Harkness tower at New Haven, so reminiscent of Antwerp Cathedral. So true it is that nothing is wasted!

When we planned a soldiers' memorial window in the church, I found myself chairman of the committee, and secured designs from leading artists in stained glass, among them Charles J. Connick of Boston, who eventually built the window. This friendship led to his designing for Mrs. Bond the beautiful chancel window in the Joseph Bond Chapel in the Divinity School group at the University, and the subsequent production by his successors at Boston of the remaining windows in the chapel. I later became a deacon and chairman of the Board of Deacons in the Hyde Park church. Mrs. Goodspeed was, as I have said, for three years the President of its Women's Society. My ever-generous mother-in-law led most generously in providing the great organ screen, and the chancel panels. And when in 1924 the church celebrated its fiftieth anniversary, my father wrote and published its history in a book of a hundred and twenty pages. Twenty-five years later, when my brother died in Los Angeles, and after his funeral in Forest Lawn his body was taken to Chicago for burial, his old church and its pastor Dr. Rolland Schloerb would not be content without a second funeral for him there, in the building and the fellowship he had so much loved, and from it he was carried by the hands of his old friends to his grave. These memories I need hardly say touch me very deeply.

My story will tell how much my student days abroad were cheered by the friends in the various American churches, and how at the end of the journey Mrs. Goodspeed and I found the happiest church relationship with pastor and people in the First Baptist Church of Los Angeles, under the ministry of Dr. Frank B. Fagerburg. Mrs. Goodspeed said to me that she had never been so happy in a church relationship, and yet she had lived under the ministeries of preachers like Dr. O. P. Gifford and Dr. Charles W. Gilkey. How much Mrs. Fagerburg, too, contributed to this pleasure those who know her will not need to be told. And in the long ago days in Chicago, Mrs. Gilkey and Mrs. Goodspeed were always very close.

The campaign for my translation of the New Testament thirty years ago and the interest it occasioned took me into the pulpits of pretty nearly every sect and denomination one can imagine, in all of which I was cordially welcomed, and found many friends. But wherever we have lived, our lives have always been integrated with that of the local Baptist church, and always been enriched thereby.

FOUR

Through Three Universities

I T WAS in 1884 that my cousin George married my cousin
Florence (no relation of his, of course) and departed for
Sonora, California, to be the minister of the Baptist Church.
A great many years later, Florence returned to Sonora, and
told the Woman's Club of those early days!

Charles and I, fifteen and almost thirteen respectively, took
our lunchboxes and our books and journeyed daily on the
Rock Island train up to what is now known as the Old University of Chicago, to continue our preparation for college. Father
showed us the original building, Jones Hall, in which he had
roomed in his college days, 1859 to 1862. It is now the fashion
to speak lightly of the old University, but even if some institutions had larger libraries, it certainly had the finest equipment for astronomical research and instruction in America.
In fact, I know of no American university even now which
can match it on its main campus, except the one to which its
equipment was eventually removed.

There were some fine teachers at the Old University, certainly for boys in our stage of development, like J. D. S.
Riggs and Lewis Stuart in Latin, Nathaniel Butler (later
President of Colby College) in English, and Edward Olson
and Oscar Howes in Greek, for now I was to begin Greek!

It was a surprisingly large class; in those days all B.A.'s took Greek. We seemed to fill the spacious room, its great windows looking out on Lake Michigan, and its walls adorned with busts of all the chief figures in Greek literature; that of Xenophon was a perfect portrait of Edward Olson himself, as all agreed. Edward Olson later became President of the University of Dakota (as yet undivided) at Vermillion, and perished in the burning of the Minneapolis Tribune building, in November, 1889.

Chief among us was Salmon O. Levinson, an irresistible young man from Indiana. He was really a sophomore, but was back with us second-year preps to begin Greek, which he needed to transfer to Yale, as he planned to do. "Solly" Levinson as he was generally called became a successful lawyer in Chicago, and a great champion of what he named the "Outlawry of War," and was active in framing the famous Kellogg Pact. He certainly gave a good account of himself. Long after, I remember, we entertained him and Mrs. Levinson at our house, out at the University. S. A. D. (for Stephen A. Douglas of course) Boggs became a missionary to India, and head of an agricultural college, teaching the Indians a sounder agriculture. Bert Veeder went to Yale and became a successful lawyer, making his home in Winnetka. Oh, I would like to go around the room. But I must relate my fearful experience in our first test. Morris Falter and I were the class children, being fourteen and thirteen respectively. When Professor Olson, whom we all admired extravagantly, as everybody did, put the results on the board, of course Levinson and the redoubtable Miss Sondericker led all the rest, and the others' marks gradually fined down through the eighties and sixties to an unfortunate man who was marked thirty. Then a dash, and, too small to compute, a gentleman named Mosler, and myself. This gave me quite a shock, after my long and peaceful tutorial experience. I think I was perhaps more incensed than injured. If the word ever reached my father, it was through me, for I remember no debate about it. But I had always had my ever-generous brother Charles' steady habits of study to keep me at my books before, and now I had to form them for myself, as he was not in this class with me.

We graduated from the preparatory department in great style at an evening commencement of our own, in the First Baptist Church, where I believe I recited an original translation of something from the *Aeneid*. I still have the certificate; it was the nucleus of my diploma collection, which I prize chiefly for the autographs of my old Presidents and Deans. What a pity the practice of signing such documents has gone out. But we candidates have grown too numerous to autograph.

This was the last commencement of the Old University preparatory department, for the whole institution expired that spring. Perhaps the effort of getting me ready for college proved too much for its enfeebled constitution. My Father and some of his friends hoped that the work of the University, to which he was greatly attached, might shortly be revived under happier auspices, and they prevailed on three or four of the professors to continue at least a fragment of its work in a University Academy, in the old Seminary building across Rhodes Avenue. There Charles and I had most of our freshman year. But by spring Father had pretty well given up his high hopes of an early resumption and sent us off to Denison University at Granville, Ohio, for the spring quarter, principally because his old friend Galusha Anderson had become its president.

At Denison, where breakfast was always at 6:30 A.M., we did not escape some boyish homesickness, but we made firm friends among our classmates, while recognizing the upper classmen as our natural enemies. This antipathy had some justification for we had been admitted to one of the best suites in the college dormitory, felicitously styled New Brick, from the fourth floor of which we looked out on a boundless view southward over the valley to the far-off hills toward Lancaster, home of General Sherman. Such suites were regarded as the rightful inheritance of the senior class, and here two small boys from Chicago, of all places, were ensconced in one, to remain there for three years to come. Chicago, too, was then regarded by our fellow students from Ohio, West Virginia and Kentucky as a remote and semicivilized precinct; no one from there, it seemed, had ever before come to Granville to study.

It was no doubt this circumstance, along with our extreme youth, that rather isolated us from the men of '88, but when they were safely graduated, we really had a very good time in college. We both had measles in freshman year, which added to our woes. And yet I now see that encountering a little opposition in college as freshmen was a valuable element in our education, reminding us that we need not expect things always to go exactly our way. It began to put a little iron into our blood.

A confirmed classical student, I gained much from my courses in languages, as well as a sympathetic approach to modern science, then only beginning to push its way into the colleges of the interior. Denison in particular was entering upon a marked scientific revival, under Clarence Herrick and Alfred D. Cole. With much condemnation from my professor of mathematics, I may be permitted to prize a remark of approbation from Professor Herrick—one of the few I ever received from my teachers—on hearing my description of the circulation of the blood. He said he had never heard it so clearly described. I may say that I have myself been a firm believer in it ever since.

Professor Herrick was later invited to the faculty in the new University of Chicago but an unfortunate misunderstanding as to his precise relation to the department led him to resign and he became the second President of the University of New Mexico at Albuquerque, 1897 to 1901. There he died in 1904 in the prime of life, of tuberculosis.

I must not omit from the cultural forces brought to bear upon me in college our Greek professor's dress suit. It was the first dress suit most of us had ever seen. Our supreme social expression was the Washington Banquet held in the parlors of the Baptist Church, and I shall never forget the sight of our professor, a fine figure of a man on all occasions, as he entered the room and moved among us in his dress suit. We instinctively recognized in him the finished man of the world. But no one owed more to Professor Colwell's instruction than I, for it was he who introduced me at fifteen to the study of New Testament Greek, to my great satisfaction and advantage.

Professor Colwell also conferred upon us our college names. The Greek classes were always small, and two Goodspeeds in the same class created a problem of classroom designation, which "Dick" as we familiarly called him (to one another) cleverly solved by the use of Elder and Younger. As thus:

"Goodspeed, Younger, you may go on."

This so delighted our classmates and the whole little college that we were at once nicknamed Elder and Younger, and so addressed to this day.

The college literary societies also did much for us, teaching us at least how to conduct a public meeting, as well as to review, debate and extemporize. They have disappeared now, but we found a great deal for us in them, and much enjoyment.

While our bitter rivals of the Franklin Society across the hall, better known as the "Franks," had only a drab bust of their eponym to rally round, we had an oil painting of Calliope, life size, and much admired, which gracefully dominated our spacious hall. The legend was that some time in the far past it had cost the Society more than a hundred dollars, a high price when most of us paid less than two dollars and a quarter a week for board. It was without doubt the principal if not the only work of art about the college, and yet it has now completely disappeared, leaving not a rack behind. Ours was, most inconveniently, a hilltop college, but the views from it in springtime, while not all that we then claimed for them, have since become so. Even then the blossomtime of the year stirred the rudest of us to writing poetry. It was, of course, highly sentimental and in May and June reached flood proportions. Perhaps it is so in all rural seats of learning. And yet none of us made the art a profession, though we all had high hopes of one another. Those same spring evenings made us cluster around the main doorway of the college, and sing lustily the college songs of that remote period; it seemed to be a college custom, and a very nice one, which I remember with unmixed pleasure. We listened with pride to our yodeler Gummy Bosler, who was also the best pitcher and orator then in college. He later became Speaker of the Ohio House of Representatives.

Of course, we got our first experiences in dealing with other men, by which we mean getting them to vote or act or give or something as we wish them to and think they should. This was richly illustrated in college elections to certain trifling offices like the president of the Reading Room and Lecture Association, or of the Calliopean literary society, which then appeared matters of positively prodigious importance. We managed to arrange it so that most of these presidencies, along with that of the Y.M.C.A., fell to my brother Charles, when we reached senior year and became eligible for such responsibilities.

Academically speaking, we were taught mostly by the textbook method, since so largely outmoded. And yet Professor Chandler, in Latin, found time to give us the gist of comparative philology, for which I have always been most grateful. What progress we made in writing was mostly made in literary society, or on the college monthly. I remember trying my hand at a short story for the latter, and a verse translation of a passage of Aeschylus, about the series of beacon fires, in the *Agamemnon*. I confess I read it still with considerable satisfaction!

And then there are the lifelong friendships one carries on from college; men and women, faculty and students, a priceless possession through the long years. Worth going to college for, all by themselves.

Of the twelve members of our class to graduate, four appeared with orations at commencement. The Goodspeed boys were not among them. This may have disturbed my father, but he gave no sign, and Charles and I were perfectly satisfied, and we returned with light hearts from senior vacation to the mild gaieties of commencement week. But if the old college did little for us that day, it has more than made up for it since, in all the kinds of consideration colleges can command.

On September 18, 1890, I found myself taking the old 5:30 for New York, on my way to New Haven, under the wing of Professor Harper with whom I was to begin my graduate work at Yale. He came to the train from the second meeting of the new University of Chicago Board of Trustees at which he had just been elected President by a unanimous rising vote, but had asked for six-months' time to think it over.

At breakfast he said to me, in his friendly, half-playful way,

"Edgar, what do you think I'm going to do this morning? I'm going to plan the organization of the new University of Chicago!"

And sure enough, at luncheon he laid it all—confidentially, of course—before me—the two-study idea, a major and a minor course; the division into academic and university colleges, of two years each, the four-quarter system, the summer quarter of the same length and caliber as the rest; University Extension, correspondence study, faculty control of athletics, the University Press—the whole layout which he later developed into that series of bulletins that in the months that followed, as someone put it, fell like bombs upon the campuses of America. Of course, it must be observed that almost every one of these new ideas he had himself tried out in other schools and situations, and found sound. He had organized correspondence teaching of Hebrew on a large scale; he had done the same thing with summer schools; he had actually organized his American Publication Society of Hebrew to publish his Hebrew textbooks and his periodical, *The He-*

brew Student, and saw the need for a University Press. It is a debated question whether the Johns Hopkins Press is older than Chicago's, but I can testify that Chicago's was first proposed by Dr. Harper in that conversation of September 19, 1890.

At New Haven I lived in the very pleasant society of my favorite cousins, George and Florence, in their comfortable house on George Street. George was then teaching in Yale and working for his Ph.D. Florence's sister Emily was there with her, as was our cousin James Ten Broeke, working for his Ph.D. in philosophy with Professor Ladd. Both James and George took their Ph.D.'s at the end of that academic year. My second cousin Harper, an active child of three, completed a very lively and amusing household.

My courses at Yale were all with Dr. Harper himself— Hebrew, Arabic and Old Testament Legal Literature. He thought it would be an interesting experiment to have me begin Arabic at the same time with Hebrew but I did not find it so. If he had written the textbook it would have been different. I had no difficulty with Hebrew and did well enough in it. In his large legal literature course, however, I did not shine; in fact, I did not find it particularly engaging, and one evening in the kindest possible way he rebuked me. He had summoned me to a midnight talk in his big study in 117 North College, in the old Brick Row. He came at once to the point:

"Edgar," he said, "I <u>am in danger of losing my reputation as a teacher on you!</u>"

My admiration for this form of reproach somewhat mitigated the force of the blow; he seemed to be accepting some share of responsibility for my unsuccess. Still I repeat, I had not failed in Hebrew, and soon could claim a large enough vocabulary to be admitted to the department's Hebrew Club. And as for not succeeding in beginning Hebrew and Arabic together, I do not know that anyone ever did. It was Sachau, I believe, who said Arabic was the Devil's language.

I most enjoyed the Doctor as he led his Hebrew class of fifty men in beginning Hebrew. I remember with especial pleasure a mnemonic proposed by a member of it; he said he could remember *Tardemah* (deep sleep) by "tardy in the morning." I am sure we all could, after that. This helpful contribution amused the Doctor very much. I also enjoyed his weekly open lecture, on the narratives of Genesis, which packed the big lecture hall in Osborn every Wednesday afternoon at five with an all-University student audience.

The Harpers very kindly asked me to dinner early in my stay in New Haven; it was a family dinner and, of course, I knew the children very well. At dinner Mrs. Harper asked me whether I rode the bicycle. I replied that I did, but admitted that I did not have one. Mrs. Harper briskly rejoined that I must have one, and suggested to the Doctor that his bicycle was lying unused in the basement as he never would ride it, and he ought to lend it to me. This put the Doctor on the spot. He thought fast, and his eyes twinkled.

"Mrs. Harper," he replied pontifically, "one never lends a bicycle!"

That autumn, to our great delight, Father had to come east to some conference in New York about the plans for the new University, and he came up to New Haven for a weekend with us. It was a fine fall Saturday, and my cousin George and I were accustomed to tramping out to Yale Field to see the football game. We suggested to Father that he accompany us. But he demurred, saying he was not interested in football, it was a brutal sport. We labored with him, however, pointing out that he had never seen it played by trained men, under definite rules, and urged him to join us. This he reluctantly did. There was no grandstand for the spectators at these minor games, Wesleyan and so on. We simply stood outside the rope that enclosed the playing field, and could even follow the teams up and down the field, to some extent, hearing their panting breath and the low-voiced signals, and watching their nimble footwork. Mr. A. A. Stagg, famous Yale pitcher of the '80's, was no longer with the team; '90 had been his last year at end, but Pudge Heffelfinger was still at guard, Laurie Bliss at end, McClung at halfback, and Billy Rhodes, the captain, at tackle, and they were playing beautiful football.

It did not take Father long to catch the spirit of the thing, and he was soon as excited and absorbed as we. That day marked a new attitude on his part toward the game, and when later he met Stagg, they became lifelong friends. At the new University Father became a staunch supporter of the team. He followed it to Madison the famous year of the unexpected victory over Wisconsin, in a post-season game with a score of 17 0, after which the Chicago rooters marched down the street to the train chanting. "Ha Ha! I told you so!"

The following Monday at the celebration in Kent Theater at the University, when Father was called on to speak, he electrified the crowd by his opening words,

"Ha Ha! I told you so!"

Some years later still, when Walter Eckersall's admirers wished to present him with a gold watch between halves at the Thanksgiving game, Father was chosen to make the presentation speech. In fact, he was known to the athletic crowd as the youngest rooter of them all.

Eager to sail the Sound, I took a weekend trip on the Old
Fall River Line down to New York to visit Harry Atwood,
then in business there, and to see the great city, then of course
in its prime. It was delightful to ride on top of the Fifth
Avenue buses, with horses to draw you, and the sociable
driver to tell you who occupied the splendid houses that
lined the stately strcct. On the homeward voyage I fell in
with Charles Foster Kent, on the upper deck, and as we
talked in the shelter of the dirty old smokestack, a small boy
joined us and amused himself rubbing the smokestack with
his hands. Charles Kent's strong social interest led him to
interfere. A lesser disciplinarian would have crudely told the
boy to stop rubbing the dirty old smokestack, but not so
Charlie Kent.

"My boy," said he kindly, "aren't you afraid you'll soil that
smokestack if you rub it like that?"

Of course, this novel approach staggered the boy. He had
not looked at the thing from the smokestack's point of view.
Charlie later became Woolsey Professor of Biblical Literature, the chair which had been established for Dr. Harper
and which he then held. Charlie went on to a distinguished
career in the biblical field.

I must not fail to record that at the end of my Yale year
Dr. Harper, who had decided to go abroad for a year before
taking up his duties as President at Chicago, very kindly invited me to go abroad with his little party and act as his secretary! How extraordinarily kind this was of him you can
imagine, from the fact that I had never been abroad, knew
nothing about secretarial duties and accomplishments, and
would only have added to his responsibilities and expenses.
So with great good sense I gratefully declined. It simply shows
the lengths to which he would go to get young men to do

the thing he felt they ought to be doing, to make something of themselves. And it is curious to reflect that many years later I served his first and second successors in the presidency, Dr. Harry Pratt Judson and Dr. Ernest D. Burton, as Secretary to the President.

I made some great friends at Yale, sitting in Hebrew beside Henry T. Fowler, meeting James Henry Breasted, Charles Foster Kent and Frank K. Sanders in the Semitic Club, Frank J. Miller and Clifford W. Barnes in the Y.M.C.A. meetings at Dwight Hall (a name since transferred to the Old Library!), and in the Divinity School Frank C. Putnam, a most engaging young man from Amherst. His father had been minister to France under President Grant, and being in New York at the time of the Grant funeral, Frank asked the management how he could witness the ceremonies. They immediately provided him with an open carriage and a place in the procession, as representing his father, so Frank became a participant in the solemnities, though wearing a light suit and a straw hat! This memory always gave him great amusement.

At the Harvard game at Springfield I met A. A. Stagg, whom I came to know so well at Chicago in after years. James Henry Breasted was in beginning Arabic with me and one day when Dr. Harper was kept away, he sent word to him to conduct the recitation. In later years it gave James much amusement on the strength of this performance to claim me as one of his students!

A year later when after twelve months' teaching of beginning Greek and Latin I was applying for a Junior Fellowship in Semitics at the new University of Chicago (I had begun Assyrian and Aramaic much more successfully in the meantime), the Doctor was a very busy man, and the only time he could give me was while he was eating a very hasty luncheon at the lunch counter downstairs in the old Chamber of Commerce building, where the University office was. He was very matter of fact.

"You have proved that you can learn," he said, "and you have proved that you can teach, but you have not proved that you can investigate, and these fellowships are for men who can investigate. And if you get one," he concluded, "it will be by default!"

Upon analysis, this was not such a serious verdict for a youth of twenty, but the Doctor said it as though I ought to have proved a seasoned investigator long ago. I think he was trying to wake me up and raise my sights. He saw about him so many men doing less than their best, and really wanted to save me from that mistake. Well, I got the fellowship, anyway, but it was plain that he meant to do his duty by me. At the end of one year I did not reapply, and the Doctor called me to his office to tell him why. I said I thought it would be a mistake to go on, for the fellowship duties, correcting Hebrew exercise books and tending the departmental library, absorbed the Fellow's time in so many little things.

"Edgar," said the Doctor solemnly, "life consists of little things!" I was amazed. I knew he was largely occupied in very large things indeed but it was nevertheless a sound remark with a lot of truth in it. But with characteristic obstinacy I stuck to my guns and resumed my prep school teaching in the South Side Academy in my leisure hours, while pursuing my graduate courses toward my degree. That the University gave me very handsomely in 1898, after seven years of resident graduate study at Yale and Chicago.

My last interview with the Doctor was just before Elfleda

and I were off for an autumn quarter in Europe, in 1905. The Doctor's physicians had given him up, and we all knew he had only a few months to live. I called on him in his study to say good-by, but of course I could not say it. He remarked,

"I understand you've got Charles to go with you. That's the best thing you ever did. He'd never have gone by himself." (How well he understood us all, and saw what we needed, and ought to do! He really did.) I tried to thank him for what he had done for me, in publishing some Ethiopic papers of mine, of no particular interest, in his Semitic Journal. He said,

"Oh, that's all right, Edgar. Universities are made for fellows like you!"

That was almost fifty years ago, but I can never think of those few words from *him* without tears.

" 'Tis sixty years since" might well have been my reflection one morning in 1951 as I sat on the platform and witnessed Yale's 250th commencement. Emotion overcame me, I confess, as that great congregation sang Bacon's Puritan hymn, as it always does at commencement;

> O God, beneath Thy guiding hand,
>   Our exiled fathers crossed the sea;
> And when they trod the wintry strand,
>   With prayer and psalm they worshipped Thee.

pilgrims.

For I remembered that among the Pilgrims was a young fellow named Francis Eaton, from whom my wife was directly descended. I seemed at that anniversary strangely near those far-off Pilgrims.

FIVE

The Island

FROM the time when at the age of nine his older brother Edgar let my father accompany him and his friends on a camping trip on Lake George in New York, nine miles' walk from Glens Falls where they lived, my father always loved the woods and waters. In his Quincy period he and his great friend and parishioner Robert Gardner went up more than once to Lake Minnetonka, and camped out on the Big Island. A pencil sketch of their tent, from Robert's skillful hand, was long treasured in the family. When Charles and I were very small, Father and Mother took their young family up to Minnetonka, and there I fell into the lake. Fortunately rescued, and taken to my Mother, I reported it to her succinctly in the words,

"O Mamma! I fell in the bluing water!"

This remark was believed by my optimistic parents to reveal powers of observation and expression of no mean order, and was so reported to me.

My father was a great oarsman and swimmer, and a capable woodsman and camper. As soon as his means and his duties permitted he began to take Mother and us boys up to such lakes as we could reach in northern Illinois. Even in my childhood I remember going with him to the Calumet River, at Blue Island, renting a boat and going for an afternoon's fishing, even though the latter part of the return journey of two miles I made on Father's back.

We had a great season about 1881 on Lake Minnetonka. We had some tents, and built a nice dry, warm house of building paper for the women and the children. It was that summer that Father, Dr. Hulbert and I got caught off shore one afternoon by one of those sudden storms that happen on Minnetonka. It swept us before it away from our shore across the lake to the Big Island where we got ashore, got into a vacant cottage, lighted a fire with Dr. Hulbert's last match, and waited to dry out and to have the lake calm down. It was almost dark when we got back to camp. We had been seen to disappear in the squall, and when it was past and we and our boat were nowhere in sight, they spent an anxious hour or two. But they knew Father and Dr. Hulbert for the watermen they were, and had not given up all hope when we reappeared.

Later in my boyhood we began to discover northern Wisconsin, and the hundreds of little glacial lakes that abound up there in Lake and Oneida counties. We went to various small resorts chiefly for the fishing, then to the Gogebic Club's camp on Tomahawk Lake, at the invitation of the club's president Henry E. Thayer, our Morgan Park neighbor. It was there we got our first muskallonge! Then for two or three years we went to the other Tomahawk lake, at Minocqua, "Kawaquesaga." At Island Lake one summer our host, who had been a missionary to the Ojibways, and who tried to teach me the language, informed me that this meant Kewayquot Sagaagon, or Tomahawk Lake. Squirrel Lake was, in Ojibway, Wabachitimo Sagaagon, and Shashibogama meant the Wandering Water. At Kawaquesaga we spent three sum-

mers. Then for three summers we went to John Mann's
Manitowish Lodge on Trout Lake.

It was at John Mann's that we came to know Captain
Edward Kemeys, the Union captain of artillery in the Civil
War who had become famous as an animal sculptor. His
ways of learning the postures and attitudes of his animal
subjects interested us very much; when possible he would
keep them in a cage in his yard to study. He afterward did
the splendid lions in front of the Art Institute in Chicago.
When we knew the Captain he was very deaf.

Father's adventurous competence reminds me of an evening after dinner at John Mann's, when somebody with a
small rifle, a twenty-two, got us all out into the edge of the
woods to try our hands shooting out a candle flame. Nobody
but the owner of the gun could do it—until Father began to
put it out every time he shot. Everyone marveled at his sudden skill. He took Charles and me aside and informed us
that something was the matter with the sight and we better
aim just a little above the flame. Whereupon we too joined
the class of first-rate marksmen and everybody exclaimed
what remarkable shots the Goodspeeds were! Father took so
naturally to every form of sport, of course, because sport interested him and he put his mind on it.

One day in our third summer there, we set off with Dr.
Franklin Miles, since famous for his patent medicines—"the
best by Miles"—and tramped and canoed by way of Big
Muskallonge Lake to the western end of Plum Lake and had
our first view of it, and the next summer when at last the
St. Paul road was built through to Star Lake, we went to
Plum Lake, and spent a summer at Sayner's Hotel, a log
building just opened for its first season.

Wishing to be by ourselves—we were seven—we would

take our luncheon with us and picnic and read over on an
island halfway down the lake. And before we left we began to
build a cabin of small upright cedar logs on the high ground
on the island. As soon as the federal government permitted
the buying of such islands we bought it, and held it most
happily for fifty years. We saw the lake gradually develop, a
few cottages go up, a golf club organized, other resorts open
on the shores, the lumbermen come and go, to our great
relief leaving unharmed the south shore facing the island,
with its noble stand of pine.

My cousins George and Florence and their son Harper
shared it with us; it was George who named it Paradise, and
that was the way we always thought of it. There we studied,
swam, fished and read to our hearts content, for a month
or more every summer. Our uncles, cousins, kindred from
far and near came to see us there. The canoes and rowboats
began to give way to the outboards and the launches and we
marched with the times. Delightful people came to the other
islands and the points. Judge William C. Hook brought his
family from Fort Leavenworth, and Mr. Robert Wilmot his
from New Orleans. Dr. Monilaw established a boys' camp
near the head of the lake, and Miss James and Miss Marshall
a girls' camp at the western end in the very grove of pines
from which we had first seen the lake with Dr. Miles that
distant summer day in 1892.

Our first house, thatched with marsh moss between the
slender upright logs, in ten or a dozen years gave way to a
more substantial one. It was built of wide cypress boards,
with a big living room, and a long hall which our architect
called the Cloister, to put the poetry, as he said, into the
house. For our architect was Mr. S. S. Beman, the famous
Chicago architect, builder of Pullman and Ivorydale, whose

daughter had become the wife of my cousin Harper Good-speed. This new house, which we enlarged in the same style from time to time, made us all much more comfortable, and brought in a new era for our island family.

Florence later built a second house a little higher up to the west of this house, and Father built himself a fine little study on the eastern corner of the hill, that is, the high main part of the island, where he could retire and smoke, and read and write undisturbed. A stone fireplace heated it when necessary. It was here that he wrote much of his history of the University of Chicago and I wrote much of my translation, and also of my mystery story, and it was here that, years later, the New Testament Revision Committee worked long hours, one week in 1938 and two weeks in 1939.

The nearest lake to Plum was Razor Back, five or ten minutes away to the westward by an easy forest trail. It contained three islands. One Father had bought, and another our University colleague Theodore Soares owned, but the great fire of 1910 that swept all that region had reduced them both literally to ashes. We were abroad that summer, but Father witnessed the whole conflagration, and actually saw the firebrands sail through the air all the way across the lake, a mile or more, and set fire to the farther shore. It was years before we could bring ourselves to revisit the place but in 1916 we went over and found the two islands (Father had bought Theodore's from him after the fire) so thickly covered with second growth that you had to cut your way through it even to land. Elfleda thought it would be amusing to take the smaller island and build a little outcamp on it, for picnics and a sort of excursion objective, and when I asked Father what he would take for it he said, dejectedly,

"Edgar, I'll sell you this island for thirty cents!"

Fortunately having the money with me, I closed the transaction then and there.

We gave our new island the grand old Indian name of Hikhookmot—as good we thought as anything in Cooper, besides honoring our Plum Lake friends the Hixons, the Hooks and the Wilmots, each of whom contributed a syllable. The name has even found a place in literature, for Judge Edward J. White, who lived on the "Little Island" in Plum Lake, and used to write endless poems to amuse his little girls, sang:

> And here, 'tis said, old Hikhookmot dwelt,
> And to the Great Spirit often knelt.
> Tradition has it that this old Brave
> Now rests 'neath the rock that is washed by the wave!

We planned to build a one-room house with a fireplace and cupboards and a brass kettle hanging on a crane, furnish it simply, drive a well, and put up a flagpole. Miss Ruth Lester, catching its spirit, sent us a trivet to equip our kitchen and in 1917 we had a housewarming. Mr. and Mrs. Joseph Hixon, Judge and Mrs. William C. Hook, and Mr. and Mrs. Robert Wilmot, the fractional eponyms of the establishment, all came over to supper.

The island was a low cone, perhaps forty feet high, and rising evenly up to the center on the top of which we built our house. It became a most useful adjunct to the main island for we could come over to fish and gather for luncheon at Hikhookmot, safe from rain or cold. There were no other houses on Razor Back and except for an occasional fisherman it was solitude.

We sometimes had little suppers over there and then came home over the waters and through the woods to Paradise, leaving the cleaning up till next day. On one such occasion, arriving with the maids to clear up after a late evening supper a night or so before, we found all the sofa pillows gone! Yet the place had been locked. We must have left a window open or at least unfastened. Our hearts were sad. It was those numerous gay sofa pillows that had given the place its cheerful air. We men went outside to reflect. Trained in the lore of the very best detectives, we surely should be equal to a problem as simple as this must be. But where to begin! What was there to detect? Who was there even to suspect?

All our best thinking could do was to steer us to the west shore of the lake, where the state had recently opened a camping ground for motorists. Arrived at which, I told my trusty operative Zero (in private life our caretaker and mainstay John Wellstein, but now my companion in this perilous adventure) to skirt the camp unobtrusively, beginning at the right side of the landing, while I skirted it from the left. On meeting at the back side of it we could report nothing. We then wandered absently through it, back to the landing. No one can fail to see and respect the subtlety of these measures, and yet at their conclusion not only the redoubtable Zero but his chief was at a loss. We were in fact baffled.

But all great detectives are dependent, to a limited extent of course, upon chance, and at this precise juncture one of those opportune incidents occurred which all great detectives know so well how to take advantage of. A canoe slid up to the dock and we politely inquired if they had had any luck. As the youth in the stern rose to clamber out, our eyes were gladdened by the sight of a familiar cushion on the seat he had just vacated.

"Hello!" we remarked. "There's one of our cushions! Where did you get it?"

He glibly explained that four young people who had left the camp that morning had thrown out a bunch of them, at the edge of the camp, and he had picked this one up. Being led to the spot, we recovered the rest of our cushions with which we returned in no small exultation to the workers on Hikhookmot, and were duly welcomed for the sleuths we were.

Of course we had our losses, such as they were. We had built ourselves a simple flat-bottomed fishing boat, which we kept on a distant lake where nobody lived, to be there when we wanted it. But once when we wanted it, it was not there. We found it later on the other side of the lake, with the name of its new proprietor carefully penciled on the bow— *Ostrander*. We recovered it, and accepted this name for it; it was always the *Ostrander* after that.

This fishing boat reminds me that more should be said in this chapter about fishing. I remember one day we took the Jared Morses over to Razor Back for a late afternoon's fishing. There were five rods in the boat. I had just gathered the minnows myself from a near-by creek, and we found the school—the thing bass fishermen are always hoping to do. We lost all track of just who caught which, stringing them just as fast as we could get them off the lines, and stopped after about an hour, when we saw we had our limit—ten fish each, of legal length. What an hour! Mrs. Goodspeed and Mrs. Morse were every bit as good as the men on this occasion. The Morses went home to their hotel with a string of twenty and we carried the remaining thirty back to the Island.

And then one day, after rowing and tramping to old Pickerel Lake, a haunt of the really big muskies, Father got his fish, a thirty pounder, and he and Charles and I were tramping homeward through the dusk, with the fish slung on a pole between two of us, when past us came hustling a Peoria man, Mr. Bourland, and his guide, the famous Reddy. Reddy had their one fish in a sack on his back, and after stopping to admire ours, turned theirs out on the trail for us to see—a fifty-three pound muskallonge, the biggest one I ever saw. Father's thirty pounder looked like a minnow beside him.

For my part, I never got beyond one eighteen and one twenty pounder in fifty years of musky fishing.

While on the subject of islands, something more should be said about the closely allied subject of boats, without which islands are of little use. Our first canoe was a dugout, hollowed out of a log by some lumberman of long ago, which Charles and I found waterlogged and sunk off the shore of Kawaquesaga. We dragged it back to our camp, dried it out, and adopted it. It was only some twelve feet long, and of course very tippy indeed, being just as round as the tree trunk of which it consisted; an excellent thing to learn canoeing in! Later, we bought one rowboat, then another, rigging a sail in the bow of each, later putting an outboard motor on its stern. Then as the years went on we added canoes, outboards, fishing boats and launches, until we had a regular fleet. For we had to keep boats on Plum, Razor Back, Rice, and sometimes Partridge and Nebish. On an island, of course, everything calls for a boat. Our first launch, which Elfleda drove with great zest, really emancipated her and made her free of the whole lake, greatly increasing her enjoyment of the north woods life. And it was a fine sight to see her in the second one, the twenty-seven foot *Elfleda II* which we bought in that year of plenty, 1929, set off down the lake of a morning in a cloud of spray, with Tom our driver at her side, at 30 m.p.h. on her way to the day's marketing.

One day a little girl in the tiny local village of Sayner—

a few houses scattered about with the station and the store—
was getting the worst of it on some petty childish mistake,
when Elfleda stepped in. She got the child paroled to her,
sent her down to a good family at a high school town, and saw
her through high school and a business training course after.
She was the first of a series of girls Elfleda put on their feet.
Later she did quite as much for some boys and young men
who wanted an education, either financing them herself, or
interesting her mother in their plans. Some of them have
gone far in educational work.

When we got to spending six weeks or even twelve at the
Island, Elfleda never left the Woodlawn Avenue house
vacant. She always gave it for the summer to some friends
with children who lived in apartments the rest of the year,
but who in the summer enjoyed the house with its enclosed
garden, especially on account of the children. It touched her
very much years later to have young people tell her how
much they had enjoyed playing in her garden when they were
little.

We went over to Hikhookmot from Paradise two or three
times every week, and oftener four or five. We developed
a flower garden with a sundial in the center, fixed up an ice
house on the back of the island, put in with our own hands
stone steps made of boulders at the waterside in front, and
in general lavished our latent talents and energies upon it.
There were still no houses on Razor Back; it was solitude.

Half an hour's walk by an old lumber road from the west
end of it was another little lake, Rice Lake. It was little better
than a marsh, being overgrown with wild rice which Indians
would come in the early fall to harvest in their quaint fashion, a squaw paddling in the stern, and kneeling in the bow
a girl with two sticks. With one she would bend a bunch

of the rice over the bow, and with the other give the abundant rice heads a sharp rap, which would shake them off into the bow of the canoe.

In the midst of all this waving field of rice was a fine pine-covered island of solid ground. This we leased from the government for twenty-five dollars a year, and built of the fallen trees an Adirondack lodge, open on one side, and with a bench across the side and back walls. We provided a movable table, and drove a well. This lodge formed another excursion objective, and could also be reached by water from Plum Lake by paddling or rowing up Rice Creek, except when the beavers took it into their wicked little heads to dam that stream!

Another excursion we enjoyed was canoeing down Plum Creek with the fast current into Big St. Germain Lake, picnicking on the way or paddling across to Chabrison's Musky Inn for lunch, then having the cars meet us, with a trailer to haul the canoes back. And another great excursion was putting the canoes into the Wisconsin River at Eagle River, canoeing down it all day with the current and the rapids, and meeting the cars about four o'clock at a predetermined point which they always seemed to find. As our steaming radius increased, we sometimes got as far as Gogebic Lake, up in Michigan, and even the nearest shore of Lake Superior for luncheon and a glimpse of the Apostle Islands, and then home again in time for dinner on Paradise. But we usually reserved these strenuosities for the entertainment of our university or city guests.

Plum Lake was enlivened in the summer of '37 by the presence at Mr. Wilmot's island of Curtis Dall and his two children, popularly known as Sistie and Buzzy. As the grandchildren of the President they were objects of official solicitude, and the Wilmot island was guarded by a redoubtable Secret Service man whom we all came to like very much. He was full of his experiences preserving the life of President Coolidge during the latter's vacation in the Black Hills. The fact that the Wilmots lived on an island had gone far to reconcile the Roosevelts to letting the children visit there for the one month their father had charge of them, and Curtis and Willis Wilmot had been great friends at Princeton. Our insular position also made it possible for us to include the children with Curtis in our festivities at Paradise, where on one memorable Sunday evening we had twelve in the dining room and eight children in the sitting room at supper tables.

Tracy Drake with Mrs. Drake came up to see us at the Island and we found him an admirable fishing companion. Zona Gale and her husband Mr. Breese spent a weekend with us and at a little dinner we gave for them, Lieutenant Clovis Byers, who was doing the horsemanship for the girls' camp that summer, sat next to Mrs. Breese. The matter of war and peace came up and we all stopped to listen when the expert pacifist and the expert West Pointer, a perfect lady and a perfect gentleman, tackled this vexed problem. Clovis has since served as chief of staff of General Eichelberger, and has later been a major general commanding the Eighth Army in Korea.

Mr. LaVerne Noyes, the inventor and philanthropist, came to see us once at Paradise and President Burton was a frequent visitor. The children of the Island as they grew up brought their children to it.

Usually some afternoon in the summer we invited the Girls' Camp, Warwick Woods, to the Island for tea and a launch ride. It was a fine sight to see their string of a dozen canoes coming up the lake and to see them make for the launch and a boat ride, or for the study, or for the house for tea. One year Curtis Dall came and brought his children, and it was good to see him take the piano bench and start right in on a community sing, which everybody enjoyed. Some of the young people explored the island to its remotest recesses, and others gathered on the highest point to study the view. Those were happy afternoons.

The cottagers on Plum Lake lived very much to themselves for the first few years, but gradually they were more amalgamated, and as the young people grew up, developed annual regattas, chiefly fostered by Dorothy Hook, Dorothy Wilmot, and my wife. It was the elder statesmen, however, who led by Mr. Fred S. James organized the golf club, which threatened at one time to transform us from a community of fishermen into one of golfers. Both these institutions contributed much to mutual acquaintance and enjoyment. Nor must we forget the skating rink, which for several seasons before it burned was a scene of gay nightly revels.

When in 1938 the Revised Standard Version project was revived and the New Testament committee reconstituted and reassembled, we all felt that we must have no more three-day meetings which got nowhere, but meet for at least a week in some quiet place with no telephones or other distractions. Mrs. Goodspeed and I at once suggested the Island, and to it in July of that year they came—Weigle, Moffatt, Craig, Grant, Cadbury, Burrows and Bowie. We would put in a long morning and afternoon and then go back for the evening too. We made one or two efforts to bring in some of our distinguished lake neighbors for dinner or to get the group away to some neighboring resort for lunch or dinner for a change. A few miles north of us on Star Lake was Oliver Lodge—no connection with Sir Oliver, of course, just Mr.

Oliver setting up his Lodge. Mrs. Goodspeed made the arrangements, and when we arrived with her at dinnertime, cometh Mr. Oliver all freshly shaved up to greet us.

"Yes, yes," he courteously observed, after meeting everybody and turning to me, "your daughter made all the arrangements this afternoon." This gave me no little satisfaction. The Lodge bill of fare boasted fourteen different kinds of dessert.

At dinner at the Island we gathered one evening among other guests Mr. Justice Rosenberry, the Chief Justice of Wisconsin, and Mrs. Rosenberry, who had been the Dean of Women at Wisconsin before their marriage. Miss Marshall and Miss James who had the fine Girls' Camp at the foot of the lake also came. I hoped Miss James and Dr. Cadbury would get on, as the Cadburys conduct a camp in the Adirondacks. Camp proprietors hold strong views on the tent-versus-lodge form of accommodation, and I found to my relief that Dr. Cadbury and Miss James both belonged to the tent school of thought. Cadbury even said that at their camp they made their own tents. I cried out in ecstasy,

"But what a point for our Revised New Testament! One of the revisers actually a tentmaker, like Paul!"

Dr. Cadbury, alas, did not respond. He briefly intimated that he did not think that was what the Greek word in the Acts meant.

This extreme conscientiousness of Dr. Cadbury's led to strange situations in the committee. He would make a motion, and everybody would say, "Why, yes, of course. What a good idea!" and after a brief discussion Dean Weigle would put the motion. Everybody would vote "Aye"—except Cadbury! He voted "No." For in the brief time since making the motion, in his effort to see both sides of every question, he had thought up so many difficulties and objections that he could not conscientiously vote for his own motion! On the other hand, Dr. Cadbury and I agreed on almost every vote that came up, though often and often in a losing minority. I remember one hot evening at Northfield when we lost every motion we made for the entire evening; yet were undismayed.

The committee returned to us the following summer for two weeks in July, and of course we made tremendous progress. President Wentz of Gettysburg was with us that summer, and added much to the geniality of the house party, as well as witnessing for the truth, for I found myself always on his side of every vote. These good fellowships were renewed later at New Haven and at Northfield. At the Island we always met in the study, about a square table, with the principal lexicons on side tables about the small room, and really within arm's reach. Typewritten records of our two summer meetings, on the native birchbark, still hang on its rough hemlock walls.

Once when Henry Justin Smith and Katherine drove up from Chicago to spend a few days with us at the Island, he sat down in the corner of the living room in the late afternoon, while we were all busy with games or talk, and wrote a poem about the Island. It was afterward engrossed like a medieval manuscript and illuminated by his gifted cousin John H. Weddell, who with his wife Marion sometimes gladdened our Island with their presence. It began:

> After the long, roaring ride, the white roads, the parched
>   meadows,
> Comes the pale, thoughtful visage of the lake,
> Colored in silver or black,
> And bordered by pines so tall and proud
> Only the upper winds dare touch them.

gives good feeling

   And so presently the Island!
There it floats against a faintly violet sky,
Its mood borrowing the twilight.
Tenderly its fronded cliff is kissed by the last bright ripples,
And the ebbing breeze, fingering the pine needles,
Thrums a coda to the adagio of evening.

It ended thus:

And the Island itself—
Would it not be as much Paradise
Were there no such word in the language of Man?

SIX

Launching the University

WHILE Mr. Rockefeller undoubtedly founded the new University of Chicago with his conditional gift of six hundred thousand dollars if four hundred thousand could be raised in addition, we students and professors who gathered on October 1, 1892, to begin its work may fairly claim to have launched it. The first definite word Charles and I had away in college at Denison that the job had really been undertaken was a telegram Father sent us on May 19, 1889, my brother's twentieth birthday. It told of Mr. Rockefeller's promise, and we shouted with joy as we raced up the stairs to our rooms. In the campaign of a year that followed Father was deeply engaged, and our letters from home senior year reported from day to day the results he and his colleague Mr. Fred T. Gates were getting. Charles for some reason preserved all our college letters from home, and when more than twenty years later, at President Judson's suggestion, Father wrote the history of the University these letters were an invaluable source on the progress of the campaign.

Returning to Morgan Park for Christmas in senior year, Charles and I joined Father and Mr. Gates in an expedition to the proposed site of the University, if they should succeed in establishing it! It was a wide sweep of almost vacant land, with few roads or houses, and we scaled a barbed-wire fence to survey it more closely. Around Christmas it was of course at its bleakest, and gave little promise of the academic paradise it was to become. We were the first scouts of the educational Israel to spy out our Promised Land, but the sight encouraged Mr. Gates and Father to renew their appeal to Mr. Marshall Field who owned the whole subdivision.

When the work was done, and the trustees on whom Father and Mr. Gates had decided assembled in their first meeting to elect officers, they at once elected Father Secretary of the Board, and he retained that office until his retirement at the age of seventy. Father and Mr. Gates were two of the six "incorporators" of the University, picked by Mr. Rockefeller, Mr. Blake and Mr. Field. And when we boys came home from college for our senior vaction, in the spring of 1890, we were much in and out of the University office.

After my graduate year at Yale I was again at home, on my first job. I was very busy learning to teach in a tutorial group which we called the Owen Academy at Morgan Park. I had come to know William B. Owen in my freshman year at Denison where he was a senior and the most brilliant figure in college. He was our best boxer and also our champion orator, winning the state oratorical contest and losing the national by what his fellow students all considered a rank miscarriage of justice. He had gone on to study theology at the Seminary at Morgan Park, supporting himself meanwhile by tutoring boys for college. The prospective opening of the new University greatly intensified the need for such work and he found himself overwhelmed with demands for tutoring. He associated two or three others with himself in the work and invited me to join the group, to teach beginning Latin and Greek, and before the year ended we had more than a hun-

dred students. It was this prospect of earning some money
for the first time in my life, in association with him, for he
was a most attractive personality, and of learning to teach
under his guidance, that drew me back to my home in Morgan Park, instead of going to Europe with Dr. Harper. And
it was a most fruitful year for me in teaching experience, and
in basic Greek and Latin. The demand was such that we
launched a new class in beginning Latin and another in beginning Greek every three months, and this rapidly repeated
hammering away at the fundamentals simply did wonders for
my knowledge of both languages. Mr. Owen was a wonderful
man to work for, the Seminary let us use such of its class-
rooms as were unoccupied any hours of the day, we had our
own chapel service in the Seminary chapel in Blake Hall—
oh, we could not have been more handsomely treated. The
experience in teaching, too, was immensely valuable to me;
the classes I had were large enough to be genuine audiences,
and included many old friends who had just awakened to
college values. In the summer of '92 President Harper's own
children were among our students, for we worked harder
than ever that last summer before the University opened. It
was really a fabulous year.

Mr. Owen shared Dr. Harper's extraordinary gifts as a
teacher. He went on to his doctor's degree in Greek at the
University, and taught Greek and education at Chicago until
1909 when he became President of the Chicago Normal College. My debt to him was very great. Eventually we published together a little book entitled *Homeric Vocabularies,*
which is still in print.

In that same year 1891-92 when the University was taking
shape and the site was being defined and planned out for
buildings, and the first ones built, Mr. Stagg passed through

Chicago and called at the office of the University. Of course I was overjoyed to see him and he met Charles and my father, all to be friends as long as they lived. Charles and I were then instructed to take him out to the site on the Midway and show him the scene of his future labors. Those were the days of the cable cars and we all jumped on a grip-car and set off visiting gaily. It began to rain, and we climbed up on the seats and stood on them to keep measurably dry. The campus must have made a sad impression on him, but he took it like a man, little thinking that one day two blocks of it would bear his name! The campus was hardly distinguishable from the adjacent Midway, then being dug into shape for the World's Fair of '93, and we brought him around through Jackson Park to the old Rosalie restaurant on Rosalie Court, now Harper Avenue. As we tramped the dreary mud banks interspersed with open water, we had once or twice to hail a passing boat to get to dry land farther on, and vainly tried to explain to the workmen-boatmen the importance of our fellow traveler. Alas! they knew him not. They were not of the Ivy League. But none of us ever forgot the adventurous good-fellowship of that rude introduction of Lonzo to the scene of his future triumphs.

Three or four years later, when the University was really established, I met Lonzo on the campus one day and he said,

"Edgar, come and have lunch with me in Snell."

Snell was the men's dormitory, of which he was the head. I gladly accepted, and presented myself at the proper time in his fine sitting room on the second floor of the building. When lo, there appeared the youngest freshman woman on the campus, Miss Stella Robertson, the other guest of the occasion.

"Edgar," said the Old Man, as we all affectionately called him, "this is Stella!"

Slow as I was in my social perceptions, I perceived that this was an engagement luncheon, and I was the chaperon. What a tribute to my propriety and discretion! I have never had a greater social distinction. And what a union that was, and still is, thank God. Fifty years after, up at the College of the Pacific, at Stockton, Mr. Stagg got into his dinner coat and introduced me to his new college, to give them my lecture, and no introduction could have pleased me more.

All in all Charles and I felt very close to the undertaking when at last on October 1, 1892, the University really opened its doors, being both enrolled in the Graduate School. I had achieved the junior fellowship in Semitics, and Charles was doing a column on the activities at the University for the old Chicago *Evening Journal.* His studies were with Professor Judson, who became the second President of the University, while mine were with President Harper, and later with Professor Burton, who became its third President upon the retirement of Dr. Judson in 1923.

I well remember my first sight of the chateaulike turrets of Cobb Hall, already rising above the dwarf oaks as I bicycled along Fifty-seventh Street in the spring of 1892, and a few months later as I walked in and out of Cobb on the plank which, until the sidewalks were finished a few days after college opened, was our only means of access to it.

And how well I remember one day when President Harper climbed the stairs to our fourth-floor rooms in what is now Blake Hall in search of Father, and looking out eastward at the rising dormitories across the campus and the World's Fair buildings far beyond, he said very earnestly to me,

"Edgar, stay in the Graduate School as long as you can!"

This advice I certainly carried out to the full, for I stayed in it for six years.

The President rightly felt that the standing of the University in the eyes of the country would be largely determined by the stature of the individual men he brought to it, especially as heads of departments. When he prevailed upon J. Laurence Laughlin and William Gardner Hale to leave Cornell for Chicago, he let the world know how he was headed, and when he got A. A. Michelson in physics scientific men were positively incredulous. When Albion W. Small left the presidency of Colby, and Thomas C. Chamberlin that of the University of Wisconsin to become heads of departments at Chicago, his critics gave up the fight. The President knew all this and smiled a little over it.

"They thought I was going to organize a theological seminary," he observed. But that too he did, bringing Ernest D. Burton, Charles R. Henderson, and later George B. Foster to strengthen the staff of the Divinity School. That was to be expected. But what astonished the country was the strength of the President's scientific staff. Whitman, H. H. Donaldson, George E. Hale, Jacques Loeb, E. H. Moore, John U. Nef, R. D. Salisbury—these were men high up in the national scientific roster whom the President had persuaded to cast their lot with the Chicago enterprise. Some of their old colleagues derided their folly; it was only a paper university, they declared. But the President prevailed. He made them see his vision and they came. A little later John M. Coulter came from the presidency of Lake Forest to head botany. The departments of political science, headed by Dr. Judson, and of sociology, headed by Dr. Small, were almost the first such departments in America. Oh, it was a stirring world that W. R., himself only thirty-six years old, was making on the Midway.

President Harper built his small department of astronomy about an associate professor, George E. Hale, aged twenty-four, who already had his own observatory with a twelve-inch refracting telescope on his father's grounds in Kenwood. This alert young man learned that a forty-inch lens for the greatest refracting telescope in the world had been ordered, and cast by Alvan Clark in Cambridge, but could not be paid for by its sponsors and was on the market. This he communicated to President Harper. Hearing that Mr. Charles T. Yerkes, the streetcar magnate, was thinking of doing some large act of benevolence, they went together to see him and lay the telescope proposition before him. He listened patiently for a while, and they began to fear they had not moved him, when he said,

"Gentlemen, you interest me more than you perhaps think, for in my school days in Philadelphia the stars interested me more than anything else I studied, and I once told my playmates that some day I was going to make a lot of money and then I was going to build the biggest telescope in the world, and an observatory to put it in!"

So it was that within a week after the University opened, my father could inform the press that Mr. Yerkes would provide the University with the greatest refracting telescope in the world, and an observatory to house it.

How it came about I do not know but I was one of the very few students who one October day five years later witnessed the dedication of the Yerkes Observatory at Williams Bay on Lake Geneva. We were a very congenial group of four, two men and two girls, who took the special train, voyaged in the yachts and launches gathered to meet us, heard the addresses, shared—meagerly—in the luncheon, and in short made a day of it. I remember the girls so well, but really I cannot remember the name of the other man!

In George E. Hale President Harper had a man after his own heart. For he went on to still greater things in telescopes and observatories, instituting the Carnegie Institution Observatory on Mt. Wilson, with its great one hundred-inch reflecting telescope, and then the far greater two hundred-inch reflecting telescope on Mt. Palomar—called the Hale telescope, in his honor. Yet the drama does not end even here. For the Yerkes forty-inch refractor has never been surpassed or equaled in refracting telescopes, and Mr. Yerkes' boyhood dream in a sense really came true. Much of this story has come to me from Mrs. Hale herself, to whom I am most grateful.

This dream of strong departments was further realized by the bringing of John Dewey to the University from Michigan in 1894 and John M. Manly from Brown in 1898, in philosophy and English respectively. And this tradition President Judson in his turn faithfully carried on with such success that when in the nineteen-twenties foundations of one sort or another took to ranking universities by the number of absolutely top departments they possessed, by two such bodies Chicago was actually ranked first in the country. Oh that W. R. could have lived to see the day!

The University was located in a rather isolated and unsettled place, and as many of us roomed in the new dormitories, a dining department was set up in the basements of the three dormitories. Charles and I thought a good deal of our enjoyment of the year would depend on whom we shared a table with, so we hurriedly cast about and among our new associates and our old college friends who had turned up at the new institution we assembled a group of congenial men. I brought in Asada, the senior fellow in Semitics, and Theodore Soares, who roomed near us in Graduate Hall and was studying with the President. He brought in his Minnesota friends Triggs and Tunell. Charles brought in J. A. Smith, a Denison friend of 1889. Clifford W. Barnes, whom I had met at Yale, and who was working in church history, also joined us. We had a most congenial group, and when President Harper had occasion to remain on the campus for an evening appointment we were gratified that he generally ate with us! My father was also an occasional visitor. The social fellowship was far superior to the food we ate and made it a memorable and most agreeable year. Soares and Asada were great raconteurs and often kept us enthralled long after the other tables were vacated.

The students of that first year were in general a remarkable crowd. Among the graduate students, who were very numerous, many were planning books they meant to write or were already at work upon. The spirit of research and publication was in the air. Most of the faculty were full of it, and the President did all he could to encourage it. There was also a great zest in the sense we had of inaugurating new things, clubs, journals, papers, traditions, songs. There is, of course, a great charm and value in tradition, and in the sense of carrying on a great past, but there is also a vivid attraction about feeling yourself one of the founders of student customs and institutions.

I found myself not only the secretary of the Christian Union, busy getting the speakers for the chapel meetings Sunday evenings, but also secretary of the Semitic Club, which met every two or three weeks at the President's House on Washington (now Blackstone) Avenue.

The President was very anxious about the first convocation in Central Music Hall, on January 2, 1893. As he stepped into the Illinois Central train, after it was over, he saw me seated in the car and said to me,

"I want to make sure your father has got the address and the statement about the convocation into the hands of the papers. Please go around to the newspaper offices and make sure." I went immediately and of course Father had duly covered them all. I knew he must have done so, but it showed W. R.'s eye for detail. He did not for a moment forget that the University was that night making its bow to the city.

When the social structure of the University was being created, the position of student head marshal emerged and I was approached as a suitable candidate for the first of what has proved a long succession. But I pointed out that as a graduate student I was no man for the post which I clearly saw ought to be the highest undergraduate honor, as it has, I think, proved. And yet it was kind of those first framers of our social structure to think of me.

Of course, the faculty there gathered for the first time was of the utmost distinction or promise, and with them many of us became lifelong friends. An extraordinary atmosphere of high hope and expectancy prevailed, a great deal of which was later realized. We all plunged with great eagerness into our several tasks. I remember I went on in Assyrian with Robert F. Harper, the President's younger brother, and later took up Syriac and Ethiopic with the President. When George Berry and I wanted to go on further in those languages and told Rabbi Emil G. Hirsch so, he generously offered to meet us twice a week in them. Yet he was one of the busiest men in Chicago, and serving at the University in Rabbinics.

The Rabbi soon after very handsomely offered a prize of $150 for the best piece of work in Semitics of the year (I believe it was the second year, 1893-94), and Berry and I both wrote long Assyriological papers in competition for it. Each of us transcribed, translated and annotated a series of ancient Assyrian letters. Professor Robert F. Harper who regarded us as about equally proficient could not choose between us and declared the prize should be equally divided. Dr. Hirsch not unnaturally waited for him to publish the winning papers in *Hebraica* of which he was the managing editor, but he was not disposed to do so. After some time, however, Robert boldly advanced Berry his half of the prize, or seventy-five dollars, on the plea that he was married and needed the money. The Rabbi was as good as his word and reimbursed Robert. But for me Robert would not take the same risk. For a long time I looked eagerly at the Convocation program from quarter to quarter hoping to see our names recorded as prize winners, but they never appeared. I do not think there is anywhere any official record of our dividing the Hirsch Semitic prize—if we did.

Very early in the history of the University I remember the Honorable Chauncey Depew, then Senator from New York, the most famous after-dinner speaker of his day, visited the campus. He was hailed by a good-sized gathering of students out of doors among the dwarf oaks of what is now Hull Court. He told us among other things how many of the presidents of the United States he had known—a surprising number, which brought home to us how really young our government was, since one lifetime could reach back so far toward its beginnings. He was born in 1834, and lived to be ninety-four years of age.

One of my fellowship duties was to correct in red ink the Hebrew exercise book turned in from day to day by the beginners in Hebrew, who were of course fairly numerous. One day I was called into conference by Professor Ira M. Price who was in charge, for having put some red ink on an exercise written by my good friend Theodore Soares; what was wrong with it? I examined it with some apprehension. But I explained that while in English we *call* the light day, in Hebrew we *call to* the light day, a point on which Genesis nobly sustained me, and I survived. This remained a standing joke between Theodore and myself for many years. He was quite unaccustomed to having anyone put red ink on his academic papers.

But much as I enjoyed doing these exercise books, at the year's end I decided to relinquish my $25 a month and take over my brother's job on the *Evening Journal*, Mayor Carter Harrison's paper. (Charles was now in law school.) Thus I became that lowest form of academic life, a student reporter. All went well at first. I wrote what I considered a sprightly column as to why the University was to have no summer session the first summer, 1893. I was well aware that the lack of funds for it was the true cause, but thought a brighter picture might be given by pointing out that the Midway Plaisance on which the University was located was to be the scene of the World's Fair concessions, and the Ferris wheel and the Street in Cairo were to face the campus, over a board fence, and the everlasting racket caused by the latter made concentration impossible. I considered this a very proper piece of student journalism, a little on the bright side, but quite unobjectionable. I learned to my regret (from my father!)

that Dr. Harper was a little displeased at such a pleasantry on what was to him a sore subject. But my journalistic labors went on uninterrupted until some miscreant put an end to them by shooting my editor, Mayor Harrison! Some political misunderstanding, I believe.

How well I remember a pep session held in my student days in Kent Theater, then the largest hall on the campus, when a popular hurdler, Steigmeyer, dressed as I remember it in a clown's costume, perilously mounted a folding chair and sang for the first time a song of his own composition, beginning,

> Oh we came here in the autumn of 1893;
> A half a dozen buildings had then the U. of C.

The influence of this song is such that many people actually think the University first opened its doors in 1893, reminding us of the man who said that he didn't care who wrote the laws of a country, if he could write its songs. But it is something to have been on hand when Steig's song had its premiere, rendered by the author in person! The effect of it, I may add, was simply electrical.

In my student days at Chicago Elizabeth Wallace, one of the chief ornaments of the Graduate School, and I quite unconsciously originated, though we did not organize, the Western Intercollegiate Tennis Tournament. It was about '96 or '97. Her brother Tom was champion at Minnesota, and I felt that Carr Neel at Chicago was unbeatable, so we brought them together on the courts of the Kenwood Country Club. When I reminded them of this a few years ago at Pasadena, Tom laughed and said that Carr had beaten him. Indeed Carr later divided national honors with Larned, some experts rating Carr, and others Larned, top man. As Miss Wallace has not included this youthful exploit in her delightful memoirs, *The Unending Journey*, I may be allowed to do so.

My only other athletic feat as a graduate student was helping to judge the hammer throw at a track and field meet. No fault was found with my proficiency in this delicate task, and I almost succeeded in keeping out of the way of the hammer as that weighty object bounced along the outfield, the handle merely tapping me lightly on the wrist as it passed. Still it does show my devotion to my duties, doesn't it? I was right on the spot where it hit the ground!

The fifth anniversary of the founding of the University was signalized by a visit from Mr. and Mrs. Rockefeller, the first visit paid by the founder to his foundation. I remember particularly their presence in Haskell Museum, which was being shown them, and Father's introducing my mother to Mr. Rockefeller. Mr. Rockefeller turned at once to Mrs. Rockefeller, saying,

"This is Mrs. Goodspeed, the wife of Dr. Goodspeed."

"*Our* Dr. Goodspeed?" said Mrs. Rockefeller simply, taking my mother's hand, and these three words, spoken in such a natural and friendly way, quite won my mother's heart.

My Assyrian studies left one deep impression upon me. Professor Harper, whom his friends always spoke of as "R. F." to distinguish him from his famous brother "W. R.," had a way of pushing back his spectacles—he was very shortsighted —and saying of this or that Assyriologist, "He's published nothing—absolutely nothing!"

This repeated remark made a deep impression upon me. I took it even more seriously than R. F. meant it. For the problem then in Assyriology was to get before the world in accessible form the vast hoard of tablets that had been unearthed, and awaited study, and how could they be studied until they were published in transcription or even photographs? His demand upon his fellow Assyriologists was perfectly just and sound. That was their first duty, to their subject and to their public. I knew this, and yet it came to mean far more to me than that. I vaguely felt that any good research man should find results worth publication, and then take the additional pains to publish them.

It must have been after my second graduate year at Chicago that Dr. Burton one day called on me and suggested that I might be interested in transferring my studies to the New Testament field. I am sure he and the President must have talked of this change, for it would have been most unethical otherwise for him to suggest it. I was much attracted. I greatly admired Dr. Burton, and in teaching preparatory Greek through Homer for two or three years, on the side, I had come to feel attracted more to Greek than to Hebrew. Dr. Burton struck me as a remarkably acute and able scholar, as indeed he proved to be, in lexicography, syntax and interpretation. So I took up New Testament Greek and interpretation, as my principal subject for my degree. Of course, this set me back two or three years in reaching it, but I had really ceased to take account of time. And when it is remembered that so many men hasten to their degrees by the shortest possible route, my course will seem the more strange. Yet in the stresses and tests that were to come, how wise this policy proved!

Not long after I joined his banner, Dr. Burton invited me to work on his Greek harmony of the gospels of Matthew, Mark and Luke, on which he was engaged. He proposed to make this a minute and exhaustive exhibit of their resemblances and differences, and laid out the work for me. I pitched in with great zest, for to work with him on a specific task I thought would teach me more about his methods than any amount of lectures. This enterprise was to occupy much of my leisure for years. For when after a year or two I showed him my results he had developed further ideas for perfecting the book and I went back to it and carried them out. After I took my degree and went abroad I returned to the task. I was now the junior man in his department. But he had hit upon a new idea for arranging the gospel materials and published an account of it that led German scholars like Huck to adopt it at once and reorganize their Greek harmonies. I proceeded to reorganize ours in the light of this new principle, which was simply to distinguish material in parallel sections from material in nonparallel sections. It sounds perfectly obvious but no previous harmonist had arrived at it. When this new improvement was introduced into our book, it was finished. But it was a very expensive book to print for it was in three columns with a deep margin, and the University of Chicago Press would not undertake it.

I then suggested to Dr. Burton that we should put the harmony into English, using the American Standard Version, and he should offer it to Mr. Lord at Scribner's; perhaps we could make the English pay for the Greek. He did so, and Mr. Lord at once accepted it. I then spent one hundred days preparing the English edition from the Greek manuscript of our book, and it is still widely used. But it required three specialists to restore me to my normal health after this frantic exertion. That was in 1917, at least twenty years after Dr. Burton had first taken the book up with me. But three years later, with the generous aid of President Judson, we were able to produce it in Greek at the University of Chicago Press. I have often said that Dr. Burton supplied the brains for this book while I supplied the brawn. But I was proud to have any part in a work which in Greek and in English still holds an indispensable place in synoptic study.

The coming of Professor Shailer Mathews to the University in 1894 greatly reinforced the New Testament department on the historical side and did much for me in most significant ways. His freshness and originality of approach made him a most engaging and stimulating teacher, and he made himself in many ways his students' friend. I can say this with more force than any of the rest of us, for it was he who in 1900 introduced me to the girl I married, and the great happiness of my life. He himself always said it was the best thing he ever did!

It was Dr. Burton's bringing of Professor Gregory to the University for a single term in the summer quarter of 1895 that gave a new direction to my studies, and opened the whole world of manuscript study to me, and my students after me. So my change of department that year definitely shaped all the rest of my life.

And when at long last I took my Doctor of Philosophy degree, in the spring of 1898, it was R. F. Harper, my professor of Assyrian, who very generously moved that my grade be *summa*. Why, for a day or two after the examination I was in doubt whether I had even passed! I remember the next afternoon seeing Dr. Burton ride up to our house on Kimbark Avenue on his bicycle to tell me the result of my examination. They signed such papers in those days and my diplomas have the signatures of Mr. Ryerson, Mr. MacLeish and Father, for the Trustees, and of President Harper, Professor Burton, my cousin George (as Recorder), Dean Salisbury and Dean Hulbert for the faculty.

The morning of my oral examination my South Side classes were dismissed and somebody asked Anthony James, one of my lively young people, where I was. Anthony was the son of Edmund J. James, our famous professor of public administration.

"He's having his Ph.D. examination," Anthony replied, "but we're all praying for him!"

I took this interest in my success very kindly of Anthony. His father soon left the University for the presidency of Northwestern, and soon after went on to that of the University of Illinois where he remained for many years. Anthony I believe entered the navy.

At the evening convocation at which I took my degree in March of 1898, President Harper quietly instructed Nott Flint, the Head Marshal, to have me head the Ph.D. candidates as they came up for their degrees, a kindness on his part that I greatly appreciated. I suppose it was in recognition of the fact that I had been in residence as a graduate student longer than the others. But what a man he was for detail and the smaller courtesies of life most men overlook.

Soon after, the President informed me that I was to be added to the New Testament department as Assistant, without salary, for two years, when I would begin to receive a thousand dollars a year as an Associate. But I must go abroad for two years to visit the German universities first. I confess that this seemed a little superfluous, as I had already spent more years in resident graduate University study than any man I had ever heard of. But my long-suffering father was willing to back me, and away I went. I have since suspected that the President was trying to get for me what he considered an ideal preparation for work on the University level. And times were coming when I had reason to be glad of every ounce of world-wide experience and seasoned learning I should accumulate.

SEVEN

Adventures with Manuscripts

IT WAS in 1895 that Caspar René Gregory came from the University of Leipzig to lecture for half the summer quarter in the new University of Chicago. I had turned away from Semitics and Old Testament to the New Testament field and joyfully welcomed his coming. I took both his courses, Greek Paleography and New Testament Textual Criticism, and that short contact with Gregory opened a new world to me, and greatly influenced my subsequent studies and students.

Gregory was an American, of French descent, and had a most boyish and winning way in his classroom. He had gone to the University of Pennsylvania and to Princeton Seminary, then to the University of Leipzig where he once saw Tischendorf across the yard. But when Tischendorf was suddenly incapacitated and Ezra Abbot of Harvard was asked to complete the introduction to his eighth edition of the Greek New Testament, upon which Tischendorf had been engaged, he suggested Mr. Gregory. Thus Gregory became the author of the great introduction, with its amazing catalogue of Greek and other manuscript sources for the New Testament text.

Gregory traveled tirelessly about the Mediterranean visiting remote convent libraries, listing and describing Greek manuscripts as no one had ever done the job before, and thus made himself the greatest expert on Greek manuscripts in the world. He had married the eldest daughter of Professor Joseph Henry Thayer, of Harvard, the great New Testament lexicographer, but he was becoming more and more German in his tastes and point of view. In my later student days in Germany I was delightfully entertained by Professor and Mrs. Gregory in Stötteritz, the suburb of Leipzig.

Greogry had an extraordinary gift, a religious passion in fact, for cultivating every sort of person. In the course of a visit to the North Side he fell in with a man who had a Greek manuscript of the Gospels, which Professor Burton authorized him to buy for the University, for twenty dollars! It was a fifteenth-century manuscript, of slight importance, but it became the nucleus of the Chicago collection of such materials, now rivaled in America only by that of the University of Michigan. It was the first Greek manuscript I had ever seen, and I pounced upon it. In text it was so ordinary that when I compared a couple of pages of it with Erasmus' third edition of the Greek New Testament, the one Tyndale translated and made the basis of the first English New Testament, there was not the difference of a single letter.

Gregory found that there was a very nice little manuscript of the Greek Gospels in the Newberry Library, and I was soon deep in the job of comparing its text in great detail with the old "received" text, the one prevalent in medieval manuscripts; in fact, I eventually made that manuscript my thesis subject. This made me a veritable habitué of that hospitable institution. Those were the days of John Vance Cheney and his mysterious and redoubtable assistant Alexander T. Rudolph, who invented the card catalogue system used there. Another man then on the staff was Dr. Karl

Pietsch, who was later brought to the University and ended his days in its service. All these gentlemen were very obliging and I was even occasionally allowed a large vacant room on the third floor for my study whenever I brought one of my Greek students from the South Side Academy up with me, to read the Greek New Testament aloud while I followed with the manuscript. My own experience convinced me that there is nothing like fresh, unpublished manuscript material to stimulate student interest in textual study.

I was vaguely aware that before the ancient world wrote on parchment it used papyrus, sheets of which the ancient Egyptians made out of strips of the pith of the papyrus plant, very much as modern plywood is made. They then pasted these sheets together into rolls of any desired length. The Greeks, the book publishers of antiquity, called this *biblos*, and a scroll of it of convenient length, say twenty-five feet, a *biblion*, a "book." The plural of this word, *ta biblia*, "the books," came to be the name of the Bible—*The* Books, par excellence.

But it was not until my last graduate year at Chicago that I saw my first Greek papyrus. I heard of it one night at the New Testament Club, when Dr. Clyde W. Votaw said there was a Greek papyrus in Dr. Breasted's office. Next morning I called on my old friend James Henry Breasted and asked about it. He got it right out and in five minutes there I was, well started on the downward path to papyrology. He had come across it in the Field Museum to which Mr. Edward E. Ayer had given it. Mr. Ayer had seen it in Egypt three years before, had paid five pounds for it and brought it to Chicago. I spent the morning on it and made a rough copy—it was not difficult—but unfortunately it was mathematical, and that was a field in which I had not shone in college! When I got up to

go Dr. Breasted generously observed that if I wanted to publish it, I might go ahead as he had no designs on it.

It turned out to be my first venture into that field and it
introduced me to a new world of scholars and interests; it
even made me a collector. For as soon as I had got the hang
of the thing, and obtained the generous and highly interested
aid of some of the men I knew in the department of mathematics, I sent a transcript of it to men whose names I knew
abroad, among others to Bernard Grenfell at Oxford, then
just breaking into fame by the discovery of the Sayings of
Jesus fragment at Oxyrhynchus. He was most helpful and
between him and my mathematical mentors I really made
quite a creditable thing of it. Best of all, it seemed to present
a glimpse of pre-Euclidean geometry for while the man's
geometrical formulas were quite like Euclid's (which we all
know from our geometry in school) the only way my author
knew for calculating the area of a plane figure was to cut it
into rectangles and right-angled triangles and multiply
height by width, for the rectangles, or half that, for the
triangles. It is all done in Egyptian arourae (the aroura was
roughly two thirds of an acre) and was evidently a portion
of a sort of surveyor's manual. But it is written in fine book
letters and the geometrical figures are very nicely done, the
length of each side of each figure being plainly marked upon
it.

It was certainly a great joke on me to be drawn back to
mathematics in spite of myself, through encountering this
papyrus. For of course I could not possibly resist it, and it
must be admitted the mathematics were of the easiest kind
imaginable. But it was my introduction to a new field, in
which no American had up to that time taken a hand, and
it also served to introduce me to a whole string of European

workers in Greek papyri, most notably Bernard Grenfell
and Arthur Hunt, at Oxford, who later became my generous
friends.

With it also I made my little bow to the world of learning,
for in 1898 Professor Basil L. Gildersleeve graciously accepted
it for the *American Journal of Philology* as making in its
very mild degree what we are all so eager to make—a contribution to knowledge. Why, I even read papers before mathematical societies about it, a thing which would have astonished my old professor of mathematics no end!

Having tasted research, I soon became a victim of it. I felt
I must have more papyri to decipher and if possible publish.
I wanted pieces that had not been deciphered to see what I
could make of them, and through my friend Dr. Breasted
I was able to buy from a dealer in Assiut a small collection
that had not been studied. Into this enterprise I poured my
modest student savings, and when the two large tin cigarette
boxes at last made their appearance, James and I repaired
to my mother's kitchen, and with a steaming kettle carefully
softened and unrolled the two sizable rolls which were the
most impressive pieces they contained. We felt as Wordsworth thought the men must have felt who unrolled the
charred rolls from the philosopher's house at Herculaneum:

> O ye who patiently explore
> The wreck of Herculanean lore!
> What rapture, could ye seize
> Some Theban fragment, or unroll
> One precious, tender-hearted scroll
> Of pure Simonides!

There was certainly no Simonides among my papyri, for
the two scrolls, though they were of noble proportions, one

being about eight and a half feet long and eight and a half inches high, the other about three feet by eight and a half inches, were columns of most painstaking accounts, in double entry bookkeeping, from the last part of the second century after Christ. They were the work of some estate managers who kept careful records day by day and month by month of every drachma they paid out or took in. The long one which was inscribed on both sides ran to no less than forty-six columns, or over twelve hundred items. The bookkeeper's reed pen sometimes grew so blunt it was no better than a stick, and then, behold! he sharpened it, and his strokes were immediately clear and fine. When I went abroad a few months later, I took both these pieces with me and at the Neues Museum in Berlin had the generous and competent aid on the hardest spots of the beloved Fritz Krebs, then in charge of the Berlin Greek papyri. He and Ulrich Wilcken of Wuerzburg were then considered the best Greek papyrus paleographers in Germany.

The months covered by the entries run from Athur to Pachon, that is, from October to April, but no year of an emperor is anywhere given, except that in one entry a thirty-second and a current thirty-third year are mentioned. No Roman emperor of the probable period of the papyrus reigned so long, but Krebs pointed out to me that Commodus, the "schlimmer Kerl," as he described him, was accustomed to figure his reign from his predecessor's accession, thus giving it what he evidently considered a gratifying length! This would make the period covered by the accounts roughly October, A.D. 191, to April, A.D. 192.

There were a few literary pieces in my tin boxes from Assiut—two nice little pieces of Homer, a column of a medical treatise—a sort of home book of medicine it seemed to be—and a meager scrap of Isocrates. But the oddest part of the shipment was a stack of grain receipts strung on the sturdy brown thread on which the systematic Roman record-keepers had filed them back in the days of Antoninus Pius, A.D. 138-161. They were receipts given by the peasants who raised grain to be shipped to Rome, and who were assigned small quantities of seed grain with which to sow their fields. These receipts, small slips mostly about two by three and a half inches, were carefully dated, almost all of them in the twenty-second year of Antoninus, A.D. 158. The office made up a sort of blank, addressed to the grain officials at Karanis, a place in the Fayum, stating what the receipt was for and giving the year; then when the farmer appeared for his grain his name, his father's name, his village (that is, his address!) and the size of his holding, in Egyptian acres, were written, or at least scrawled in. The form part of each document was also usually much abbreviated, and this, taken with the careless and uneducated handwriting of many of them, made their decipherment a discouraging undertaking.—Until Professor Frank Tarbell of the Classics department, who had heard of my labors, discovered that my subsequent friend Krebs and his colleagues in Berlin possessed forty-three of these bewildering little puzzles and had deciphered and published them in their archive.

This was great good news and much needed for I was the fortunate possessor of no less than ninety-one of these papyrus riddles of which only one was carefully spelled out in full to the last letter! Evidently the Arab who had found them, or bought them from their finder, had hoarded these strange little slips and when opportunity offered had sold about one third of them to some German representative, saving the majority for a rainy day and perhaps a better price. I accordingly worked out my string to the best of my ability, and later in Germany reread the forty-three at Berlin, revised my own with Krebs's aid, and published the whole collection of one hundred and thirty-four in the Chicago Classical Studies. It was an amusing reunion.

Another tiny slip of papyrus of about the same size proved to be a boat ticket, being the second one that has been found. The first was in Lord Amherst's famous collection, now in the Morgan Library in New York. Mine gives the passenger's name, his father's name, describes him as "Passenger from Karanis," and gives the name of the pilot, and his father's name. Thus:

> Ptolemy son of Psenomgeus
> Passenger from Karanis
> Isidore son of Isidore pilot
> Even full.

This last line, which has given rise to many a ribald suggestion, probably means that the boat was full and evenly loaded and was all in the charge of the said Ptolemy, who was evidently what we would call the supercargo. The Morgan ticket is without this fourth line. My ticket was shown at a University affair at Chicago and President James R. Angell, then Vice-President there, held it up to the light and exclaimed,

"Why, of course it's a boat-ticket! You can see where it's been punched!" and it does exhibit plenty of perforations, the effects of time.

Back in the early days of the Hyde Park Y.M.C.A. before it grew up and built its present imposing building, it occupied a large old frame house and to it I sometimes accompanied my brother on his way to its committee meetings.

There I made the acquaintance of the janitor who turned out to be a Syrian. I soon learned that he had brought with him from Syria a New Testament manuscript in Syriac which I prevailed upon him to lend me. I explored it with great interest, for my Semitic studies had included Syriac. I made a study of its text—it was, of course, of the ordinary Peshito version, of twenty-two books—and this I offered as my thesis for my B.D. degree.

Incidentally, I learned from my Syrian friend that there was a Syrian student, Mooshie Georges, at McCormick Seminary who had a Syriac manuscript, so I searched him out at his room there and inquired about it. The poor fellow turned pale at my question. It was his secret and he feared to have it known for it was I suppose the family fortune. But he let me study it in his room and even photograph a leaf or two.

It was impossible for me in those days to capture either of these manuscripts, and they floated on by me, and disappeared. But one day many years later, Dr. Burton summoned me to the Library to look over a Syriac manuscript that was being offered him. After examining it I said it reminded me strangely of one I had seen years before in the hands of Mooshie Georges, at McCormick Seminary. He drily observed that it was Mr. Mooshie Georges' son who was now offering it for sale. It's a small world. In the end I believe Mr. Cyrus H. McCormick bought it for the McCormick Seminary.

One brief footnote may complete the story of my Syriac holiday from Greek manuscripts. It was well known to such researchers that a Syriac New Testament manuscript belonging to the Syrian Protestant College in Beirut was preserved in the safe of the Union Theological Seminary in New York. So one day in New York I called there and asked to be allowed to see it. But it was vacation time and the person who would have been authorized to open the safe to let me examine it was absent. My disappointment over this lost opportunity was allayed when a few weeks later the Seminary through the kindness of Mr. D. Stuart Dodge, sent the manuscript, a magnificent thing, all the way to Chicago for me to study at my leisure. This was generosity indeed.

I soon found out that while most of it was Peshito text, the gospels had been explored by Professor Isaac H. Hall twenty years before and were believed by him to represent a pre-Harclean text, probably the long lost Philoxenian. I thought it more probably represented the Harclean revision of A.D. 616 and published my views, with the Syriac text of the first twenty pages of Matthew, in the *Journal of Biblical Literature* in 1906, a view which British study of the manuscript made by F. C. Burkitt, of Cambridge, confirmed thirty years later. All of which puts the manuscript in a very distinguished class indeed, for only some fifty Harclean manuscripts of the gospels are thus far known. But to this day I never meet a Syrian of high or low degree without sounding him on manuscripts.

These experiences with ancient manuscripts, Greek and Syriac, parchment and papyrus, formed only my introduction to the subject and to the field which was to prove so highly adventurous for me for at least forty years. But my subsequent adventures with manuscripts are too deeply interwoven with my later life to be anticipated here.

EIGHT

Foreign Shores

THROUGH all my graduate years at Chicago after the first I was also steadily engaged in teaching beginning Greek, Xenophon and Homer to the young people in the South Side Academy, an experience which of course did wonders for my basic knowledge of the language. I felt the absurdity of reading the splendid narratives of Homer in the piecemeal fashion that seemed unavoidable, so I organized a Homer Club among the better students. We would meet once a week and one of us, carefully prepared, would smoothly and rapidly translate one whole book of the *Odyssey* or the *Iliad* while the rest of us followed the reading with the Greek text before us. We met around at one another's houses, one evening, I remember, through the kindness of President Harper's daughter Davida, meeting around his library table in the President's House. So while I was reading the Hebrew Bible through at the University, I was covering the *Iliad* and the *Odyssey* with my young people. I afterward introduced this method with my graduate students, reading patristic Greek with those so inclined, over our after-dinner coffee for half an hour or more before the New Testament Club meetings. I still possess a beautiful silver-mounted cane they presented to me as a souvenir of the Patristic Club, as we called these informal gatherings.

The President, as I have said, felt that two years abroad would be necessary to fill out my preparation for my life-work, as he saw it, and I accordingly journeyed to Germany, and spent a semester at Berlin, taking Adolf Harnack's lectures and attending his seminar as a visitor. I took most of my papyri with me and worked them over with the generous aid of Fritz Krebs at the Neues Museum, on Unter den Linden, where I shared the workroom with W. Schubart. At the University I heard the lectures of Bernhard Weiss, Otto Pfleiderer, and Hermann Baron von Soden, and occasionally of Ulrich von Wilamowitz-Moellendorf and Paulsen. I also belonged to Schoene's seminar in Greek paleography. In the American church and colony I made some delightful friends. It was altogether a memorable semester. There were some fine American students in Harnack's lecture audience, Gerald B. Smith, A. A. Berle, whose son has since been active in the State Department, and D. I. Coon, among them. I made great progress at the Museum, with Krebs's aid, on my last problems in deciphering my long papyrus scroll, and my ninety-one grain receipts.

In February I broke away for a tour of the Luther country, Eisleben, Erfurt, Wittenberg, and the Wartburg, and went on to the chief universities where serious Greek and biblical research was carried on. First, Halle, where I met and heard Friedrich Blass, whom Oxford rated the foremost classical scholar in Europe; Willibald Beyschlag, the veteran New Testament theologian; and E. Kautzsch, the great authority on Old Testament history and the Apocrypha. At Göttingen I heard and met Emil Schuerer, the great historian of the Jewish people, stopped at Weimar for its associations with

Goethe, and went on to Jena, where I met and heard Ernst von Dobschuetz and H. H. Wendt, two of the leading New Testament men in Germany. At Leipzig I renewed my acquaintance with Gregory, and met Oskar von Gebhardt, who had done so much in patristics.

I had a delightful stay in Dresden, where I heard Ysaye play, and of course saw the pictures. I went down to Prag, and Brünn, where the frowning prison of the Spielberg reminded me of Silvio Pellico and I Miei Prigioni! And so on to Vienna where I had a rendezvous with the Archduke Rainer papyri, and saw them with their chief interpreter, Franz Wessely, who had helped to train most of the Greek papyrus scholars of Europe. I met Professor Josef von Karabacek, who told me of the death of the Archduke Ernst, the emperor's last brother. The state funeral a day or two later was a most impressive sight.

It seemed a pity not to run down to Budapest for a few days and I found that city and the Danube full of interest. I turned back through the Tyrol—Salzburg and Innsbruck—and then on to Munich with its wonderful galleries. Here I found some delightful Americans, and also a Scottish couple, the Archibald Smiths, of Edinburgh. At Tübingen I had a memorable visit with Carl von Weizsaecker who among other things had made a modern German translation of the New Testament. Then down through the Black Forest to Strassburg, another great center of New Testament learning. But how could I know that a young man of great promise named Albert Schweitzer was just taking his degree that year—perhaps that very month—and was destined to win such extraordinary fame in philosophy, criticism, music and medicine? Why, I may have brushed against him in the halls of Strassburg, that May 17, 1899!

I met Theodor Noeldeke, who was retired and met his small classes in his house, and these groups served to revive my interest in Ethiopic. I hastened on to call at Heidelberg, visit the library, and have the sunset hour in the Schloss garden. Then on by Mainz and Frankfurt to Giessen, where Gustav Krueger has always been my friend. At Marburg I found my Berlin friends the Gerald Smiths and H. B. Carré, and we had a marvelous reunion, comparing notes on the German universities as we had seen them.

Touching at Bonn, my fifteenth German university, on my way down the Rhine, I settled down at last at The Hague, where the genial librarian of the Royal Library sent back to Dresden for a manuscript I had discovered some value in, and borrowed it for my use. I also caught up with my Scottish friends the Archibald Smiths, and from The Hague as a base saw Holland with them.

It was at Mainz I think—I had hardly finished the arduous course in German universities that President Harper had coveted for me—that I received a letter of great importance. It was from Mr. Joseph Bond of Chicago, whom Dean Mathews had interested in my further education. He very generously offered me five hundred dollars to enable me to visit Egypt and the Holy Land the following winter. Of course I welcomed the opportunity. But as it turned out Mr. Bond's gift was to do infinitely more for me than take me to Palestine.

From The Hague I went on to London and Oxford for a wonderful summer. I found my way speedily into the manuscript room of the British Museum and soon got hold of some promising patristic pieces in Ethiopic. Mr. F. G. Kenyon and Dr. E. A. W. Budge were most obliging. I ran down to Oxford one day in June to see it on commencement day and was rewarded by seeing two great Englishmen, Cecil Rhodes and Lord Kitchener, walking together in the procession into the Schools Quadrangle to receive the D.C.L. With an American friend I went out to Henley to see the regatta. Some other American friends took me on a bicycle tour to the Isle of Wight and at Queen's Club I witnessed a Yale-Harvard-Oxford-Cambridge track meet which resulted Oxford-Cambridge 5, Harvard 4, Yale, alas! o. Naturally, I suffered. But I saw, from afar, Walter Camp, and the Prince of Wales, afterward Edward VII.

An old University friend, Fulton Coffin, and I then went to Oxford for a University Extension meeting. We were to live in New College, hear all sorts of lectures, see the colleges, and absorb Oxford generally. It proved a most interesting experience.

The young Duke and Duchess of Marlborough received all of us extensionists at a garden party in Blenheim Palace, a few miles from Oxford. She was Consuelo Vanderbilt and was a beautiful and gracious figure, and as I write has just published as Madame Balsan, *The Glitter and the Gold,* the rather somber story of her life. We heard and met Canon William Sanday, the leading New Testament man in Britain, and his leading student Kirsopp Lake very kindly took me to his seminar; Lake and I were to be lifelong friends. At Queen's I called on Bernard Grenfell, who had been so very helpful about the Ayer papyrus, and he and Hunt welcomed me cordially, had me to dine in hall, and told me of their plans of excavation for the following winter. Grenfell also offered to take me about to call on anybody I wanted to meet in Oxford. His recent discovery of the Sayings of Jesus at Oxyrhynchus had of course made him a well-known man though he was only a year or two my senior. They even went so far as to say that if they found very much in their next digging in Egypt I might come back to Oxford and work on it with them, a most handsome offer. Canon Sanday very kindly told Professor R. H. Charles of Dublin of my interest in Ethiopic, and this led to some very helpful interviews with Charles the following summer, in his big study in Oxford.

Meantime, my old friend Professor W. D. MacClintock of Chicago had arrived with Mrs. MacClintock and a tandem bicycle, and when she did not care to ride he took me on long jaunts into the literary country about Oxford, reciting the poetry of the region most fascinatingly as we swept along.

Two Chicago University men, the Wallings, Willoughby and English, came along and asked MacClintock to row down the Thames with them but he passed the invitation on to me, and we had four wonderful days together on the river, rowing as far as Windsor. With the beginning of September I found myself in the spacious house of the Archibald Smiths in the suburbs of Edinburgh and for ten days they did nothing at all but show me the beauties of Scotland. This visit was an oasis in my travels; at last I was in somebody's home again.

Returned to England I had a memorable hour with Rendel Harris at Cambridge before setting out for Rome and the Oriental Congress where Breasted, Dr. Clark E. Crandall of the Chicago Semitic Faculty, Stratton the Sanskritist and I were to represent Chicago. We also put in a good deal of time at Frascati in the Albans to escape the heat and study the manuscripts at Grotta Ferrata near by. We saw the antiquities of Rome under expert guidance—I remember Boni himself and Platner of the American School showed us the Forum.

But my eyes, of course, were on the East and early in November Dr. Crandall and I sailed from Naples for Alexandria. On the boat we met Arthur Mace, Professor Flinders Petrie's nephew, on his way out to Abydus to build the one-story mud brick house that was to accommodate Petrie's expedition. We had met the Professor in London at his exhibit of his recent finds, and he had most hospitably invited us to stop at his camp at Abydus, so we were glad to meet Mace. Mace lived to become a distinguished Egyptologist, assisting Howard Carter twenty years later with the wonderful discoveries in the tomb of Tutenkhamen.

At Cairo, of course, I found Grenfell and Hunt at the Gizeh Museum, and they introduced me to the two lions of the place, Gaston Maspero, the director, and Emil Brugsch Bey, the conservator, of the Museum. It occupied a former Khedivial palace in Gizeh, in spacious grounds. Grenfell very kindly arranged that I was to be allowed to copy any Greek papyri I pleased and thus established my position with the Museum. It was of course for Egyptology the richest museum in the world and has since been further greatly enriched. But we made no effort to exhaust the sights of it or of Cairo, being in haste to get away on the first boat of the season up the Nile.

The season had hardly opened and there were only six of us on the upper deck, four Britons, Dr. Crandall and myself. After the great ride along the pyramids for half a day the scenery became very dull and monotonous; just the low mud banks of the Nile with an occasional shadoof and very infrequent stops at towns or ruins. Our one excitement was seeing Dendereh where we arrived after dark but all went resolutely ashore hoping to find some boys and donkeys to take us up to the temple and then to get the custodian to open it for us.

Well, we did! And what a ride it was. The dust rising, the lanterns tossing, the boys yelling, the donkeys running—and then the beautiful temple, more fascinating than ever I am sure in the uncertain light of moving lanterns.

We had a few hours at Luxor and Karnak but postponed Thebes across the river until our return journey. We reached Aswan and the First Cataract—the cataracts of the Nile are numbered from the bottom up, the last one being the first, because it is the first one you come to—and saw the great dam then under construction. We went down the river by rail to Luxor where the University of Chicago now has a fine headquarters house and paid our visit to Thebes and the Valley of the Kings, where Carter twenty years later found the tomb of Tutenkhamen!

Then we came down to Baliana and our long-anticipated visit to Professor Petrie's camp, at Abydus across the valley. Petrie had only lately married and it was Mrs. Petrie's first season in the "field" which was very much like camping out all winter. She was a very attractive and capable hostess and there were several young people in the party. Petrie was digging for the lost tomb of Osiris and it was interesting to go about his diggings with him, a powerful masterful man, with a great record as a working archeologist.

Arrived in Cairo I settled down for a few weeks at the Museum, doing pyramids and mosques between times, and it was almost Christmas before we set out for the Holy Land, the real goal of our endeavors. We traveled over to Port Said to take the steamer to Beirut, where we were shown over the Syrian Protestant College, as it was then called, by Dr. Daniel Bliss himself, the virtual creator of the institution. We made a hurried trip over the Lebanon and Antilebanon to Damascus, where we greeted the new year of 1900. Then

back in Beirut we took the boat down to Haifa. We spent
the night on deck watching the lights first of Sidon, then of
Tyre, and then of Haifa, beside Mt. Carmel, where we landed
between three and four in the morning.

And here began our horseback tour of Palestine. We found
a good dragoman, and a muleteer, and four horses, and rode
through the Holy Land over rough trails; there were no
roads, except a few about Jerusalem. We visited Nazareth
and the Sea of Galilee, and spent a memorable week in making a journey modern travelers do in a day. And yet the
country as we saw it, so thinly populated, so untouched by
civilization, brought us nearer to Bible times than visiting
it can bring the traveler now.

In Jerusalem I spent a wonderful month under the eye
of Dr. Selah Merrill, our American consul there, and perhaps
the foremost Palestinian archeologist of the day. Hornstein
of the English School very generously took us visiting Americans off on trips to the Cave of Adullam and the Convent
of Marsaba, and we went out to the Dead Sea to try its waters,
little thinking that a near-by cave on its rocky shores held
such treasures of Hebrew manuscripts as John Trever identified in Jerusalem almost fifty years later.

Then back to Cairo and the Museum where a letter from
Grenfell awaited me. He invited me out to their excavation
camp at ancient Tebtunis in the Fayum, and there they told
me the now-famous tale of finding scores and even hundreds
of mummified crocodiles wrapped in Greek papyri and
stuffed with them! It was the University of California expedition and it was a great success. I was now definitely invited
to return to Oxford for a summer's work with them deciphering and editing the Tebtunis papyri, and of course I gladly
accepted.

As I sailed for home after two solid years abroad, what had they given me? A wider and more immediate knowledge of scholarly personnel and opinion, German and English, for one thing. Closer acquaintance with the Greek papyrus documents of ancient life, for another. A working alliance with Grenfell and Hunt, for a third. Wider social experience, and fuller mastery of familiar spoken English, for a fourth—no small matter, though many translators seem to think so! And a firsthand acquaintance with the Holy Land which is, of course, the first and greatest commentary on the Bible. What was I being fitted for, anyway? I rather wondered, myself.

NINE

Growing up with the University

AS SOON as I returned from Europe, about the end of August, 1900, I joined the family at the Island, and we had ten days there before going back to Chicago. It seemed wonderfully good to find the Lake as of old though the family got much amusement from my unconscious Oxford accent. How I had longed for those sights and sounds and faces.

Once more in Chicago, I promptly called on Mr. Bond to express my appreciation of his generosity. I found him a most gracious and friendly gentleman, and he kindly invited me to call at his home. Soon after this occasion, as I have said earlier, Dean Mathews introduced me to Mrs. Bond and her daughter Elfleda, and while he escorted Mrs. Bond to her carriage, I followed with Elfleda. This was the beginning of a friendship that soon became a courtship and on May 5, 1901, we were engaged. Mr. Bond was away on business and so we addressed a joint telegram to him. On his return I took up at once the matter of his consent which he very graciously gave.

Mr. Bond was the head of the American Radiator Company, the foreign business of which he had just established on secure foundations in England, France, Germany and Italy, organizing boards and building factories, and everywhere making lifelong friends of the English and European representatives he put in charge. His generous friendship for the young men in his immediate employ was a source of the utmost inspiration to them, as it was to me.

My fiancée and I immediately formed the praiseworthy habit of attending University convocations which were often amusing as well as informing. It was in 1901 that Wu Ting Fang, the Chinese Ambassador at Washington, was asked to give the convocation address at the University and did so in excellent English, dressed in his magnificent Oriental robes. He almost brought down the house, however, when on taking his seat after giving his address, he unostentatiously thrust his manuscript into his boot! This greatly entertained the audience and rendered that particular convocation forever memorable.

Our engagement received an announcement and endorsement of a most gratifying kind at the great University reception given two or three months later for Mr. and Mrs. Rockefeller in a huge tent on the campus, when they paid their second visit to the University. Mr. Bond was out of town again and I escorted Mrs. Bond and her daughter in the long procession of Chicagoans paying their respects to the founder of the University. President Harper introduced Mrs. Bond to Mr. Rockefeller and then drew me past Miss Bond, saying to Mr. Rockefeller,

"This is Dr. Goodspeed's son, Edgar, and this," said the Doctor, turning with manifest satisfaction to my fiancée, "is the girl he's going to marry. And it's *all right!*"

This recollection never ceased to give Elfleda great amusement. She was particularly struck with the fact that he did not even mention her name.

At eighteen Elfleda had been prepared for Vassar and was

planning to go there but a serious illness upset these plans.
On her recovery the family took her abroad for a long tour.
She would have been sure of a welcome at Vassar because,
as she used to say, the matron there (they had matrons in
those days) was her mother's sister's husband's first wife's
father's brother's wife. She would reel this list off with the
greatest zest, but it was many years before I could manage
to recite it.

Elfleda sought to improve the months of our engagement
by introducing me to the sacred precincts of Onwentsia and
the mysterious game of golf of which she had already mas-
tered the elements. We were to pursue such studies later at
Plum Lake where the new sport was introduced by Mr.
James, who first created a golf course of his own and then
got us all interested in it. Of my later attainments in golf let
it suffice to say that in after years, when at the top of my
form, I rose to be for a short time first vice-president of the
Plum Lake Golf Club. How many golfers can say as much?

On December 3, 1901, Elfleda and I were married in her
father's house, with her sister and my brother in the wedding
party, and my father performing the ceremony. It was a small
wedding with a supper following, and then a big reception.
We left in a storm of congratulations and drove in a carriage
to the Auditorium Hotel where I had made our reservation
for the night. The perfidious clerk told me, however, that
he had not been able to keep the room I had reserved and
I was forced to rush into a telephone booth and seek other
quarters, while the out-of-town wedding guests kept arriving
and going to their rooms! Most inauspicious, you would say,
but we kept out of sight and I managed to get the bridal suite
at the Virginia, up on the north side. There we had a hall,
a sitting room, a bedroom or two, a dining room and kitchen—

a sumptuous setup, which we had to leave early next morning
to journey off to Madison, Wisconsin, for a week—all we
could afford in time or money.

We took up our residence in a brand-new apartment at
5627 Madison Avenue (now Dorchester), first floor. I remember the Angells were on the third. Our apartment was fur-
nished entirely with our wedding presents, some of which had
fortunately been in the form of cash.

My first class in the University was in the Apostolic Fathers,
and I prevailed upon my small group of students to undertake with me the making of a practical concordance of its
Greek words and forms. This was a most burdensome job,
which they and their successors carried out and Hinrichs
published at Leipzig in 1907. How heroically my wife worked
with me on our trip abroad in 1905 at arranging these thousands of slips for me to copy, practically learning Greek to do
so! The fact that three months after Hinrichs had begun to set
the type, Harnack's assistant Erwin Preuschen turned up at
Hinrichs with a manuscript of a similar work—too late!—
probably did me no good in that quarter. The way Mrs.
Goodspeed now entered into my undertakings made me feel
she was giving up too much of her own individual life in
doing it, and I resolutely urged her for her own sake not to
become just my research assistant.

Her coming into the University circle at the age of twenty-
one and appearing as chaperon of various fraternity and
other affairs won her a host of friends of her own age, nine
years less than mine, and the Sigma Club very graciously
made her an honorary member. This gave her a certain
campus standing which was delightful. Young people of the
college and of the department were very much in our home,
especially Sunday evenings when we had gay informal sup-

pers, which many of them still remember, singing joyously later around the piano.

Elfleda made herself useful in the church, not only helping me with the social life of the large Bible class we organized in it, but in the Women's Society, of which as I have said she eventually became President. She was also active from the first in the Settlement League of the women of the University, led by Mrs. Charles R. Henderson, whom Elfleda greatly admired. She herself in after years became the President of the League, retaining that post for three years. She carried these responsibilities with the greatest ease. She saw at once how a thing was to be done and who were the best people to do it, and while most of us would be still puzzling over a situation she would have it solved and done. This is no conjugal exaggeration of her capacities; it is simply the way her mind worked.

When the Settlement League presented the Dance Festival in the Bartlett Gymnasium she was given charge of the sale of tickets, of which there were some twenty-two hundred. It was a notable affair, with authentic national dances on a stage by genuine nationals of most European countries and even by American Indians. As we took our seats an usher hurried up to report two people had arrived without their tickets, and what was he to do with them? Not at all flustered, Elfleda managed or happened to remember where they belonged in her distribution and they were quickly taken to their seats.

Mrs. Goodspeed's position as chairman of the sale of tickets involved her in a difficult situation, for the tickets had gone so well that some eager Settlement League women wished additional seats put into the gymnasium, beyond the twenty-two hundred on the blueprint of the hall; they felt that more tickets were positively demanded. But Mrs. Goodspeed felt that while this would undoubtedly bring in more money, it would be an injustice to some who had already on the basis of the chart bought seats which would now be blanketed by the new additions. The matter was referred to the Acting President, James R. Angell, since President Judson was absent on one of his foreign assignments. Mr. Angell, after hearing both sides, declared in favor of Mrs. Goodspeed's position and no additional seats were provided. It was a good illustration of her keen sense of justice, as well as of his. Certainly she never lost her zest for fair play. Through the years she had no difficulty in making friends with the wives of my students, sharing their problems and finding ways of being of use to them. She did this with all her characteristic zest and interest, whether it was helping with the rent or taking them to some current play which they had expressed a wish to see.

While my wife never actually enrolled for any courses in the University, she was keenly alive to its intellectual stimulus and found great satisfaction in the work of Dr. Charles R. Henderson whose principal course in sociology was at the time the most popular course given in the University. Talking matters over one day he invited her to attend it as a visitor, which she did with great delight. When prison reform was up Dr. Henderson proposed that the class visit the City Prison, and Elfleda was one of the first to follow out his suggestion. In fact, on a later morning, knowing that she had done so, and to help the rest find their way over there, he called upon her to explain how best it could be reached, facetiously saying,

"Perhaps Mrs. Goodspeed can help us about directions; she has been there," which occasioned considerable merriment at my wife's expense.

The untimely death of Mr. Bond in 1902, at the age of fifty, broke up Mrs. Bond's home at 2733 Michigan Avenue, and she and her younger daughter went abroad for the year. Elfleda and I had given up our apartment on Madison Avenue, and lived for a time on the North Shore, boarding in Highland Park. This made us most pleasantly acquainted with Mrs. Folsom and her young people, Mrs. Carl C. Bullock and William R. Folsom, and they, with Mr. Bullock and Mrs. Folsom, became our lifelong friends. They had married a brother and a sister, Carl and Bertha Bullock, of a family that had lived on the North Side since before the fire and been long identified with the business life of the city. Meantime, we had decided to build a house as near the campus as possible, and secured a lot at 5706 Woodlawn Avenue, from the estate of Mr. Field—the first such transaction carried out by his executors. It was very funny to buy our lot at Marshall Field's Wholesale, as we actually did.

It was one wintry afternoon at the old Del Prado, at Fifty-ninth and Blackstone, when the snow was falling thickly, that we suddenly felt the need of a home, and decided then and there to build a house. Meeting John Putnam later at Highland Park, we learned that he was building, and with the other boarders at Mrs. Goodridge's we made frequent inspections of John's new house. We asked him who was his architect.

"Well," said John with great resignation, "whoever you have, you'll be sorry!" Charging this off to mere pessimism, we got the name of Mr. Howard Shaw, and we were never sorry. We found a very able architect in Mr. Shaw and in the spring of 1906 we moved into what was said to be Mr. Shaw's last small house. We later improved it with a terrace outside the dining room and a door from the dining room onto the terrace and garden, and eventually erected a three-car garage at the alley end of the lot, which completed our developments.

Many years later, a group of religious people of quite another denomination from ours was dining at our house, and as one of them, a very able business woman, came down the stairs she said to me earnestly,

"There is peace in this house!"

I was deeply touched, and said to her,

"How true that is! But how did you know?"

"I feel it," she said, and from her it was something more than a mere pleasantry. I have often thought how right she was. The happiness and harmony of our home life were extraordinary.

But it was not all smooth sailing. Soon after our marriage our oculist assured me that in three months' time I would lose my sight. What a blow this pronouncement was may be imagined for my wife and I were already full of plans and hopes. We talked with Dr. Burton, the head of my department, and he advised me to see his oculist, Dr. Cassius D. Wescott. Dr. Wescott was encouraging. He said I must stop all my work for three months, not even reading the newspaper, and follow his medication directions. And for the future I must do no work or reading by artificial light.

These stern directions, with my wife's aid, I carried out and for the rest of my active life did no work by artificial light, making the most of the daylight. This gave us our evenings together, for games, reading aloud, entertaining our friends, and conversation, which proved to be a great boon and delight to us both. There remained in Chicago's short

winter days a time after four or four-thirty when any reading had to be by artificial light, and to tide me over this dull
two hours of inactivity, Mrs. Goodspeed invited in our close
friends Dr. Soares and Dr. Burton, one or both of whom
would come in day after day to play pool with us on a port-
able table we set up in my study. This all seemed perfectly
natural then, but as I look back upon it I can see what a
sacrifice it was on the part of those two busy men. Such is the
power of friendship.

Another disaster of our early married life was the failure
of the Hyde Park Bank in which we had our checking and
our savings accounts. As we were quite literally counting our
pennies this was a major disaster to our establishment, as it
was to many neighbors and colleagues. When we were at
length able to bank anything again, we chose the largest bank
we could find.

In August, 1909, George Milligan, then minister of Caputh,
in Scotland, but afterward Regius professor of biblical criticism and Vice-chancellor in the University of Glasgow, visited Chicago and stayed with us. We very much enjoyed
showing him Chicago. He was already deeply interested in
Greek papyri, and in writing about them. One evening we
were speaking of the old story that the first such scrolls found,
back in 1778, the Arabs burned to the number of fifty "for
the aromatic odor they exhaled," evidently supposing they
were tobacco. I had some tiny scraps of papyrus with no
writing on them, and I suggested that we experiment with
them to see if when burned they possessed any such aromatic
qualities. We did so, burning them on a fire shovel and
eagerly sniffing the fumes, which smelled just like burnt
brown paper. I have tried this experiment since on dried
papyrus from my California garden, with the same result.

No, the Arabs who burned those fifty first Greek scrolls were disappointed, that is all. Milligan recorded this experiment in his *Greek Papyri,* in 1910. He had just published his admirable commentary on Thessalonians, and his *Vocabulary of the Greek Testament* done in collaboration with James Hope Moulton, in 1930, has proved a valuable supplement to the lexicons. Dr. Robert J. McCracken, of the Riverside Church in New York, tells me he was one of Dr. Milligan's student assistants in its preparation.

Mrs. Goodspeed kept open house and enjoyed doing so, and a remarkable series of guests passed through the Woodlawn Avenue house in the more than thirty years of our residence. The New Testament Club always ended its year's meetings with a dinner there. The residents of Goodspeed Hall used to take Thanksgiving dinner with us, with Father, while he lived, as guest of honor since the hall was named for him. Besides our Chicago colleagues and friends in the city, a series of interesting personalities of those days, visiting the University to preach or lecture, came our way, few of whom the world has forgotten—Christopher Morley, Ellery Sedgwick, Thomas Whittemore, Archbishop Horsepian, Martin Dibelius, George Milligan, Louis Betts, James Hope Moulton, Franz Cumont, Arthur S. Hoyt, Cornelius Woelfkin, Henry Sloane Coffin, William Mitchell Ramsay, Kirsopp Lake, "Ian Hay," "Ralph Connor," Francis J. McConnell, James Moffatt, Glenn Frank, T. R. Glover, Gustav Krueger, Charles J. Connick, Adolf Deissmann, William Craigie, Alfred North Whitehead, William Gillette, Irving Babbitt, Werner Jaeger—oh, a goodly company of artists, authors, preachers, scholars, whose mere names I find fragrant with memory.

Elfleda's readiness and courage were shown in a conversation she once had with Uncle Henry, Father's only living brother. He was remarking that when he died there would be a thousand dollars in his will to provide a portrait of "that young man," meaning Father, for the University. She said,

"Why don't you do it now, Uncle Henry, and then you can get some satisfaction out of it yourself?"

He liked her spirit and directness.

"All right," he said. "You get the artist and have it done, and I'll pay for it."

She did. We asked the advice of Mr. Charles L. Hutchinson, the President of the Art Institute, and he suggested Louis Betts who was just coming to the front. The portrait was painted in our music room where the light suited the artist. Mr. Hutchinson and Mr. Martin A. Ryerson, Chairman of the Board of Trustees, came to see it and gave it their approval. Louis gave it his, calling it "a stunning portrait." It was his first picture in Hutchinson Hall and I think his last thousand-dollar portrait. As Elfleda had said, it gave Uncle Henry much satisfaction. In his youth, long before his publishing business in New York, he had been a soldier in the Civil War and was brevetted Captain for gallantry in action on the battlefield of Shiloh. I remember well his calling on us, one Sunday morning, in our flat; it was April 6, 1902, forty years to a day since the opening of that battle. He told us how the battle began, the rebs as my uncle called them rudely interrupting them as they were cooking their coffee for breakfast. He was in fact for a while that morning a prisoner in the hands of the Confederates.

When Professor Burton was called upon to make his journey of inquiry to China in 1909, he closed his house and stayed some weeks with us before setting out. From his interesting journey up the Yangtze he faithfully sent us copies of his journal letters, which we had bound and ready to surprise him with when he came back to us for some days on his return. Guide, counselor and friend of those years he certainly was.

Dr. Burton was a difficult man to surprise but I think I did it on one occasion. We were canoeing together and I suggested to him that the strange nonacquaintance of the Synoptic Gospels with the letters of Paul, abruptly succeeded right after the appearance of Luke-Acts by everybody's knowing them, would be explained if it was precisely then that they were first collected and published. He was immediately interested.

"If that position could be established," said he, "it would have some very important consequences."

Of course I felt strongly that it could and would, and I was later able to pursue this thesis to what I believed to be a demonstration.

Our famous Arabic professor James Richard Jewett, who was such an ornament to the Semitic department, once received and long treasured a letter addressed to him in care of the "Lunatic Department, The University of Chicago," beside which I would humbly place one that reached me through the Faculty Exchange, though plainly addressed in typewriting to "Edgar J. Goodspeed, Sacristy Exchange, University of Chicago." After all, what does the first syllable or two matter, if you have the right ending? -Tic or -ty, that is all you need.

A favorite lecturer in the University circle from the very first was Richard Green Moulton who came to the University from Cambridge, England. He became the creator of *The Modern Reader's Bible.* His brother W. F. Moulton was a famous New Testament grammarian and Richard was a delightful and impressive lecturer on the English Bible. To hear him actually recite the whole book of Job, or the book of Deuteronomy as the oration it is, was a great experience for any audience, such was his dramatic power. When his distinguished nephew, James Hope Moulton, visited him in later years at Chicago—it was in 1914—the two couples dined with us. It was a tempestuous spring evening with the thunder rolling most of the time, and as Richard sat down to write in the guest book, he remarked, but did not write, "A thundering good time!"

A few years later, James Hope Moulton died of exposure in an open boat on the Mediterranean, at the side of J. Rendel Harris; they were returning from India, when their ship was sunk by the Germans.

It was Richard Green Moulton who brought to America the Cambridge story of the don who fell in love with the rich American widow, which led his associates to say of him that "such time as he could spare from the embellishment of his person, he devoted to the neglect of his duties." It is quite forty years since I first heard Dr. Moulton tell this, and recent efforts to place its origin in Columbia University in New York City are much mistaken.

One day in our early years in the new house—in fact it was in April of 1910—Dean Mathews called me into his office to ask if we would entertain a visiting English clergyman, the Reverend William Gascoyne-Cecil, and his wife who were to visit the University. I interrogated Elfleda and she readily agreed. It seemed that the President was to be away and Mrs. Judson was otherwise occupied. We accordingly received them and took them about for their stay, presenting their letters to the Harold McCormicks and other leading Chicagoans. The fact was, Lord William was the son of the

Marquess of Salisbury, so long Queen Victoria's prime minister, and his beautiful wife was the daughter of her Lord Chamberlain, the Earl of Lathom, who managed both her jubilees.

Lord William told us a remarkable story which I have not seen in print. When Sun Yat Sen was a young man he studied in Edinburgh but was rather looked down upon by the Scots as a mere Chinaman. Coming down to London and passing the Chinese Legation one day, he was pounced upon by the legation police and hustled inside where he was held incommunicado, and with his revolutionary ideas had every reason to fear the worst. Through one of the servants he managed to get word of his plight to the outer world and it reached Lord Salisbury, who was then Secretary of State for Foreign Affairs. Lord Salisbury, as Lord William put it, took a strong line and demanded the release of the prisoner as he was on British soil. The legation protested that his being in the legation placed him on Chinese soil, but Lord Salisbury ruled that as it was merely a legation and not an embassy, it was British soil. So the Chinese released him.

Lord William and Lady Florence had just been through China and when they left they were given the freedom of the port for their luggage in consideration of this long-ago service done by Lord Salisbury to the Chinese emancipator.

We found ourselves invited with the Cecils to a distinguished luncheon at the Harold McCormicks. Lord William preached at the Sunday Evening Club in the Auditorium, and we took him to Hull House, and tea at President Judson's. He was much impressed with his interview with President Judson, at which I was present, and told me his talk with Mr. Judson was the most important one he had had with anybody in this country.

The Cecils were delightful guests; they called each other by their youthful nicknames, he being Fish and she Fluff. Lord William became Bishop of Exeter, and one of King Edward's chaplains. Seventeen years later the Cecils passed through Chicago again, and spent a few nights under our roof. Lady Florence and Elfleda exchanged letters as long as Lady Florence lived. They sent us his book, *Changing China*, which came out in 1910 soon after their first visit. The saddest part of their later story is that they afterward lost three of their four sons in the Great War.

In 1912 the University dedicated its great memorial to Dr. Harper, the stately general library building and Dr. Edwin H. Lewis read another of his noble poems on the great occasions in the life of the University. When in 1923 he read his third, in honor of Mr. Ryerson, it occurred to me to suggest to the President that the Press should collect and publish these poems, and he ordered it done. I only wish these deeply imaginative pieces might be published again accompanied by Dr. Lewis' later poem in honor of the medical fraternity. They fairly belong to our Chicago literary and spiritual heritage.

The great reading room of the Library was on the third floor, as is so often the case, and one morning soon after it was opened an eager young man who seemed to have missed the elevator addressed me earnestly on the stairs.

"Pardon me, sir," he began politely, "but where is the Library—the open part where the students may sit down?"

I was happy to direct him, marveling too at the accuracy of his definition. Freshman though he was, he already knew what the reading room was for.

Sam Harper, the President's eldest son, used to tell a very amusing story of how when he was motoring east with his mother, passing near Mr. Rockefeller's great summer place, they stopped to call and remained to lunch. After luncheon, Mr. Rockefeller accompanied Sam out to see his car, and asked him how many miles he got out of a gallon of gasoline. It was a Franklin, I believe, and Sam was able to give him a surprising figure, some fifteen or sixteen miles.

Mr. Rockefeller evinced consternation.

"Young man," he exclaimed, "you'll ruin me!"

I well remember when in 1913 Sir William Mitchell Ramsay lectured at the University, we had a group of scholars to meet him at luncheon. I knew Professor James Henry Breasted had received an extraordinary letter from a man in Kentucky, on the stationery of the Ramsay Family, asking James if the name Ramsay might not be derived from Ramses, and pointing out that an earlier member of the family in Kentucky had been named Pharaoh Ramsay! While regarding this idea as historically unlikely, I thought it might amuse Sir William. But it did not! No, he took it very seriously, and informed James and me that Ramsay was not derived from Ramses, but from Ram's Ey or Island. Then for good measure he kindly explained to me that Goodspeed and all names beginning with Good, such as Goodwin and the like, were of Danish origin, and corrupted from Godspeed, Godwin, and so on. This I found seriously interesting, and on the strength of it have ever since claimed a Danish strain in my ancestory, going back let us say to the days of the Danish invasion in the ninth century.

As a luncheon guest, however, Sir William had another side. The luncheon as planned was a particularly good one, beginning with soup in cups, but Sir William waved his aside, declaring that before lecturing he never took anything but a cup of tea and a poached egg. This sounded very simple, but what with preparing the luncheon, it turned out there was not an egg left in the house. My wife's place at table commanded the garden, and she beheld the cook going first to one neighbor's and then to the other's, to borrow the necessary egg. All this was lost on me, however, absorbed as I was in the problem of Pharaoh Ramsay. In the end, of course, his simple wants were duly satisfied, and after his lecture and a long wait at the Englewood station for Sir William's train east, which we spent discussing the views of Professor James Moffatt, another Scotsman, whose views Sir William did not share, we parted, I hope on the best of terms.

To the First World War days (it was in January, 1917) belongs the visit of Captain Ian Hay Beith to the University. He was to speak at the University Club, and as my friend Thomas Wearing, who was working for his Ph.D. in the University, was anxious to hear him, I took him to the meeting. We met the Captain after his stirring address and Tom invited him out to the University to speak in Mandel Hall before the Canadian Club, of which Tom was president. He very obligingly accepted. After stopping at our house for tea before the lecture, he was given a spirited introduction by Tom, who was by way of being quite a literary man himself. The Captain's book, *The First Hundred Thousand,* was one of the notable books of the First World War.

Another visitor of great renown was Cardinal Mercier, who came to Chicago in 1919. He was to visit the University and be welcomed by the assembled faculty. Dr. Frank W. Gunsaulus had among his rare books a famous work of Balbus, *The Catholicon,* in the printing of 1466, the Louvaine copy of which had been destroyed when the library was burned in the war. Dr. Gunsaulus generously proposed to present his copy to the Cardinal for the library, as a gesture of reconstruction. I was sent down to the city to guide the cortege out to the quadrangles. But after waiting an hour at the appointed corner of Michigan and Monroe for its appearance, a thoughtful friend resorted to the University Club close by to telephone for information, and told me the Archbishop had decided the Cardinal should take a nap after luncheon, and the procession would therefore be one hour late. I had been hardly inconspicuous, standing for an hour and a half just after the luncheon hour at the corner of Michigan and Monroe, wearing an Oxford cap, with an academic gown on my arm—the Archbishop's little joke! My own sufferings had been slight, however, compared with those of the expectant faculty lined up in caps and gowns in readiness to welcome the Cardinal and escort him across the campus to Mandel Hall. When at length the procession reached my down-town corner, one hour and a half late, it stopped as prearranged at sight of me, and the police car opened to receive me. I managed, however, to meet the Cardinal in the end, and conduct him to the President's presence. But such are the uses of us utility men.

Dr. Gunsaulus was an extraordinary personality. One glimpse of him I cannot leave out. Mrs. Goodspeed and I had bought an interesting Persian tile at Nice, and had begun to collect them in a small way. Seeing a fine Rages tile down at Marshall Field's art room one day, and being staggered at the price, I ventured to ask his expert advice. He met me at the exhibit and proved to have been one of the sponsors of the Persian in charge.

The room was empty at the moment but when the Doctor got Mr. Kuhli Khan, the proprietor of it, to get the tile out and put it in his hands and then began to expound it to me, it quickly filled up. Before the Doctor had finished explaining the rabbits on the tile and their manifest connection with the Rabbit year in China, he had a very good and most attentive congregation, one saying to another.

"It's Dr. Gunsaulus! Listen! He's lecturing!"

The Doctor closed by asking Mr. Kuhli Khan the price of the tile and giving him the following instructions:

"Do not sell this tile to anyone but Mr. Goodspeed or myself." And so we parted. I was not at all encouraged by this experience, but my amiable mother-in-law on hearing the story went down and bought it for us. I think she thought the story was worth the price. But where did all this nonsense about mothers-in-law come from? I have often wondered.

A few days later Dr. Gunsaulus limped up the steps of our house attended by his chauffeur. The latter was carrying two cast-iron rabbits, reminiscent of the Rabbit year in China, which he left with us. I have never fully understood whether they were a loan or a gift, but I have them still.

When Seymour de Ricci visited Chicago in his great task of listing and cataloguing the medieval manuscripts in America, it became my duty to call for him down town and drive him out to the University. As we set out he expressed his surprise that American scholars who would undertake to catalogue the manuscripts of the hill towns of Italy would not do as much for their own manuscripts. I replied by handing him the printed catalogue of the University of Chicago manuscripts which Dr. Martin Sprengling and I had produced for the opening of the Harper Library in 1912. I was glad to observe that he made use of the book in preparing his catalogue and spoke generously of it. It was a pleasure to meet de Ricci and to welcome him to the University, as I had heard so much of him from Grenfell and Hunt.

I remember so well the visit of General William Booth of the Salvation Army to the University, and how after his address Dean Mathews had us all stand and sing "Onward Christian Soldier" to him in farewell, a simple gesture, but a very moving experience for us all.

Clayton R. Bowen, our near neighbor in the Meadville Theological School and a stimulating counselor in so much of my research, brought back to us from his journeys abroad our first knowledge of earlier Elfledas. He was interested to find that at Romsey Abbey, founded by King Edgar, Elfleda, or Ethelfleda, daughter of the noble Ethelwold, became abbess about a thousand years ago, and then a saint. And then he brought us word of Elfleda, or Ethelfleda, the eldest child of Alfred the Great, who married the Lord of Mercia and ruled there for many years. I find that there was also a St. Elfleda of Glastonbury, and in the Old Saxon Calendar, October 27 was "the Feast of St. Elfleda." We were both pleased that our names were such old Saxon ones, and that they had been associated so long ago.

TEN

I Begin to Enjoy Travel

MRS. GOODSPEED had inherited from both her parents a fondness for travel and I soon found travel in her society a far better thing than I had found it by myself. She had greatly enjoyed seeing Colorado a few years before, and our first summer together managed to entice me out there among the Rockies. But in the autumn of 1903 we set out together for Europe. We took the southern route, stopping over at Gibraltar for a few weeks in Spain, about which we had been reading that summer in George Borrow's inimitable book, *The Bible in Spain*. She was an enthusiastic traveler and extremely good at it.

From Gibraltar we ran across to Tangier for a day or two, then up the Andalusian coast to Cadiz, for a glimpse of that historic spot—all this in a tiny coasting steamer of no great tonnage or comfort. From Cadiz we journeyed inland, to Seville, Cordova, Toledo and Madrid. I sought admission to the principal manuscript libraries hoping to discover something, and at any rate had some interesting experiences. .

Fortified with letters from the Archbishop of Chicago and Professor Henri Hyvernat of the Catholic University at Washington, I approached the authorities at Toledo, seeking admission to their famous Chapter Library. I was put

off by one office after another, but after a few days reached
the presence of the Bishop of Toledo, a kindly man with a
fine spirited face—the very image of my old Greek professor,
Edward Olson, and his more famous double, Xenophon! We
soon found my Spanish unequal to the task and fell easily
into Latin conversation which served our purposes perfectly.
From him I was passed on in the course of a week—there was
nothing hurried about these negotiations—to the presence
of the Cardinal Archbishop himself, who had very recently
married the young King and Queen. He spoke to me graciously in French, saying I could study in the library an hour
a day *"tous les jours."* His staff then wrote me an order to
that effect, blotted it with sand in the medieval manner,
and showed me where to await the coming of the librarian
who would emerge from a certain doorway at eleven. He did,
and I presented my paper. He read it without enthusiasm
and curtly directed me to meet him in the cloister next day
at four.

There I found a young Frenchman named Marcel Robin,
from the École des Chartes in Paris, who had been hanging
about for ten days trying to get into the library. The librarian
appeared promptly and told us briefly that there was a chapter meeting he must attend; we might return the next day
at eleven. He then turned on his heel (I had never seen it
so perfectly done) and disappeared. My French friend was
inconsolable. He was now sure he would never get in. I told
him my letters would get us in; I would see that they did.

And next morning, after a week's work on my part, and
two on his, we got in. The librarian appeared with a bunch
of keys. He opened the cloister door to the hall, then a door
into a farther hall, then a farther door—and after unlocking
five successive doors, we entered the library! At the end of

an hour the librarian turned us out and locked up again.
But he found existence in the library very boring and after a
couple of days of supervising us, he turned over the job to a
young nephew of his. He was a lively boy of fourteen, who
found it even more boring than his uncle did, and in a day
or two brought a young companion along to play with. They
soon wearied of the musty old books, but finding some old
music manuscripts they practiced singing them to their own
great entertainment. But out of hours Marcel Robin was
cultivating the librarian's nephew, taking him for long walks
and amusing him generally, and we soon found this boy
was allowing us an hour and a half daily!

In the end I found nothing of great worth at Toledo,
except this experience, which so stood out against the welcome given me at Escorial, for example. But afterward it was
explained. Not long before an American scholar (oh those
Americans!) had been admitted to the library for a while
and this nefarious man had found there a third manuscript
of one of the minor works of Tacitus, the Agricola, I believe,
of which only a few manuscripts had been previously known
in all the world—and had gone and published it. This service
to learning had somehow annoyed its custodians.

In Madrid, at the National Library, I simply presented
myself, showed my letters, and went to work. The very agreeable and willing attendant went off to bring me what I had
called for but seemed unable to find it. I wrote more cards
for it but with the same result. An hour passed. Finally I said
to him,

"What is the trouble here? I am ordering the Codex Toletanus, a well-known manuscript of the Latin Bible. I know
it is here because they told me at Toledo where it used to be

that it had been brought here. That is the manuscript I want to see."

He threw up his hands despairingly.

"Señor," said he, "I have brought you every manuscript from Toledo in this library except a Hebrew Bible."

I saw a great light.

"Then bring me the Hebrew Bible," said I, and he did. It was the Codex Toletanus, which is written in such a strange Latin uncial script that he thought it was Hebrew.

Of course we were really happiest in Granada, browsing about the Alhambra, with Washington Irving in our hands.

When on November 2 we rejoined our ship at Gibraltar, bound for Naples, Mark Twain with Mrs. Clemens and their two daughters was on board, but he was having little to do with the other passengers, he was so preoccupied with Mrs. Clemens' illness. She was seen on deck occasionally, in her chair, carefully watched over by her household, and he was of course conspicuous about the ship with his well-known features and his great halo of white hair standing out around his head. Mrs. Clemens died early in the following June, in Florence.

We went on to Naples, where we found our ideal hotel in Bertolini's. After some weeks in and about Naples we took the *Hohenzollern,* disrespectfully known as the "Rolling Billy," up to Genoa. We went right through to Paris where Mrs. Bond and Elfleda's sister Louise were spending the winter, for a fortnight there with them, then home by way of Boulogne on my old ship the *Pennsylvania.*

Two years later we were off again for Europe, having persuaded my brother Charles to go along for a month anyway. We showed him England and Scotland, and some of my old friends over there. Grenfell and Hunt very kindly had

Charles and me to dinner, and as they could not include ladies in such college occasions, they had all three of us for luncheon in Hunt's rooms in Queen's, gracing the occasion with the college plate. We in turn had them to dine with us at my old High Street lodgings. While Charles returned to Chicago, we went on to the Italian lakes and put up for three memorable weeks at the Villa Serbelloni, above Bellagio, in the very middle of the Lake of Como. We had been told of it by Henry Ives Cobb, Jr., when we met him on the dock at Tilbury where he was meeting his mother, a very charming woman, who had been on the ship with us.

As it grew cold we fled southward to Naples and continued the tedious task of preparing the Patristic Index for publication. What a way to spend one's time in Bellagio and Naples!

Then five years later in 1910, we sallied forth again for the Mediterranean. On the ship were some very pleasant young men bound for Beirut and the Protestant College, with whom we played shuffleboard (which I am told the British hideously describe as horse billiards!). We took them to dinner at the old Bristol at Gibraltar, and again at Bertolini's in Naples, while the ship lingered in those ports, but hearing rumors of pestilence in Italy we sailed right on to Genoa and took the next train for Nice and the Riviera.

There in spite of bondage to another Index, of the Apologists this time, on which Elfleda helped me manfully, we managed to do the marvelous drives of the Riviera and see its principal points, from Cannes to Monte Carlo. We got in a few days at Florence before sailing on the *Berlin*—another of my old ships!

Our motoring experiences began with a tour of Kentucky and the neighboring states with the Folsoms, before we rejoiced in a car ourselves. Then in California in 1915 Joe and Louise Rhodes (Elfleda's sister was now Mrs. Joseph F. Rhodes, Jr.) drove us over most of the state, with longer stops at San Diego and San Francisco for the Expositions. We went over the Stevenson country, the Bret Harte country and the Jack London country on our way. Years later from Provo, in Utah, we made week-end visits to the national parks in Utah, Bryce and Zion, and later covered most of the great national parks, including Yosemite, Yellowstone and Glacier.

It was then while I was lecturing in Provo that Mrs. Goodspeed and I made those memorable week-end excursions to the marvelous canyons, Immigration, Bryce, Zion, and the rest, of which I speak elsewhere. On one of these week-end journeys into the mountains, we were approaching the entrance to Zion National Park, just when the governors were having a meeting at Ogden, and seeing the Utah sights in the meantime. A ranger stepped out of the little office building to hand us our permit to visit the Park, and receive our fee. He gave us this flattering greeting:

"Are you delayed dignitaries?"

Having read the Park classic "O Ranger!" and learned how much amusement the Park staff gets out of us tourists, I made a guarded reply. It seemed that some of the governors had gone astray, and he was hoping he had found them.

Thomas M. Williams came to drive for us in 1925 and remained with us most acceptably in that capacity. A Pennsylvanian of Welsh ancestry, he had been in aviation in the First World War, in France, and his knowledge of boats was also very complete, making him invaluable at the Island which he came to enjoy as much as any of us. We did not neglect New England or the south, making Florida one Christmas vacation, San Antonio and Houston another, and the Gulf coast on more than one. Charles and Father accompanied us on some of these trips. Latterly as the roads and the cars grew better, we would drive up to the Island in a day. Of course lecturing, particularly about the Chicago area, was greatly facilitated and made much pleasanter by driving, especially as we did not do the driving ourselves, and consequently arrived at our destinations ready for the fray. And the lives saved by my simply giving up driving the moment I had learned how, are literally incalculable. This is where so many men make their great mistake.

Arriving at Lake Forest to lecture one Sunday afternoon, after a dizzy ride of more than thirty miles over what was practically glare ice, I was introduced to the audience as not only an experienced lecturer but a driver of no ordinary skill, or I would not have been there at all. But Honor to whom Honor, and I hastened to explain that while I had indeed come over the ice from Hyde Park, it had required a better man than I was at the wheel. We decided that the next time we went to Europe, Tom and the touring car must not be left behind.

ELEVEN

Skimmings in the Atlantic

THE seasoned reader will well remember how that *Atlantic* veteran Oliver Wendell Holmes collected his *Atlantic* papers, or some of them, under the impressive title, *Soundings from the Atlantic*. In comparison with his Olympian profundities, I would venture for mine a more modest name. I will not pretend that my very first offering to the *Atlantic* was eagerly welcomed and published; that would be to palter with the truth. Though I do not remember exactly how many articles I had vainly volunteered to Mr. Sedgwick's reconstituted monthly, when the impossible happened.

It was up at the Island. We had run impatiently through the mail, and I had returned to my job of making a chest of drawers for the Cloister, a monumental piece of cabinet work, simplified by taking grocery boxes of the same size for drawers and nailing a false front on each one. Mr. James Hopkins was later fascinated by this achievement, pointing out that there were even names such as "Mackerel" still on the sides of the boxes to indicate what they contained! Absorbed in this creative work I was interrupted by my wife flying out into the dooryard crying.

"Why, this is not an advertisement from the *Atlantic*! They've accepted your article!"

This pleased me very much, especially as having been first discovered by my wife. Mr. Sedgwick's letter he will, I hope, forgive me for quoting:

"It is seldom now that we can accept contributions written by friends of the *Atlantic* for which no plans have been made in this office, but such a paper as yours disarms all possible opposition. I read it with great delight. . . . I fear it marks some moral delinquency in your habit or in ours, that in all these years you have not before contributed to the *Atlantic*."

This made it plain to me that my earlier efforts had, doubtless for very good reasons, never found their way through to the Chief.

But what a delightful welcome! I continued to write for the *Atlantic* as long as Mr. Sedgwick held sway, and found it a very happy experience. The Sedgwicks became our friends and even visited us in Chicago, and through the *Atlantic's* columns I reached a lot of old friends and made many new ones.

As soon as the proof arrived I read the article, such as it was, to the Island household. It was "The Life of Adventure." A few days later, Charles arrived at the Island. As we were going down the hill, he said to me,

"Edgar, what is your *Atlantic* article about?"

"Ask Father," I guardedly replied.

"Father," said Charles patiently, "what is Edgar's article about?"

"Well, Charles," said Father, with manifest restraint, "it's light, very light."

Father then asked Charles,

"What did Edgar get for that article?"

Charles replied,

"He got sixty dollars."

"Good Lord!" exclaimed Father.

I fully sympathized with Father's view of the article. He had not brought me up to be a humorist. Mother's reactions interested me even more. She said to me,

"Edgar, I like your *Atlantic* articles. You don't talk about a subject till I get tired of it."

This butterfly quality I did not disclaim or regret. For in this field as soon as I found myself laboring over a subject I dropped it.

Seeking to be of some use in World War I (the War to end War) I had joined the faculty company, and drilled assiduously. I had also joined Mr. George Creel's Four Minute Men, who spoke for that length of time nightly on civilian duties of the week, as the government viewed them, in the moving picture theaters of the South Side. Along with movie houses, we also got into vaudeville, burlesque, and even legitimate shows, and it was certainly some discipline. One night I spoke between shows from the runway of the White City, another I followed Jenks's Mules on the stage of the old Majestic, and once between the acts of Joseph and His Brethren, I found my way through the steel curtain onto the stage of the Auditorium. But my greatest satisfaction was writing it all up for the *Atlantic,* faculty company, Jenks's Mules and all.

Meeting one of my military colleagues on the campus soon after, he denounced me for having written him up in the *Atlantic.* He admitted he had not yet read the paper, as somebody else in the Quadrangle Club reading room had it, and there were five men waiting to read it after him. When at last he did get his turn to read it, however, he was reconciled.

Upon seeing my article my Chief, Professor Burton, wrote me a most amusing farewell, as I set forth on seas where he said he could not follow. And from Marion Angell, vacationing with her husband President Angell in Essex County, New York, came a delightful letter, gaily ending, "It is out of sight. Do it again." So we expressed ourselves in those days.

Mr. Sedgwick crowned his generosity by putting it in the new *Atlantic* anthology, *Atlantic Classics,* "intended primarily for use in schools," though I could not see what use it could be in schools.

But I followed this airy trifle shortly with another entitled "Do One and One Make Two?" showing the narrow limits within which this familiar affirmation is true. I was rewarded by a very handsome note from Mr. Ralph Adams Cram, saying how penetrating and constructive he had found my engaging article. And my old friend Edwin H. Lewis, the poet, went so far as to compare "The Weekender" with the labors of the late Charles Lamb! When I sent Mr. Sedgwick a little paper called "Things Seen and Heard," he replied, "A paper of the distinguished inconsequence of 'Things Seen and Heard' is a great comfort to an editor. I have enjoyed it greatly, and our readers will too."

But of all these generous reactions the one that pleased me most came from New York when Mrs. Goodspeed was meeting with the members of the Y.W.C.A. National Board and found that "The Weekender" had been read among them and had even enhanced her welcome. My heart was really touched.

But enough of this. Only, my brief career as an essayist was one of the happiest experiences of a long life. Professor Small, our great sociologist at Chicago, even thought he discerned a philosophy peeping shyly through my paragraphs, and teachers of English have included some of them in volumes of select essays for student use. One on "Buying Happiness" was even translated into Spanish, for an international monthly, I don't see why, and—oh yes, best of all, "The Art of Being Outshone" reappeared as leading article in *The Reader's Digest,* no less! What more can I say? The force of nature could no farther go. Mr. Sedgwick sent me a small check—ten dollars—"your part," he said, "of the modest loot." This disposed forever—at least as far as I was concerned—of the popular delusion that vast sums are paid for these reprinted articles.

The generous hospitality of the *Atlantic* extended also to graver pieces on "The Ghost of King James" when I sought to repel some of the cruder slanders on my translation of the New Testament, from the heights of the *Atlantic.* There was also one in later years on "The Original Language of the Gospels," on which it struck me a good deal of nonsense was being written.

Among the new friends that article writing brought me were the members of the Chicago Society of Midland Authors, a genial body of middle west writers founded by Zona Gale, Hobart Chatfield-Taylor, Hamlin Garland, and kindred spirits whose companionship I greatly enjoyed. Later, the P.E.N. was also established in Chicago chiefly through the efforts of Fanny Butcher, the *Tribune* columnist. This organization brought us many pleasant social opportunities. I remember I once had the honor of taking Victoria Sackville-West in to dinner. As for the Midland Authors, when I was Vice-President of them, I was once called upon much against my will to introduce the Sea Raider, Count von Luckner, to a luncheon meeting but found him to my amazement a most agreeable old fellow. He told us how in youth he ran away from his father's fine house in Dresden to find Buffalo Bill. Proceeding by way of Australia to San Francisco, he hitchhiked over the Sierras and the Rockies to Bill's home in Colorado Springs, only to learn that the great man was away, in Germany, Dresden in fact, where he was being entertained at von Luckner's home! This was certainly a most edifying tale, for a Sea Raider. I have no doubt it's in his memoirs but I heard it from his own lips. Fanny Butcher produced a telephone book, and he obligingly tore it into sixteen equal parts (one of his well-known accomplishments) and thus brought the meeting to a close.

Rising to the presidency of the Midland Authors I had the pleasure of introducing to them one of the founders, our dear friend Zona Gale, and of seeing Mignon Eberhart join our ranks. And one enchanted evening I brought to the society William Gillette, the genuine Sherlock Holmes of the stage. I had never seen the Midland Authors so moved. Before the speaker's arrival, one veteran member approached me almost with tears in his eyes. Did I really think Mr. Gillette would come? He had been a worshiper of his for a generation and had a great collection of Gillette theater programs covering many years which he wished to show him. As Mr. Gillette took his place at the table, he recognized Miss Edith Wyatt and went around the end of the table to speak to her. They had last met at the London dinner in honor of Mark Twain.

I persuaded Mr. Gillette to come out to the Quadrangle Club of which I was President that year, to speak at a luncheon, which he did, to the great delight of as many of the faculty as could crowd into the second floor. I had tried in vain by letter to secure him for these speeches but I had the good fortune to meet him at a dinner at Tracy Drake's apartment in the Blackstone, and when I took it up with him personally he promptly reconsidered.

Our genial secretary, Mr. Arthur Meeker, called me up one day to ask me to pick up Theodore Dreiser at his hotel, the Annex, and bring him up to the P.E.N. luncheon at the Casino, as I was, he observed, the only person coming from the South Side. Though stung by this remark, which seemed to be doubly barbed, I paused for Mr. Dreiser and brought him along. Neither of us had ever read a line of the other, and there seemed to be nothing to talk about until I thought I remembered something about his attitude toward life in general, and asked him if he still felt just as hopeless about things and he gloomily replied, Yes, he saw no reason for any encouragement. As we entered the Club, I seemed to remember that he was lecturing around town and so I asked him, as we went upstairs, whether he made very elaborate preparations for his lectures. Glancing back at me over his shoulder as we mounted the stairs, he replied,

"Oh no! I never give it a thought beforehand."

Startled by this observation, I followed him upstairs and upon reaching the P.E.N. group, I sat down beside a most agreeable North Side woman, at whose house the other guest of honor, Abbé Dimnet, was being entertained.

She had taken him the evening before to hear Mr. Dreiser, who she said had spoken for some two hours most uninterestingly, just talking about himself. She said she had told the Abbé that abroad the audience would have simply walked out long before the end and that she and the Abbé had agreed to keep each other awake till he stopped.

Of course I had the key to this experience fresh in my mind, from an authoritative source. Should I then betray a brother lecturer, or should I respect his fatal secret? What would you have done?

But encompassed by literary influences as I now was, was

it strange that I grasped at the leading literary vehicle of modern life, and wrote a mystery story? All the more, since Mrs. Goodspeed proposed the idea, and for a subject referred me to a colophon I had found in a manuscript I had "discovered," as we call it.

We were down at Urbana for a Sunday evening lecture at the University, and she said to me,

"Why don't you write a mystery story about that curse you found in the colophon of the Rockefeller McCormick manuscript?"

I jotted the idea down on a sheet of the hotel paper—it was February 24, 1934—and followed it out that summer. After all, all a writer needs for a book is the idea. Nay, had I not the example of that impeccable man, James Moffatt, and his express advice to do so? Why, I was simply, as the politicians say, "drafted." A divinity colleague in Chicago speaking of it inquired wistfully whether I just "wrote it right off." I could not bear to tell him that the hopeless mess into which I got our hero and heroine one day I spent the next laboriously extricating them from. That would have destroyed his illusion! But as Moffatt said to me, firmly clutching the lapel of my coat,

"Most people have to pay to get their first mystery story published, but mine brought me a hundred pounds." I may say that following his example closely, so did mine, but then for some inexplicable reason, instead of taking its rightful place among the classics of its field, went out of print and became a collector's item.

I did not think it necessary to declare on the flyleaf of my book, as the manner of some is, that all the situations and characters in it were entirely fictitious. Where would such a method have left *Uncle Tom's Cabin,* for instance—if you've ever read the *Key* to it? That declares that practically none of them are. Nor could I say that any resemblance to any actual persons or incidents was purely coincidental, since the very reverse was true. Mine was, if I may say so, the highest realism. All the characters were drawn from life, of course with their names slightly altered for propriety's sake. Nor was I afterward deeply offended to hear them calling one another by these thinly disguised sobriquets. Of course I did not undertake in this work to associate any of them with any high crime or misdemeanor though there have to be such things in any lively work of this description. Yet my villains too were drawn from life no less faithfully; give the devil his due, I say. But I knew them to be safely located in remote parts of the earth, definitely beyond my publisher's fatal spell unless he should have the hardihood to put the book into foreign languages other than the Scandinavian. One work of mine, my agent declared, was to appear in the Finnish tongue but it has never reached me. I do not think I could bear to look upon it and say,

"Can this be I?"

One afternoon after luncheon I picked up a little book called *Julia Newberry's Journal,* published by two spirited Chicago women, the Ayer sisters, Harriet Ayer Barnes and Janet Ayer Fairbank, both of them accomplished novelists. And as I read the journal entries of a lively American girl in the eighties rushing about Europe and its gaieties with her mother, and then suddenly struck down in Rome and buried in the English Cemetery, I thought, "Why! This is Daisy Miller, of course!"

For it is just the story of Henry James's heroine and her flirtations so startlingly cut short—by Death. Could anybody doubt that James, coming to Rome just after Julia's death,

used her and her fate for his story? This was about my last
offering to the *Atlantic*. In response to an inquiry Mrs.
Walter Lowrie kindly sent me a photograph of Julia's tombstone from Rome, and Harriet Ayer Barnes wrote me her
full agreement. James was tireless in his search for literary
material, and Julia Newberry's story was almost ready-made
to his hand, when he reached Rome, early in the following
season.

We had the pleasure of entertaining Mr. and Mrs. Sedgwick for a few days in the midst of the Hoover-Roosevelt campaign, and while they were with us, we gave a small dinner
for them to which we asked President and Mrs. Hutchins and
other University people. It was an election year, and Mrs.
Goodspeed could not help exclaiming at finding herself,
a good Republican, seated between two Democrats, Mr.
Sedgwick and Mr. Hutchins. Mr. Hutchins, however, stoutly
denied that he was either a Democrat or a Republican.

"I don't know whom I'll vote for," he gloomily remarked.
"Sometimes I think I'll just have to vote for myself!"

Hoping to interest a benevolent friend in the University,
we once invited Mr. Hutchins to meet her at luncheon. He
was out of town and accepted by telegraph, ending his message, "Thanks, thanks, forever thanks! The exchequer of the
poor."

I suspected this came from one of the World's Great Books
and soon found it in substance in *Richard II*. I told him he
was the only university president in the world who taught his
faculty Shakespeare by telegraph.

I once had occasion to inform him of the discovery of great
deposits of potash in Texas along with the oil that was so
enriching the state university there. He gaily dismissed it as

"A mess of potash?" which for years I considered exceedingly good repartee, and highly original—until I found it in the *Complete Works of Artemus Ward*. I then transferred the credit from the President's wit to his erudition, an even more suitable line for a university president. But my researches have since led me to believe that Artemus originated most of the principal types of American humor. Even Mark Twain did not escape his influence, for when his reception committee showed him Niagara Falls, he exclaimed,

"Gentlemen, it's a success!"—just what Artemus had said on first seeing the Tomb of Shakespeare! Surely, in simple justice, the *Complete Works of Artemus Ward* must be added to the list of the World's Great Books.

When Mr. Hutchins was once dining at the White House in the bad years of the depression, he found Mr. Hoover silent and preoccupied, and striving to impart a little gaiety to the conversation he told the Chicago story of how at some student affair Mrs. Hutchins, who was very young and looked younger, just like a college girl, heard a student reviling her husband, the President.

"Do you know who I am?" she haughtily inquired of him. "I'm Mrs. Hutchins!"

"Do you know who I am?" the student rejoined sharply.

"No," she replied.

"Thank God!" exclaimed the young man and fled from her.

This roused President Hoover from his lethargy. He burst out laughing.

"That old chestnut?" he exclaimed. "Why, they were telling that around Stanford when I was a student!"

While I do not find this in Mr. Hoover's Memoirs, such at

least is Mr. Hutchins' account of the incident, and I must say if anything could furbish up a well-worn anecdote, this does it.

When my four nephews were very little boys in the nursery, their mother would sometimes take supper with them, to their great delight, and there was often much rivalry as to who should sit next to her. One evening as they were having the usual debate about it, one child asked her,

"Mother, who sits next to God in heaven?"

Though considerably startled, she collected her thoughts sufficiently to say,

"Why, Jesus, I suppose, of course."

"Well, I know who sits next to Jesus," cried another. "Hoover does!"

Those were the days when we were all being trained by Mr. Hoover to waste no food so that there might be enough for the starving people of Europe, and he was much in the children's minds.

Years later, after a speech of Mr. Hoover's in Chicago, when he was Secretary of Commerce, I told him this story. He was much amused and laughed heartily.

"When was this?" he inquired.

I told him it was when he was Food Administrator.

"Well," said he, "I'm afraid I've gone off a good deal since then!"

TWELVE

A Romance of Translation

MANY other men have translated the New Testament into English and published it, but I don't believe any of them has found the experience such an exciting and bewildering romance as I did. And yet I found my way to the task and performed it without the slightest expectation of any such result.

It may seem ungracious to revive a controversy thirty years old, when the international verdict has gone so sweepingly in one's favor, and yet it has such instructive and amusing aspects that one cannot pass it over. For it was in the year 1923 that I performed the horrendous deed of publishing an American translation of the New Testament. This simple act, obscurely done, in my own field of specialization, on the basis of many years of close study, with no expectation of any publicity at all, and quietly published at the University of Chicago Press, called forth from the public press a nation-wide, indeed world-wide and vehement protest, though now, when Jews, Catholics, and Protestants, yes and the Jehovah's Witnesses also are engaged upon modern speech translations or revisions of the Old Testament, or the New Testament, or the Old and New Testament and the Apocrypha, hardly an editor dares lift up his voice against these dreadful undertakings. And not one of these who does, will face the dreadful responsibility of commanding people to show their faith by drinking poison and picking up poisonous snakes! Yet that monstrous and totally unchristian precept is in the very heart of their favorite scripture version, Mark 16:18, which they brazenly urge upon the ignorant pious, with such awful results. It is time we had an authorized version, that is, one recognized as to be read in public worship, that has the intelligence and courage to disown this spurious interpolation, Mark 16:8-20, which is absent from the oldest Greek manuscripts and the earliest versions, and so flatly contradicts Jesus' own experience and teaching, recorded in his second temptation, Matthew 4:7.

But thirty years ago, as I soon saw and frankly said, the fault was basically ours of the biblical profession, for we had so long been silent about the progress of biblical studies and discoveries that the general public was unaware of what was going on, and the newspapers of course had the standpoint of the public, not of the scholars. I therefore made it my business to inform the public, and through them the journalists, of the real situation in biblical research. The lesson of it is, never again to let the public fall behind in these fields. For the sake of that lesson, perhaps the whole quaint story is worth reciting. And not a few of these critical papers, the *Chicago Tribune* for example, have since become, editorially and personally, my cordial friends.

At the regular fortnightly meeting of the New Testament Club, at the University of Chicago, on February 24, 1920, I read a paper on modern-speech translations, discussing the three leading ones, as they were then regarded—Twentieth Century, Weymouth, Moffatt—and criticising them freely. In the discussion that followed, one of my colleagues, Dr.

Shirley J. Case, drily remarked that if I saw so many flaws in these versions, perhaps I had better do one myself, which called forth some laughter at my expense.

But young Mr. Guy C. Crippen of the University of Chicago Press happening to be present, found a serious suggestion in this remark and lost a night's sleep over it. Next morning he laid the idea before Dean Gordon J. Laing, the accomplished editor of the Press, and Gordon lost no time in inviting me to undertake the task for the Press. How well I remember getting his letter one noon, at the Faculty Exchange, and reading it hastily as I crossed Ellis Avenue on my way home. I smiled a superior smile. Every translation of a masterpiece is a failure and why should I labor to produce another? No, not for me! Or so I thought, and it was with some amusement that I read the letter to Mrs. Goodspeed at luncheon.

But she to my surprise seemed to take it seriously. She advised me not to say No too hastily but to think it over. To have the Press actually invite me to undertake it, she thought, might really be an opportunity. So I fenced with the invitation, and tried my hand at the easiest and most familiar part of the whole task, the Gospel of Mark. And how right she was! Without her restraining hand I would have declined Gordon's invitation that afternoon and closed another door in my own face, a thing we all do all too often.

That spring whenever I was called upon to speak in Divinity Chapel, instead of preparing something original to give them, I simply read a few pages from my new translation. And invariably I was listened to with an attention—an almost breathless attention—I had never before had from any audience I had addressed. At the Island too, during those years of preparation, encouraged by my wife and my parents I would read the scripture reading we always had before our Sunday evening sing from my translation manuscript.

So from the beginning my translation was geared to public reading, a course so different from Dr. Moffatt's. I remember once, long before, I was acting as chaplain for the Sunday morning service in Mandel Hall when Dr. Moffatt was the preacher. I asked him before the service whether he would like to have the scripture lesson read from his translation. He replied almost with horror,

"Oh, no! I never read from my translation in church!"

Still, the rest of us often did. I remember especially dear Bishop Williams of Michigan, who prefaced his reading the scripture lesson in another preaching service in Mandel by saying,

"I will read the lesson from Dr. Moffatt's translation. Perhaps the new words will make the old truth bite deeper!"

So it came about that I undertook the task of making a new translation of the Greek New Testament. I had little knowledge of earlier translations made in America of the New Testament or the gospels by scholars like Andrews Norton of Harvard, 1855, H. T. Anderson, 1864, George R. Noyes of Harvard, 1869, F. S. Ballentine, 1902, and A. S. Worrell, 1904, though Chaplain Ballentine entitled his *An American Bible in Modern English, for American Readers.* I felt, however, that as there are more readers of the English Bible in America than in any other country, their especial needs should be taken account of and terms peculiarly British should be given up. I saw no reason, for example, to carry on the illusion that the sterling currency—pounds, shillings, pence and farthings—was in use in the Roman world in the time of Christ, more especially as purchasing power has so greatly altered. Thus a penny is set forth as a reasonable day's wages! This merely confounds the American reader. As does also the British way of speaking of wheat as "corn," which means something so different in this country. This may seem an insignificant point, but as a matter of fact it reduces the familiar story of the apostles finding a path through a field of standing wheat to a positive absurdity; picture them plucking ears of corn—no easy task!—husking them, which requires a good deal of exertion, and then of all things eating the kernels! If it was dry enough to shell, it was too dry to eat! Of course what we call "corn" was unknown in Palestine in Jesus' day, and is planted in rows, or hills, not sown broadcast. The disciples were simply pushing their way, as they had a perfect right to do, along a familiar path now overgrown with the broadcast wheat, and as they went they unconsciously rubbed a few kernels free of the chaff and munched them. An American reader would never get this picture from the King James or any British translation. He would miss the point of the story, which is that the slight, perhaps even unconscious act of rubbing three or four grains free of their tiny husks would be to the Pharisees' way of thinking, threshing, and hence working, on the Sabbath day!

The full modern paragraphing of my translation, a feature I shared with Dr. Richard Weymouth, making every new remark of a speaker in the action a new paragraph, as in modern books, though bitterly criticised and even derided in some quarters (one theologian declared he had never before seen a book so paragraphed!), had the value of revealing to me at least the dialogue character of the Gospel of John. Unlike the other gospels, John develops Jesus' teaching by the conversational method so familiar from the *Dialogues* of Plato. This is in fact a marked Greek trait, which has not received the attention it deserves, as a feature of John.

Unlike Dr. Weymouth, on the other hand, I proposed to keep the margin free from footnotes since there were none in the original New Testament. They distract the reader's attention and they inevitably introduce a technical, non-literary feeling into the aspect of a book. Had Dr. Weymouth lived to see his translation printed he would doubtless have greatly reduced the space given these footnotes, as his publishers have recently done. In the third edition it is sometimes as much as half a page, and in the earliest editions I believe whole hymns are quoted in the footnotes. They probably represent Dr. Weymouth's own working notes from which he meant to make a selection for publication. Dr. Moffatt's few notes, on the other hand, are wholly textual, but even these are generally of little use to the reader.

It is difficult for me to conceive a translation of the New Testament designed only for private meditation and study since every part of it so unmistakably addresses not the solitary Christian but the Christian public, religiously a most significant feature of the book. Religion is a social experience! Such use is indeed definitely contemplated in the very origins of the New Testament books; Paul's letters were of course written to be read before the church groups to which they were addressed and the gospels were made up of materials which had been used in preaching. The Revelation of course particularly requires reading before each of the seven churches to which it is addressed and no doubt was meant for the widest church hearing.

My first serious acquaintance with the Greek New Testament began in 1887 in sophomore year in college—I was not quite sixteen—when Professor Richard S. Colwell had us provide ourselves with a convenient student's edition of the Westcott and Hort text, then comparatively new; it had come out only six years before. We read the Gospel of John, in reasonable instalments, for our Monday recitation, and I became so taken with the work that I continued it by myself at odd hours or moments so that before I was graduated at eighteen I had read the New Testament through in Greek, though of course in a most careless fashion. So the translating of it was an old practice of mine. And of course in my graduate work I had pursued it critically and made something of a specialty of its syntax and lexicography. My work on papyri also now came into focus with my New Testament studies and proved of great assistance, as did my Greek indexes of the Apostolic Fathers and the early apologists, published at Leipzig in 1907, 1912. Greek syntax studies with Dr. Burton and Dr. William Gardner Hale fortified me on that side. I had taught elementary Greek, Xenophon and Homer for a number of years, and for twenty years had taught reading the Greek New Testament and New Testament grammar every year at least once, on the University level. All this was to prove of the utmost value to me in this new undertaking. I recite it all here, because my preparation was soon to be vigorously called in question, in every part of the country, and overseas.

One thing in particular I got from Professor Hale, one of the great Latinists of his day, and a man of very wide culture.

"Cultivate your English feeling," he used to say to us, and how very important that is, especially in language study where so often almost no attention is paid to English, and all attention riveted on the language studied. Translation English is mostly no English at all. And how much there is of this careless English in the Bible. "Whom do men say that I am?" "Whom do ye say that I am?" Both these sentences are grammatically wrong as English. This blunder occurs six times in the King James version. But a translation must be made into English, and English just as sound as the Greek you translate from.

I was never busier in the University than during the three years I worked on my translation for beside my teaching in the New Testament department, I had in the autumn of 1920 undertaken the duties of Secretary to the President, Dr. Harry Pratt Judson, and those were not duties which could be slighted or postponed. I spent the day in the office, and as my oculist had long before forbidden me to do any close work at night, my time for the translation was very limited. I tried to make up for this lack of time by working hard when I did work, but I soon learned that after I had done fifteen or sixteen verses I found myself saying, "Oh, that is good enough; let it go at that," and I observed that what I did after that had lost its edge and quality. So I made it a practice to do no more at that session.

The most difficult thing, I found, was to forget the old translations, King James and especially the Revised Versions, English and American, which I found I knew better than I did King James. The familiarity we all have with the English Bible was my greatest obstacle. For of course I did not wish merely to reproduce that, but to give my version something of the force and freshness that reside in the original Greek. I wanted my translation to make on the modern reader something of the impression the New Testament must have made on its earliest readers, and to invite the continuous reading of a whole book at a time. That was what I was striving for.

It is often assumed that the familiar style, the style of modern speech, is an easy, careless style to write. Quite the opposite. True, it is not learned in the study or in the class-room, but in social contacts with well-bred men and women who can talk. There is a kind of churchman and a kind of scholar that has no general social contacts; and such men do not learn the familiar style, and consequently cannot write it. They may think themselves above it, but the result is the same. When they try to write it, they lapse into all sorts of barbarisms. To point some of these out would be ungenerous. It is simple enough to write the stiff formal style of the old translators, but it is far more taxing to write in the familiar spoken English of today. We must remember Hale's old maxim, "Cultivate your English feeling!" Many present-day translators would not even see what he meant!

The last of the manuscript of the translation I turned in at the University Press the last week of May, 1923, but we were already deep in the proof of the gospels. On the fourth of June I had luncheon at the Cliff Dwellers with my old boyhood friend Henry J. Smith, managing editor of the Chicago *Daily News,* whom President Burton wished to bring to the University as "public relations" or publicity man. I had been doing that work as best I could, as Secretary to the President, but I rejoiced at the prospect of turning it over to such a capable individual as Harry Smith. He seemed to think favorably of our proposition, which he later accepted. As we walked down Michigan Avenue after luncheon, he said to me,

"Edgar, why aren't you writing any more articles for the *Atlantic?*"

He was famous for stimulating literary work among his

associates, as men like Gunther and others of his staff will
bear witness. No wonder so many of them achieved fame for
their books.

"Oh," said I, "I'm too busy translating the New Testament."

He was much interested at once.

"Are you translating the New Testament?" he said eagerly.
"That'll be news when it comes out."

"I don't think so," said I. "For a New Testament man, it's
just part of the day's work."

"I do," said Harry, "if a University of Chicago man does
it!" And we dropped the subject.

I spent my weekends up at the Island, with Elfleda and
Father, and one Saturday afternoon, as we were lazily fishing
over on Razor Back, she said to me,

"How do you expect your translation to sell?"

"Oh," said I, "about a thousand a year, I suppose; about
like my Story of the New Testament." I was entirely serious
in this; I saw no reason for any large sale for the book. There
was nothing whatever sensational about it, and there were
several other modern-speech New Testament translations on
the market. Little did I think it would introduce me to a
thousand audiences in the years ahead.

It was a few days later, in Chicago, when the book was in
galley proof, that the excitement began. On the afternoon
of Wednesday, August 22, 1923, a pleasant young man from
the *Daily News* called at the office to interview me about the
translation. I felt that it was too soon to say anything, as the
book would not appear for a month or more, and any publicity now would be forgotten by that time, so I fenced with
the young man and tried to put him off. (His name was John
Gunther, but this meant nothing to me then.) He hung on,

however, evidently resolved to have an interview, and I finally sent him over to the University Press to talk with the Manager, Donald Bean.

Toward five o'clock Mr. Bean telephoned that the *News* was determined to print a statement and we might as well give them what they wanted, although he too felt it was much too early for the publicity to do the book any good. I reluctantly agreed, but stipulated that I must cover the Associated Press which had always treated University news very fairly, so I dictated a brief account for my friend Mr. Cutter of the A.P. and put it in the mail. We also gave him and Mr. Gunther a galley of proof as a sample of what the book would be like.

Next morning the papers began to call up about the book— *News, Post, Journal*—and an *Examiner* reporter came to the office with a photographer—all very novel experiences for me. I began to feel that something must be going on. Of course, August is notoriously the "silly season" with newsmen, and there was so little real news—war, crime, disaster—that anything that promised a paragraph was welcomed—one reason Harry had sent John out when he did. When I reached the office that afternoon I found Mr. Herman G. Seely of the Chicago *Evening Post* awaiting me. He said that Mr. Shaffer, the publisher of the *Post*, wished to publish the translation serially on his editorial page, and would we consent?

This was really fame, but I was so staggered that I did not know what to say.

"Why," said I, "your Old Man has not even seen my translation! How can he possibly know whether he wants to publish it or not?"

"He has seen the two hundred words the Associated Press has put on the wires, and that's enough for him!" said Mr.

Seely. I could only thank him and refer him to Mr. Bean at the University Press for a decision. Even there, the experience was so new that it took them some time to decide to accept it. But it was a goodly sight, for us, that autumn to see the horse-drawn delivery wagons of the *Evening Post* with their sides covered with announcements of the American Translation, which could be read daily in the *Evening Post!* Mr. Shaffer remained a good friend of the translation through the trying days that followed when it so often needed a friend.

The *Examiner* had sent out a reporter, Bruce Grant, for an interview and I gave him a long one, talking steadily for nearly two hours. He did not take a note but seemed to be listening closely. I read his interview the next morning with grave apprehensions but it was admirable. He got my points and presented them clearly and fairly in what I believe is called a six-column spread. This was about the way the papers handled the matter, the news columns generally fairly and informedly. The excitement was provided by the editorials.

On Thursday I parted with the last section of the final proof, and in the afternoon I was interviewed for an hour by Duncan Clark, for *Success* magazine.

Friday the 24th began early, for at 7:45 the United Press was on the wire. Somehow or other it had become possessed of a galley proof of the eleventh chapter of Luke, with its somewhat abbreviated form of the Lord's Prayer, and the U.P. man, one H. E. Caylor, mistakenly supposing that that was where the Lord's Prayer came from, leaped to the conclusion that I had shortened the Lord's Prayer. Now if there is one thing the English-speaking world will not tolerate, it is shortening the Lord's Prayer, and the U.P. proceeded to make the most of it.

In Philadelphia the *Bulletin* recorded the unanimous disapproval of the clergy. In Boston it so aroused the old Boston *Transcript* that it devoted two editorials to excoriating me for abbreviating the Lord's Prayer, and the long shadow of this altogether groundless accusation reached even to Capetown, South Africa, where further editorial disapproval was evinced. Of course, it is actually from the Sermon on the Mount in Matthew that all churches derive the Lord's Prayer, as well as the Beatitudes and the Golden Rule, of all of which Luke has variant forms. Certainly the charge made against me can be made just as truly against every serious New Testament translation or revision from Alexander Campbell in 1826 down to the Catholic revision of 1941, the *Revised Standard Version* of 1946, and the Jehovah's Witnesses New Testament of 1951. Not one has transferred Matthew's Lord's Prayer to Luke; that is, as the U.P. puts it, they have all shortened the Lord's Prayer!

The fact was, nothing could have been more mistaken than to say I had tampered with the text. I had taught textual criticism for twenty years, and had the utmost confidence in its results. No translator had been more rigorously faithful to them, to the very last, minutest detail. I had deciphered, collated and published half a dozen Greek manuscripts of the gospels. The United Press was attacking the book on the point on which it was strongest, in fact unassailable, by any truthful means.

That Friday afternoon Underwood sent its photographer around to take my picture, and at 10:30 Friday night the *Tribune* telephoned for my translation of the Beatitudes to print side by side with those of King James next morning. And then on Saturday morning the *Examiner* gave its views of the translation in a leading editorial by Oswald F. Schuette, whose very limited education and Roman Catholic faith explained his aversion to all private translations of the Bible.

Most amusingly this editorial appeared in the Hearst papers generally, especially the little *Americans* all over the land. What must Mr. Schuette think of the current Catholic movement, with headquarters in Kansas City, and with the Pope's approval, to put the Old Testament into familiar modern English for American Catholics? He can hardly have anticipated such a complete victory for the modern-speech school of translators. Some of his criticisms are too good to be forgotten. "In music," said he, "a gentleman of such limitations would jazz a Beethoven sonata." This vigorous sentence which so well summarizes Mr. Schuette's review, I have had the pleasure of reading to hundreds of lecture audiences to their immense gratification. With it we may contrast Cardinal Gibbons' delightful introduction to Father Spencer's *Modern Speech Gospels*, 1898: "Father Spencer," said the Cardinal, "has endeavored to represent Our Lord and the Apostles as speaking, not in an antique style, but in the language they would speak if they lived among us now." Surely the aim of the modern speech translators has never been better put.

Monday morning I was awakened from a troubled sleep by a friend calling, "Have you seen the *Tribune*?" It was Ernest Wilkins, afterward President of Oberlin College, who thus introduced me to the *Tribune*'s tribute, entitled "Monkeying with the Bible." The *Tribune* spoke up strongly for the King James version. "Tampering with it," it declared, "is chipping a cathedral." It regarded the King James version as a seamless coat, a perfect version. I was reminded that the King James version, the first issue of the first edition of which I have before me, underwent a lamentable amount of chipping after the appearance of Samuel Johnson's dictionary in 1755, to which of course it had to be conformed. The current forms of it, as we all know, go back without exception to Professor Benjamin Blayney's revision of 1769. These alterations have so far as I know never been counted, but it is safe to say they are not less than eighty thousand, and they may reach a hundred thousand. But as I hastened to inform the *Tribune*, this was all done a hundred years before my birth so that it is unreasonable to hold me responsible for any part of it. Worse yet, the Apocrypha, the whole transept of the *Tribune's* noble cathedral, has long since disappeared from the King James version, and the *Tribune* has never missed it!

This admirable editorial, in far better taste, of course, than that of Mr. Schuette (I only wish I might reprint them both), appeared a fortnight later in Paris in its European edition and was sent me from abroad by delighted friends. For after all both papers were simply trying in their own ways to help us along, and that was no doubt the end result of all their striving.

Not a whit behind the *Tribune* was *The New York Times* of the same date, August 27. Its editorial was cuttingly entitled "The Bible A La Chicago." "When it comes to the substitution of 'lamp' for candle," said the *Times*, "and 'peck-measure' for 'bushel,' and 'stand' for 'candlestick,' one is struck by the absurdity of endeavoring to 'modernize' language. Had the translator been willing to 'go the whole hog,' he would have written 'electric light' instead of 'lamp,' and 'fixture' instead of 'stand.' "

No doubt the effort to modernize language, which the *Times* found so absurd, is involved here, but it was not on my part but on that of William Tyndale, who started the whole business by translating the Greek word "lamp" by what he saw all about him, that is, candles. This brought candlestick in its wake, of course, and deceived the *Times* into thinking that the Greco-Roman world was lighted by candles, in candlesticks, which is far, far from the truth. Perhaps the *Times* has never seen the commonest souvenir of Greco-Roman antiquity, the tiny lamp of bronze, iron, or clay, perhaps an inch and a half high, which had to be set on a stand to give any light to speak of. Tyndale, in a world of candles, sought to modernize the picture for his generation. Of course, had not my old friend John Finley, the editor of *The New York Times,* been in Palestine that summer, this would never have happened.

For what a man John Finley was! In his early years with his friend and mine, Victor Elting, he had followed the track of La Salle and Tonty by trail and canoe through all their wanderings over Northern Illinois and Wisconsin. And one summer afternoon in New York, when his wife was away and nobody was at the apartment, he came down from the office and feeling like a good long walk, he walked to Princeton! Arriving there in the small hours, he got a cup of coffee at an all-night stand, caught a stage back to New York, had a shower at the apartment, and so back to the office again for the day's work. I shall always wish he had been in town to review the translation, for his reactions I should have welcomed and valued.

George Eliot once said that you cannot examine the middle aged. How wrong she was! Offer the newspaper editors a new translation of the New Testament and they will send in their examination papers in the greatest possible hurry. How many of them I have in my files.

The editors were totally unaware of the rise of the science

of comparative philology, chiefly in the last century, and what it has done for the study of Greek; and of the discovery, chiefly around 1900, in countless thousands of the Greek documentary papyri, which have proved that the New Testament was written in the language of everyday life. The Greek of the New Testament has always perplexed New Testament scholars; it is not classical Greek, and yet it is not like the Greek version of the Old Testament. One German theologian, in evident desperation, once declared that it was a miracle language, especially devised by Providence for purposes of revelation! It remained for the Greek papyrus documents of common life—letters, contracts, invitations, accounts, deeds, leases, receipts, wills, business settlements of every kind—to settle the question fifty-seven years ago.

Not only the American press was disturbed over the translation; the New York representative of the London *Telegraph* cabled the London office a strange jumble of my translation with King James and his own vocabulary, which that paper published as my version of the thirteenth chapter of I Corinthians. The New York office later explained that this jumble had been necessitated by the expense of cabling to London! The editor had felt obliged to condense and paraphrase. Based upon such misinformation British opinion was naturally unfavorable: "Heaven preserve us from Chicago professors," one editorial began, going on to compare me unfavorably with a Hottentot. It seemed to me strange that a paper so averse to the expense of telegraphing should call itself the *Telegraph*; it was so frankly more concerned about getting the news cheap than about getting it right. Might it not better be called *The Pony Express*? The Romans had an expression for it, in their ancient joke about the false etymology—*lucus—a non lucendo!* This notion of the illiterate character of my translation still reappears from time to time, in Berkeley, Boston and London.

Yet on October 23 Mr. Doran wrote to inquire as to the availability of the translation for publication by Hodder and Stoughton in London. And on the same day my father touched me very much by writing me, "Many congratulations and good wishes on what should be your happiest birthday."

The London *Times Literary Supplement* now came along with a brief and rather guarded review. It only objected to my translation of Matthew 1:18, professing to prefer the King James reading, "Now the birth of Jesus Christ was in this wise." This was an unfortunate example for that is not the reading of King James but of the Rheims New Testament of 1582, the first Catholic version!

The immediate local reaction to the newspapers' announcement of the translation was recorded in the Chicago *Daily News* on August 24. Dr. Carwardine thought the undertaking most absurd, but of course we do not know what the reporter asked him, and the book itself was not to appear for more than a month. Dr. Duncan C. Milner was prepared to welcome the translation, as was Dr. Ernest A. Bell, of the Night Church. Dr. Keene Ryan, however, hailed me as the Mr. Dooley of the University, and offered this observation, which was destined to go far:

"Theologians and laymen alike will await with awe for God to strike him dead for thus laying his calloused hands upon the Holy of Holies."

He added that nobody much would read the book, which was just what I had always expected.

But it helped me in this strife of tongues to remember that in colonial times a minister who could not in the pulpit translate the text and lesson for the day from the Greek New

Testament was not thought fit to minister to a Christian congregation.

All my critics, it is interesting to note, had no other idea of retranslating the New Testament than to take the King James version in its current commercial form and rephrase its meaning! Indeed one would not even need to know Greek to do what they envisioned.

The Monday of the *Tribune*'s editorial I had thirty-two letters about the translation: One, from a Negro in New York, touched me. He said the book would be refused by the rich and educated, but welcomed by the poor and ignorant. I was sincerely pleased by this. Another from another New Yorker, said the writer was sorry he had not known of my undertaking, for he could have been of great assistance to me. He said he was the reincarnation of the apostle Paul, also of the Archangel Michael, the prophet Jeremiah, and even the Patriarch Noah! He must have led a very interesting life. Of course, crank letters are innumerable, but this was one of the quaintest I had ever seen.

That Monday was also signalized by the column-long editorial in the St. Louis *Globe-Democrat*, ending with these immortal words: "It is as much of an anachronism to put the gospels in colloquial American terms of to-day as it would be to put pants on the twelve Apostles." We can only hope that the editor of the *Globe-Democrat* will never translate the New Testament.

Twenty more translation letters came on Tuesday. I remember I heard from thirty-one states in five days. Some, of course, were mere crank letters, some were hostile, but most were cordial and commendatory. It was especially nice to hear from old friends of earlier years who were pleased at what I had done, and at the interest it had aroused.

Late in September the Columbia *Record* and another paper in South Carolina, stung by the elimination of candles from the New Testament, declared in almost the same words that if we are to have lamps instead of candles, we might as well give Ruth a McCormick harvester in place of a scythe. One wonders what scythe. She had no scythe. Do these editors, in their retrospective moments, picture Ruth as she

> stood in tears amid the alien corn

(meaning wheat, of course)—as leaning on her scythe? How did she ever come to be possessed of a scythe?

The scythe is totally unknown to the Bible and to the archeology of Palestine and the adjacent country. Of course, there is no mention of one in the book of Ruth. Is it the difficult word "glean" that has misled these seasoned editorial writers? They think gleaning is something you do with a scythe, instead of an apron! And yet "glean" is one of the twenty thousand commonest words in the English language, according to Dr. E. L. Thorndike of Columbia University and his famous *Junior Dictionary,* for children from ten to fifteen years of age.

One poor fellow, writing an editorial, cried out, "How can anybody hope to improve on such a sentence as 'Blessed are the pure in spirit'?" He really thought that was something from the Bible, when as a matter of fact, he had thought it up himself, but felt that it was so good it must have come from Holy Writ.

The *Deseret News,* the leading Mormon paper of Salt Lake City, in its issue of August 31, 1923, under the discouraging heading, "Little Chance for Success," could think of no other reason for my translation than a desire on my part "to give it a personal interpretation or construe its language to

meet his own private conceptions." Of course, it had no idea
how shockingly revealing this comment was. But seven years
later the Mormon Church invited me to Utah to teach half
the summer in Brigham Young University, and one Sunday
afternoon even put me into Brigham Young's pulpit, at the
great weekly meeting in the Tabernacle. The young seminary
men in my class became so attached to my translation that
they tried to interest the Church authorities in publishing a
special edition of it but this neither the Presidents nor I
could approve.

Canadian editors were loud in their allegiance to King
James. Of course that version is a royal monopoly and cannot
be printed anywhere in the British empire without a license
from the royal printers. A Guelph editor professed himself
familiar with the "writings" of Socrates and Homer (neither
of whom ever wrote a line), which perhaps sufficiently shows
the depth of his culture. Others talked loosely of the absurdity of altering Shakespeare, altogether unaware of the
extent to which this has in fact gone! How many people,
one wonders, have ever seen an unaltered Shakespeare? And
others spoke as though the King James version had never
before been altered, quite innocent of all that has happened
to its text since it used to speak of Marie, charet, moneth,
fornace, middes, thorow, ancres, fift, sixt, moe, fet, creeple
and Hierusalem. They naïvely suppose that their department-
store copy is an accurate reproduction of the edition of 1611,
and are totally unaware of all that Benjamin Blayney did to
improve and modernize it in 1769. Indeed one Chicago paper,
the *Defender*, declared that the Lord's Prayer had existed
in its present form unchanged ever since the time of Christ!
This unfortunate man, too, supposed the New Testament was
written in English. It seemed to me that when newspaper

writers from coast to coast made such preposterous statements as these, it was time for scholars to speak up.

A priceless editorial was that in the Indianapolis *Star*, of September 2, which accepted the U.P. story that I had shortened the Lord's Prayer:

"Nothing stops his devastating pen. He has even abbreviated the Lord's Prayer, a petition not so long originally but that hustling, hurrying Chicagoans could find time for it, if they ever thought of prayer. It is a petition that in its present wording has been held sacred for nearly two thousand years, for the King James translators are said to have made no changes."

One rubs one's eyes at this extraordinary statement, but there is no escaping its meaning: The writer actually thought the Lord's Prayer was originally uttered in English. One hardly knows where to begin with such a mind. He must suppose all men everywhere have always spoken English. There is no other way to understand his words.

Of course, the Lord's Prayer is well known today in two forms, one with, and the other without, the fine doxology, which is absent from the Latin Vulgate and from the oldest Greek manuscripts, having been evidently made up from David's prayer in I Chronicles 29:11. The Prayer Book (The Book of Common Prayer) to this day includes two forms of the Lord's Prayer, one with and one without the doxology. And, of course, Protestant churches vary from one fold to another as to whether to say "debts" or "trespasses." But all ancient manuscripts agree that Luke's Lord's Prayer is several clauses shorter than Matthew's and Christian liturgy has always preferred Matthew's to Luke's, just as it has preferred Matthew's Beatitudes.

So far from my being the first modern translator to give

the Lord's Prayer of Luke, chapter eleven, with only five petitions, Moffatt had done so in 1913, the *Twentieth Century*, in 1905, Weymouth, in 1903, the *American Standard Version*, in 1901, the *English Revised Version*, in 1881, printed in full in New York and Chicago newspapers, and widely recognized as an Authorized Version—not to mention George R. Noyes of Harvard, in 1869, Andrews Norton of Harvard, in 1855, and Alexander Campbell, in 1826. All subsequent manuscript discoveries—and it has been an era of unparalleled manuscript discovery—have confirmed the soundness of their procedure. Of course, this irresponsible misrepresentation did the translation irreparable harm—Indianapolis, Boston, London, Cape Town! It is utterly untrue that the King James revisers made no change in the Lord's Prayer as it had stood in the Bishops' Bible, revised edition, of 1572, on which they rested, and every preceding reviser had altered it from the form his predecessor had given it. The idea that it had ever possessed any English fixity is a complete delusion. But when this English fixity is pushed back two thousand years, it becomes mere delirium.

I remember well going out to the University on a bus in the dusk that Tuesday evening in '23, after dinner at the University Club. I had a long time to reflect, and I felt deeply injured. The editorial criticism that was beginning to pour in from all over the country hurt me. I had done obscurely and in all good conscience a painstaking piece of work in my own field. No man among my critics had had anything like the preparation for such a task that I had had; I now began to understand why President Harper had insisted that I have so much; I was in a most favorable position to defend my version. And after all, as I soberly reflected, what had I to complain of? They had burned William Tyndale at the stake! And he was just the first of the "private translators."

Friday night after Convocation I took the old Fisherman's Special for Northern Wisconsin and the Island, and there at last laid the situation as I saw it before my wife and my father. Of course, they had had my letters and had seen the papers and were pretty well abreast of things, but I had not seen either of them since the Gunther interview broke on the 23rd. What I complained of was that the editorial writers all over the country, east and west, wrote just as though King James himself or his ghost were at their elbow; they used almost the same phraseology in their attacks.

Father finally got up and stood with his back to the fire-place, and his hands clasped behind him in a characteristic attitude.

"Why don't you write an article for the *Atlantic*," he asked, "and call it 'Laying the Ghost of King James'?"

He knew that doing this would at least soothe my wounded spirit. Anyway I jumped at his suggestion.

"Father," said I, "that's exactly what I'll do!"

Mr. Sedgwick welcomed the proposition and later accepted the article which came out in January. I called it "The Ghost of King James," and you may be sure the last thing my editor-critics had expected was to find themselves answered in the columns of the *Atlantic*. A gentleman in England liked it so well that he had it reprinted as a pamphlet to circulate over there.

One of the early letters I received about the translation gave me an inordinate amount of entertainment, which I did not fail to share with my lecture audience. It came from a place in New Jersey, and was dated September 29, 1923. The writer had seen the translation of the Sermon on the Mount in the New York *Herald*. He had formed the notion that I proposed to bring the Gettysburg Address up to date, and desired me also to revise the Emancipation Proclamation and the Constitution of the United States and bring them up to date. He was evidently laboring under intense excitement. I wrote him a soothing letter, assuring him I had never expressed any such intention as to the Address, but adding that if he would send me the original Greek of the Gettysburg Address, the Emancipation Proclamation and the Constitution of the United States, I would do what I could for him. This may have been ruthless treatment of his request, but I thought it might convey to him the fact that the New Testament was originally written in Greek.

Less than a week after the translation was so prematurely announced, in fact on August 29, the George Matthew Adams Syndicate asked for the rights of serial publication in the newspapers outside of Chicago, and a contract was made with the University Press which resulted in its appearance in daily installments in newspapers all over the United States. What this did for it in the way of publicity can be imagined. There had been nothing like it since the day in May, 1881, when the Chicago *Times* and the Chicago *Tribune* both published in full, as a part of their daily issue, the Revised Version of the New Testament, copies of which had reached New York from London the day before.

Twenty-four newspapers in as many cities and in a dozen states from coast to coast, as well as Canada published the translation that autumn. One at least of them, the Cleveland *Press,* printed it in uniform pages, so that it could be clipped and put into a scrapbook. This was an unprecedented welcome for a new translation. Some of them printed it in full-page installments that were little short of magnificent.

Very soon after the translation made its appearance, on October 1, Mr. William Ziegler Nourse, a well-known radio broadcaster in Chicago, asked to be allowed to broadcast selections from it over KYW and of course we were happy to have it so intelligently read to a radio audience. So the translation soon found generous allies in the radio as well as in the press. As I write of its reception now, thirty years after, it all sounds very much like a dream.

So long before January the plot had thickened. Of course, old friends of each of us had written—old teachers, fellow students, and friends of other days. President Faunce of Brown wrote beautifully, "Like Scott's Old Mortality, you have carved anew the old sentences, obscured by time and overgrown with misunderstandings, and we are all your debtors."

On November 14 Professor A. T. Robertson of the Baptist Seminary at Louisville, veteran New Testament scholar of the south, sent me his congratulations, and ten days later, Professor Robert A. Millikan, of Cal. Tech., former colleague and neighbor in Chicago, sent me his. One man about whose opinion I cared greatly was my former colleague and friend Richard Green Moulton, famous editor of *The Modern Reader's Bible*. He wrote me to my great relief that he liked everything about it except the name! "An American Translation" displeased him, for it seemed to build up the old wall between Britain and America he had spent his life tearing down. But I could not recant; experience has proved that British and American English are definitely divergent. Other great ministers of my acquaintance supported me cordially, Dr. Coffin and Dr. Woelfkin in New York, Dr. Ashby Jones in Atlanta, Dr. A. W. Wishart in Grand Rapids, Dr. James Gordon Gilkey of Springfield, Massachusetts, Dr. Charles W.

Gilkey, Dr. E. S. Ames, Dr. W. C. Covert, Dr. J. G. K. Mc-
Clure and Rabbi Louis L. Mann, of Chicago.

The University too stood by me handsomely not only by
giving me a hearing on the Moody foundation, and before
the Philological Society and the Quadrangle Club, and inviting me to speak at a meeting of friends of the University
down town (which I felt obliged to decline), but also by many
most generous personal messages. One from Mr. Ryerson I
greatly prized. Mr. Ryerson said, "It has seemed to me so well
done, and so well worth doing." No comment I received
pleased me more than this.

Another old friend of my father's who wrote me at great
length with his own hand was Dr. Frederick T. Gates, who
had played such an important part in the founding of the
University, and subsequently as Mr. Rockefeller's adviser
in his philanthropies. Some of his New York colleagues wrote
us that for a time he carried the book around with him and
read passages of especial interest aloud to them when they
met! This did me a great deal of good, on Father's account.
"You have done a great service," he wrote, "I congratulate
you, and I congratulate still more your father." In March
Professor George Holley Gilbert, one of the deans of American New Testament scholars, wrote me from Dorset, Vermont, his "heartiest congratulations" on the translation. A
generous letter of really wonderful commendation and understanding came from Bishop Francis J. McConnell, at
Pittsburgh. In short, the encouragement I received far outweighed the editorial slurs I had sustained and more than
restored my equilibrium.

The greatest thing about a book is the friends it makes you
and certainly the translation did nothing more delightful for
us than that it brought us the friendship of Mme. Louise

Homer, then such a star of opera. One afternoon, the telephone rang and a beautiful, gracious voice said,

"This is Louise Homer."

Really, I could not believe it. I thought it must be her daughter, but with some amusement she set me right, and expressed her pleasure in the translation. (How much editorial abuse do you think that outweighed? Why, all of it, of course!) We at once invited her out to the University for the Saturday game, which she declined, but agreed to come out to the house for tea after it.

We had two young couples with us for luncheon and the game, which was just around the corner from our house, and they were only too glad to come back to the house for tea after the game to meet Mme. Homer. Her brother Mr. Beatty came with her. This was the beginning of a long friendship and correspondence. She immediately invited us to come and hear *Samson and Delilah,* and come back stage afterward to see her, which we were only too happy to do. Driving east one summer, we called on her at her beautiful home on Lake George, and were graciously received.

The popular response to the translation was such that within a very few weeks the University Press was raising with me the question of a similar treatment of the Old Testament. Of course, I referred them at once to my Old Testament colleague, Professor John M. P. Smith, and he presently associated with himself three other competent Hebrew scholars, all Ph.D.'s of the University's far-famed Semitic department, and in 1927 they produced their translation. Alone among such versions, it is throughout the work of thoroughly competent and highly trained experts not only in Hebrew but in the related languages. And so in 1931 we were able to publish the Bible, in the limited Puritan sense, of the Old and New Testaments.

This aroused a fresh wave of criticism from the professional champions of King James, who as before really showed very little acquaintance with him. Among them was Gouverneur Morris, a Yale man, of distinguished colonial descent, a journalist and author of *The Seven Darlings*. He objected vehemently to the expression "a tempestuous wind" in our Old Testament version, scornfully asking why not take a short cut and call it a tempest? "Not enough difference to justify a waste of eight letters," he writes.—Forgetful that what wrecked Paul's ship was, according to King James, "a tempestuous wind, called Euroclydon." The King James scholars, according to Gouverneur Morris, "approached their task with the reverence and faith of little children"—having himself evidently never read a line of their own great preface, the attitude of which is as far from that of little children as can possibly be imagined. How little these journalistic champions of King James really do know about it! Each one of them in turn gets up and gives himself away. They reveal so much more than they convey. Certainly, if any of them ever read the King James Bible, it was a very long time ago.

Other contemporary journals like the Higbee, Missouri, *News* and the Paris, Missouri, *Mercury,* shuddered at "the dissonance and the naïve pedantry of the word tempestuous" —never having read the long and difficult book of Jonah, nor how it was only when "the sea wrought and was tempestuous against them" that the sailors took extreme measures against that prophet, in the greatest short story in the world. But if these country editors have not found time in the rush of modern life to read the greatest short story nor the most famous shipwreck in literature, what can we possibly believe of their loud protestations of lifelong devotion to the King James Bible? They are strangers even to its vocabulary.

Yet from a saner, sounder point of view, one's common sense must triumph over one's sensibilities, and recognize that if wholesale criticism is the price of reaching the public with one's message, the end is worth the price many times over. So I have learned to be grateful for all that was said for good or ill of my translation since it has all tended to further that enterprise. One must learn to view these utterances with a vast good humor as simply the way of the world.

In 1926 at Mr. Bean's suggestion I shared with the Press the expense of providing two sets of plates of the translation to produce an edition of the New Testament in India and another in China. Our missionary friends felt that they would be very useful for their students of English for whom the antique style of King James was difficult. Mr. A. J. Appasamy wrote an admirable introduction for the Madras edition, which was produced by the Christian Literary Society of Madras. The Chinese edition was published by the Commercial Press, Ltd., of Shanghai, and did surprisingly well for a time. It soon fell under the guns of the *North China Daily News* which attacked it bitterly, demanding that it be at once withdrawn from circulation. Mr. Green, the editor, went on to say, "By every religious and aesthetical standard, the thing is a horror."

I felt called upon to take up the cudgels on its behalf with the editor, pointing out to him among other things that in referring to the King James version as the "original" English Bible he was very wide of the mark, as its preface alone was enough to prove. He retorted that I should not have made so much of that slip on his part, especially as he had only said it twice. I could only conclude that he was closely related to Alice in Wonderland;

"I said it once—I said it twice—if I say it three times it's true!"

The China edition survived the attacks of the *North China Daily News,* but soon after fell a victim to the Japanese, who in their war with China bombed the Commercial Press, destroying not only its plates of the translation but its uniquely wonderful library of Chinese manuscripts. But strange to say the missionaries in Japan had begun to use the China edition of the translation and missed it so much that in 1936 a new edition, slightly reduced in size, made its appearance in Tokyo from the press of Kyo Bun Kwan.

A later incident in the Oriental story of the translation may be added here. For when our Bible appeared in 1931 and in revised form in 1935, the monetary exchange was so unfavorable to China that the Chinese could not possibly buy it, so they produced what would ordinarily be called a pirated edition by getting one American copy and by some ingenious process offprinting from it fifty or sixty copies on a thicker paper. I was deeply touched when a missionary to China, Victor Hanson, upon returning on the *Gripsholm* after a year in a concentration camp, showed us his copy of it which was the only book he was allowed to take into the camp with him and which he had read through again on his long homeward voyage on the *Gripsholm.* He even presented it to me and I cherish this volume, along with all my old original sixteenth-century Bibles, as a book of great price for it has been the companion of men who went through great tribulation. Another of these offprinted Chinese Bibles reached me later from Dr. W. B. Nance, of Shanghai, who had also carried it with him through a long confinement in a Japanese concentration camp.

It is a well-worn saying that one thing leads to another, and this was never more abundantly true than in our work with the translation. I think it was Mr. Bean who suggested that Dr. Smith and I should produce a volume of selections of the most useful and vital parts of our translation with short introductions to the books from which each was taken—in fact another of those numerous Short or Shorter Bibles of which such a number have appeared since Lucy Rider Meyer's, two generations ago. We assented with no great enthusiasm, I confess, and we set to work to make a list of selections and to write our brief introductions. Dr. Smith had turned his contribution over to me, and gone abroad, but on his homeward journey he died very suddenly while still on shipboard in New York harbor.

It remained for me to complete the shaping up of the book. It then occurred to me, Why print these selections in the traditional order, Genesis to Revelation? Why not print them in the order in which the books containing them were written? I was debating this question in my mind and one day I laid it before a large class I was teaching in New Testament Introduction. I asked their candid advice: In what order should we arrange the selections?

They were not children, or even young people, many of them. In fact they had taught the Bible around the Seven Seas. And one woman immediately said,

"Well, Professor, if you don't arrange it historically, we'll have to do it ourselves, when we use it."

My doubts dissolved at once and that is the way I arranged it, revising Dr. Smith's introductions where necessary to suit this development, which became the chief distinctive feature of our Short Bible, albeit one loudly denounced by some, who found the ideas the selections embodied now shockingly arranged in the order of their historical emergence! A further edition of this book, in the Modern Library, has sold more than fifty thousand copies, quite apart from the edition sold by the University Press.

Another footnote to the translation arose in quite a different way. At the annual dinner of the Theological Faculties Union in the winter of 1936 I found myself seated next to Frank M. McKibben, the professor of Religious Education at Northwestern. He began to tell me of the lack nowadays of any first-rate Bible for children and expatiated upon the theme. I was but mildly interested, and as we reached dessert I asked him why he did not produce the right kind of book himself. He replied promptly,

"I thought perhaps *you* would do it!"

This at once arrested my attention. I begged him to repeat all that he had been saying and took some careful notes as he very kindly did so. The next morning I laid the plan before Mr. Bean at the Press and we were off. Aided by some questions I asked some Sunday School groups in the Hyde Park Baptist Church, I settled upon the main passages to be printed and then wrote the necessary introductory statements. The Press offered the book to Macmillan for their excellent juvenile department and it still has a large sale.

I dedicated it to three little girls I knew, children of old friends of ours, and of just the age for which the book was intended. One publisher ventured to rebuke me for dedicating a form of the Bible to any mortal creature but I was able to mollify him by pointing out that the first printed English Bible was dedicated to King Henry VIII and Queen Anne, and the third Authorized Bible was dedicated to King James I. And if to a king, why not to a child?

One final chapter in the story of the translation remains. When I retired from the University in 1937, my friend and former student, Professor Selby Vernon McCasland of the University of Virginia, suggested that I should translate the Apocrypha. I had nothing else immediately in hand and set about the task. I was about halfway through the job and was in the midst of Ecclesiasticus when I came upon a verse so utterly different in the Greek from the standard translation of it in the Oxford Press Revised Version, that I exclaimed,

"How could anybody ever get that English out of that Greek?" and it came over me, Why, of course, no one ever did! The Revised Version, the best English form then available of the Apocrypha collection as a whole, was made in 1894 from the King James version, which rested on the second edition of the Bishops' Bible, 1572, which was a revision of the Great Bible of 1539, which was a revision of John Rogers' of 1537, which was a revision of Coverdale's Bible of 1535, which was, as its title page candidly states, "faithfully and truly translated out of Douche and Latyn, into Englishe." While the title page mentions only "the scripture of the Olde and New Testament," as thus translated, it is plainly intended to cover the whole book, which included the Apocrypha. Of course, Coverdale meant by this to say that he had not used the "original tongues," as later Bibles called the Hebrew and Greek, but only the German and Latin versions, two of each of which he employed.

I had recited this fact often enough in my lectures to have grasped it, one would think, but it was only then, in 1938, there in the Town House in Los Angeles, that its full signifi-

cance reached me. Most of the Apocrypha in the Oxford
Revised version edition rest not on the Greek at all but upon
the fourth revision of Coverdale's translation not of the
Greek but of the best German and Latin versions he could
find. Was it then possible that the Apocrypha as a whole had
never before been translated throughout from the Greek,
except of course for the Latin II Esdras, for which the Greek
has not yet been found?

The idea astounded me. When I made my translation of
the Greek New Testament, I was well aware that it had been
done at least a hundred and fifty times before. And had the
Apocrypha never been so treated? Incredible! I thought at
once of Charles Thomson, the Secretary of the Continental
Congress, who in 1808, encouraged by his friend Thomas
Jefferson, translated the Septuagint, the Standard Greek version of the Old Testament, into English. I sought out his
book, and found to my amazement that he had confined
himself to the books of the Septuagint which are included in
our Old Testament, carefully leaving out all the Apocryphal
books when he encountered them.

But the Septuagint has had another translator, Sir Lancelot
Brenton, who made his version, independently of Thomson,
in 1844, and he too scrupulously omitted the Apocrypha.
But one must also reckon with our old friend Archdeacon
Charles and his great edition of the Apocrypha and Pseude-
pigrapha, 1913. Surely his contributing scholars must have
translated the individual books assigned them for comment!
And certainly some of them, like James Moffatt, more con-
scientious may we say than the others, did so. But not by
any means all of them; others had been content to accept the
very imperfect revision of the English Revisers of 1894, who

were so indifferent to their task that they actually let such things as "Artaxerxes his letters" and "Darius his pillow" stand unmodernized.

It is true the Geneva Revisers of 1560 retranslated some books of the Apocrypha, and individual books here and there have been translated directly from the Greek, but putting all this together (and it has never been put together!) does not make enough to constitute a complete translation of the Greek Apocrypha into English. It had never been done! And here I had stumbled blindly into it, never dreaming (as I should have known) that it was a new undertaking. Needless to say, I proceeded with my task with renewed energy, and it was duly published in 1938. This, of course, enabled us to publish in 1939 the first complete English Bible ever translated throughout from "the original tongues."

Writing now in 1953, I am interested to observe that British Protestants of all groups are uniting to make a new translation of the whole Bible, including the Apocrypha, into modern English.

In the Second World War the Association Press distributed two hundred and eighty thousand copies of a pocket edition of my New Testament translation among the young men in our army and navy, and when the University of Chicago Press celebrated the twenty-fifth anniversary of the translation, in 1948, a total circulation of over a million copies of it, in all its forms, was reported. It has also had some modernizing influence on subsequent American versions and revisions, and on the whole I have reason to be very glad that I accepted my wife's advice at luncheon, that February day in 1920.

THIRTEEN

Escape to the Platform

IT IS all very well to say with Mr. Barnum that every knock is a boost, and that all this abuse would help circulation. No doubt it did. But that is after all a very imperfect compensation for the deep sense of injustice and injury such attacks produce. And it is curious to reflect that of all the men who do this malicious work not one ever actually experiences anything of the kind himself. What could one do? With the *News,* the *Evening Post* and the Associated Press on one's side, one was perhaps in a strong position, whatever editors in New York, Indianapolis, Bloomington, St. Louis, Paris or London might say.

But a better way was soon to show itself. Back in Chicago, we got our first copies of the translation on the evening of September 26, 1923, and on the 28th I spoke before the Midland Authors in defense of it. On October 11 I spoke again before the Friends of American Writers in the south parlor of the Auditorium. On the 17th I spoke before the Philological Society at the University and on the 28th I spoke for my good friend Irvine Goddard in the beautiful La Grange Episcopal Church at the Sunday morning service. This was as many public addresses as I had made in the previous nine months, for I was in no great demand for public lectures, nor was I any marked success at them.

The invitation of the Quadrangle Club to address a ladies' night on the evening of November 1 alarmed while it gratified me. I had a perfectly sound and clear argument— a better Greek text to translate, a better knowledge of Greek gained through the new science of philology, a knowledge of the colloquial character of the New Testament gained from the Greek papyri, and the need for a translation into the kind of English intelligent people use in America, not the old British kind.—But how dull! All our faculty friends and their wives would be there, and a speech that was good for the Philological Society would hardly answer there. I should bore them to death! These grim facts faced me that afternoon of November 1, as I ran over my pedantic notes, and imagined giving them to our friends and neighbors. Could nothing be done to lighten the thing up, and give it an entertaining quality?

It was now that my mother's sense of humor came to my aid. Yes, of course! The very thing! The letters, the editorials! But could I rightfully use them? Certainly, I above all others. Why, they were addressed to me. They were mine. And properly considered, these attacks were not so much infuriating as highly amusing; why, some of them were really dreadfully funny. I exploited them unsparingly from that point of view, and found them richly rewarding.

I hastily ran over some of the best, from this new angle. The *New York Times* editorial entitled "The Bible A La Chicago"—the one so amused because I had read "lamp" for "candle," which inquired, "Why did he not 'go the whole hog' and say, Press a button, so that all would know an oil lamp was not meant?" The letter from the Texas engineer, challenging me to get around the tabernacle candlestick! The Bloomington *Pantagraph* editorial entitled "Jazzing the Bible." The South Carolina editorial entitled "Let the Bible Alone"—that was what the editor meant to do and that was what he wanted everybody else to do. The St. Louis *Globe-Democrat* proposing to "put pants on the twelve Apostles." The *Tribune's* unforgettable "Monkeying with the Bible." The South Carolina idyl of Ruth gleaning with a scythe. And the *Examiner's* conclusion that "in Music, a gentleman of such limitations would jazz a Beethoven sonata!" Why, there was no end to them. I would have to hurry through my main argument and give my four points twenty minutes, and then let fly with the editorials, for forty minutes of good hearty fun. It was certainly worth a try and I gave it one.

James Weber Linn was President and in the chair that night—one of my oldest friends. Besides teaching English in the University he had a column in the *Examiner*. When I read the *Examiner's* editorial charge that I was without proficiency in English, I pointed out the fact that so far was this from true, I had actually during the War taught Freshmen English in the University of Chicago, and taken them as far as page 157 in James Weber Linn's *Essentials of English Composition*. This allying myself with the chairman did not displease him and was generally well received, the more particularly as he had in his column joined in the chorus of derision at my expense. But as one who had taught his English Composition to the troops, I now claimed the right to shoot a slender arrow from under his shining shield.

If these newspapermen had done me any wrong in uttering these strictures upon me, I got it all back with interest that night and on at least a hundred other nights in the year that followed. For I had found the remedy; it was the lecture platform. It seemed that there were clubs of all kinds, not to mention churches and schools, that were constantly searching for speakers or lecturers, and one who had been mentioned for good or ill in the press was especially desired. In a few weeks I was lecturing six and sometimes seven times a week. Churches, schools, clubs—groups of every kind gave me a joyous hearing. I became aware that the newspapers by their news reports had given me a public, and by their editorial attacks had provided me with a cause. For I was concerned not just with the fate of my translation—that was a small matter—but with the whole problem of retranslating the New Testament from time to time for each new generation, for that was what was being denied; the editorials denouncing it were continuing to appear here and there over the land. No wonder I now plunged into public lecturing, and with considerable zest. I must also admit that not far back in my ancestry was an Irish strain which my critics had awakened and it now came into play.

On October 25 my old friend James Breasted, speaking on the William Vaughan Moody foundation, gave one of his great lectures on Egyptian history and culture. Always a master showman, he filled the Mandel Hall platform with tablets, statues, busts and paintings illustrating his discourse. I was to deliver the next Moody lecture one month later and his procedure gave me an idea. So many people, I was beginning to see, believed the King James to be the sole and original English Bible; why not simply show them before their eyes its seven famous predecessors, in actual copies, with their dates conspicuously placarded above them? Such a display would powerfully reinforce my mere words and perhaps impress the fact indelibly upon their minds.

In the Divinity library I found the old books, in early editions if not always first ones, and these I prepared to exhibit on the stage of Mandel on tables and easels, duly dated and open for subsequent inspection. This plan proved so effective that it became a regular feature of my lecture. The University obligingly improved its collection from time to time as earlier editions came on the market and when it was reluctant I bought the books myself. It was a bulky exhibit to set up and to transport from coast to coast, and up and down the interior, but its effect was beyond description; it was simply unanswerable. At Birmingham, Alabama, where I spoke in a large high school auditorium for the Birmingham *News,* the audience stayed for forty-five minutes after the lecture to file up on the platform and have a look at these old Bibles before King James, a huge copy of the first issue of the first edition of which occupied the last easel, at the right of the audience.

My Moody lecture at the University was enlivened by an observation from the Columbus *Journal* which remarked that "improvements on the New Testament and the American flag will hardly appeal to very many people"; the editor seemed to think the flag a symbol of fixity instead of being just the opposite. Perhaps he was acting on Mr. Arthur Brisbane's famous counsel to journalists, "Never lose your superficiality." I was especially interested in reading before a William Vaughan Moody audience the statement of a New York newspaper: "Our age is no more competent to revise the King James version than was Sir Philip Sydney to adjust the valves of a gas engine." We wondered what he thought Moody wrote.

By the first week of November more thoughtful attitudes to the translation were beginning to show themselves. On November 3 *The Baptist,* the national weekly of my own denomination, used as its front cover-page my translation of I Corinthians 13, so caricatured by the London *Telegraph*. And on November 28 *The New Republic* published a full-page review by Philip Littell which pleased me very much. He was good enough to say: "Professor Goodspeed has taken the New Testament figures out of their frames. He has endowed them with motion and life. It is as if he had given us back a lost power to wonder."

In December I told the story of the translation—I called it "Why Translate the New Testament?"—before the Baptist ministers meeting, then before the Presbyterian ministers meeting, and a little later before the Methodist ministers meeting; these bodies warmly commended my undertaking, and the Methodists in particular received it with unparalleled enthusiasm. The Baptist ministers, on December 10, took formal action, congratulating me on the translation, which touched me deeply. These proceedings must have startled my press critics who had expected just the opposite reaction.

The Theological Faculties Union, consisting of the theological seminaries in and about Chicago, which enroll more divinity students than those of any other metropolitan area in the world, took action on December 22, very graciously and generously commending my enterprise. This action was instigated by George L. Robinson of McCormick Theological Seminary. We had been fellow students in beginning Assyrian under Professor Toy at Cambridge in 1891.

As the autumn advanced invitations to lecture became more numerous and significant. My old friend Clifford Barnes generously invited me to speak to his Sunday evening Bible Class in Orchestra Hall, and at Gordon Laing's suggestion President Burton proposed that he and I should share an evening in Orchestra Hall before the friends of the

University. For various reasons it did not seem wise to accept either of these generous propositions. Various bodies at St. Paul's, St. James, the Fourth Presbyterian, the Hyde Park Baptist, and the leading churches in Winnetka and Evanston opened their doors to me and gave me a generous hearing. It is enough to say that I spoke one hundred and eight times by the middle of June. The translation had in short made a public lecturer of me and introduced me to a new phase of my existence.

My audiences were of a pleasing variety but I proposed to follow wherever the newspapers had led and supplement their missionary efforts as best I could. Fortunately we are a lecture-loving people and the daily paper is not our only source of instruction and information. I found myself addressing the Chicago Woman's Club, the Woman's City Club, the Woman's Press Club, and the Staff meeting of the Chicago Y.M.C.A.—a body which presently took a special edition of a thousand copies for the Y.M.C.A. Hotel.

In January I spoke to the Saturday afternoon assembly of the University Club with a crowded house. I read them parts of the *Tribune* editorial and tried to show them how guiltless I was of ever having chipped the *Tribune's* cathedral. To my amazement the whole audience laughing heartily turned and fixed their eyes on a man in the back row—the author, I suppose, of the editorial. This was not the only time that winter that we caught up with the writers of those damaging editorials.

If one's education were ever completed, mine should have been by the variety of my audiences that winter. I remember one supper audience—the After-Dinner Club—in the downstairs restaurant in the Wrigley Building, right on the river. A part of the restaurant was shut off with sliding partitions to give privacy to the club audience I was to address. But when I was introduced these doors were opened, and I found myself addressing the whole restaurant! The diners offered no overt objection, but ate quietly on, undistracted by my reflections, and no doubt happily occupied with their own thoughts.

Most of my speaking on the translation was, of course, done in the general Chicago area—the city, suburbs and outlying towns. That it soon began to reach a wider circle was largely due to a suggestion of the Chicago Alumnae Club, and resulted in sending me and my lecture in the spring as far as the Pacific coast. I had spoken to the alumnae on December 28, 1923, and their chairman, Alice Greenacre, thought she discerned in my remarks an interesting and concrete example of research in the humanities, in which the western alumni might be interested. She made this suggestion to the University Press and the alumni. Mr. Bean was interested and the trip was arranged for early May.

The December pace of ten lectures a month rose to twelve and thirteen in January and February, but reached a new high of twenty-four in March with eight lectures in a single week. I began with the Evanston Sunday Evening Club and ended with the Piano Club in the Illinois Athletic Club. I ranged from a single appearance before the Dill Pickle Club, in a commodious barn on the near North Side, to four appearances before the Fortnightly, the most conservative of Chicago women's clubs.

The Sunday evening with the Dill Picklers, as they called themselves, was a crowded house, mostly churchgoers of the most respected kind, who had turned out to see the famous Dill Pickle Club at home, as it were, and how they would take an address on the New Testament. But after my address, and refreshments, when the redoubtable chairman Bill Jones called on the Dill Picklers, a pretty psychopathic lot if you remember, they fell strangely silent, and he had to call on them by name to get them going at all. They were huddled on the floor at my feet for the place had filled up before they got in, and as I stood right among them the whole affair had a very pleasant, informal feel. Altogether it was one of the great evenings.

It was in March that I really began to tour for the Press and the translation. One of my first stops was Cleveland, where I was in the hands of a Big Ten committee who thought so well of my lecture as to charge one dollar admission to it. They secured the ballroom of the Winton, a place provided with at least nine hundred gilt chairs, but as only some fifty of these were occupied by 8:30, it seemed best to proceed. This was not an encouraging start. But the next week, at Columbus where Bill Harmon, our alumni chairman, had secured the use of University Hall at O.S.U. to accommodate my listeners, the place was literally packed. I could only conclude that Bill had telephoned everybody in Columbus. We dined before the lecture with President and Mrs. William O. Thompson at Professor Alfred D. Cole's, a memorable occasion as the Coles had been at Granville in my college days and had been generous friends of mine ever since. I especially appreciated the presence at the lecture of Dr. Thompson, who retired a year later after being President of O.S.U. for thirty-five years. After the lecture old friends from other years surged up to the platform and altogether it was one of our most memorable evenings for Elfleda too had many friends and relatives in Ohio and as always fully shared the excitement of the hour. The evident success of the Columbus lecture reassured us a good deal about the proposed western trip.

That morning Bill's son very kindly and expeditiously drove me out to Granville, twenty-five miles away, where I had the pleasure of giving my lecture to the whole student body of my old college gathered in the Baptist church for morning chapel. The President, Dr. Clark W. Chamberlin, who introduced me, was an old college friend.

After a day in Chicago in the office and speaking before the Fortnightly I was off again Tuesday night for the lecture in Birmingham before a splendid audience gathered for me by the *Birmingham News* which had been publishing the translation serially. It was this audience that showed such remarkable postlecture interest in inspecting the exhibit of sixteenth-century Bibles on the platform.

In April the chief feature of my fourteen lecture appearances was our visit to Kentucky where I had been asked to give a series of addresses before the Disciples' Congress at Lexington. On the way to the Congress we paused at Louisville for a church lecture there. At Lexington, President and Mrs. Frank L. McVey of the University of Kentucky gave a great luncheon for the Congress, which was a brilliant affair, and I had an opportunity to speak at a University convocation and at Transylvania College in Lexington. The Congress coincided with the races in Lexington and in the elevator one evening a man asked me if I had had a "good afternoon." I assured him that I had.

Early in May there were lectures in Peoria, Indianapolis, Cincinnati and Milwaukee, the University of Cincinnati audience in particular being one of the most alert and responsive I had ever faced. All this was most significant and delightful and also good preparation for the California trip which was to begin at Aurora on May 11 and end on June 2.

Dr. Henry van Dyke was preaching at the University that spring and was staying with us as our house guest the week between his two sermons. He had suggested it himself as he was not very well and much preferred being in a private house to the preacher's room in a dormitory. He made a delightful guest and we enjoyed his stay very much. We had planned a small bridge party for some faculty friends before we knew he was coming and of course invited him to join it. He said he didn't play bridge but would be glad to meet the guests with us when they came and if he was still up when the bridge was over he would come down for the subsequent visiting and refreshments.

Well, it was the most successful bridge party we ever gave. After meeting him people would take me aside and ask, *sotto voce,*

"Is that *the* Dr. van Dyke?"

And when he joined us for refreshments he entertained them all inimitably with stories of his youth and his adventures out west among the "whiskey tents" in mining days on the frontier.

One noon I brought home a *McCall's* magazine with a long article on my translation by Gene Stratton Porter, criticizing it unmercifully. I think it was eighty-two inches long scattered along through the magazine in the regrettable modern manner.

"Well, Doctor," said I at luncheon, "I have decided to withdraw my translation from publication."

"Why?" he inquired.

"Because Gene Stratton Porter doesn't like it," I replied.

"Who is Gene Stratton Porter?" he inquired.

"Why, Dr. van Dyke!" I cried, "You are a professor of English in Princeton University and do not know the works of Gene Stratton Porter, the author of *Freckles,* and *Laddie,* and ever so many more?"

"I never heard of her in my life," said Dr. van Dyke. And after luncheon he took *McCall's* and plunged into the article, which he roundly condemned as altogether unjust to my effort. For though a professed admirer of King James, he understood what the modern translator was trying to do. I still possess that May, 1924, issue of *McCall's,* annotated by Henry van Dyke.

A few days after our memorable visit with Dr. van Dyke, Elfleda and I set off on our journey to the coast. We took with us beside our ordinary luggage two large cases which the porters aptly described as our "samples," containing the sixteenth-century Bibles. After stopping at Aurora for a few remarks, we proceeded to St. Paul, Des Moines, Kansas City, Lawrence, Los Angeles and Pasadena, San Francisco and Palo Alto, Denver and Wichita, after which June 2 found me bright and early at the office again. My largest and most enthusiastic audience was in Los Angeles at the Bovard Auditorium of the University of Southern California where I was eloquently introduced by Miss Eva Jessup, the president of the local alumni. The next day I spoke at Occidental College and in the evening at the Valley Hunt Club in Pasadena, before a group of friends of Mrs. Bond and Mr. and Mrs. Joseph F. Rhodes, Elfleda's brother-in-law and sister. Dr. O. P. Gifford, long the beloved pastor of Mr. and Mrs. Bond, very graciously introduced me and nothing could have touched me more deeply than to be introduced by him.

With her wide acquaintance with the alumni, her social gifts, her experience and zest for public speaking and reaching audiences, and her deep concern for my translation campaign, Mrs. Goodspeed was a constant source of encouragement and suggestion through this western journey. One midnight, halfway to the coast, when we got into our drawing room for the next stage of our journey, she sat down on the edge of her berth and with great amusement began to recite the opening sentences of my principal lecture; "Four hundred years ago the Bible of the English-speaking world was the Latin Vulgate," and so on, and so on. No one could have entered more enthusiastically into the purpose of our long and arduous journey or have given me more intelligent and useful support. Her company in fact made the journey to the coast one long holiday.

This long series of one hundred and twenty-five lectures, almost all of them in defense of the translation, scattered from Cleveland and Birmingham to Los Angeles and San Francisco, in as many as thirteen states, called forth a considerable amount of local publicity, mostly of a generous and understanding kind.

This trip should of course have marked the end of the translation story but what it really terminated was my connection with the President's office. I told the President on the morning after Convocation that I felt I was of little use to him any more; he now had two vice-presidents, an assistant, and a full-time publicity man in Henry J. Smith, and I had better pull out and devote my time to lecturing and to the chairmanship of the department of New Testament. He demurred and said he would like to have me stay on if only to retain charge of public exercises, but I thought it better to make a clean break and eventually we did so, though naturally our relations remained close and cordial, as he was still head of the New Testament department, and any serious department problems I took up from time to time with him.

The lecturing for the translation continued undiminished. In June I spoke before the Presbyterian Synod of the state at Jacksonville. Six weeks later, I was to give my lecture before the Gideons at their annual meeting, in Madison, Wisconsin, and on August 28 I was to make the address for my old friend President George Norlin, at the summer convocation of the University of Colorado, at Boulder.

We were settled at Paradise Island for the summer as usual, and motored from Plum Lake to Madison for the Gideons' meeting. It was a hot Sunday afternoon, and we reached the hall early in order to set up the old Bibles on the platform before the audience arrived. But the hall was locked. Finding an open window however, we gained admittance and opened the stage door. The hall was in confusion, the floor strewn with programs from the previous evening and the stage with mattresses, evidently left from some athletic exhibition. My staff pitched in to pick up the main floor while I reduced the stage to order and set up the exhibit.

A large attendance of Gideons soon filled the hall and before I finished a cool breeze and a shower of rain had put an end to the intense heat. The Gideons streamed up to shake my hand. But one evinced anything but pleasure.

"Couldn't you find anything better than that to give us today?" he bitterly inquired. "I believe the Bible from cover to cover. What was that miserable little verse in Revelation you made so much of and what difference does it make what it means, anyway?"

I answered him I am afraid none too patiently; I had gotten very warm sweeping the platform and the lecture had not cooled me off. But I presently asked him what church he belonged to. He mentioned a well-known Baptist church in Boston.

"Boston?" said I. "Do you know Henry Bond?"

"Henry Bond?" he cried. "I should say I do. One of the finest men in this world!"

This was better. "How right you are!" I exclaimed. "He's my wife's uncle!"

This mollified him completely.

"He is? Well, well, well!" We shook hands on Uncle Henry, and parted the best of friends.

We disliked leaving Father on the Island for a week while we went to Colorado for the Boulder Commencement; and wondered if we could inveigle him and Charles into going with us. Elfleda conceived the idea of motoring to Estes Park, for the Boulder engagement, and then up to the Yellowstone which none of us had seen, and so home, and this we proposed to Father. He never even hesitated, and so with Father and Charles we set off with John Wellstein, our seasoned Island man, to drive.

It made a great excursion. We drove over from Estes to Boulder for luncheon and the convocation. At luncheon President and Mrs. Norlin of course entertained the Regents and as Father was deep in the affairs of the University of Chicago Board of Trustees, of which he had always been the Secretary, he was perfectly at home with them. Charles was the Secretary of the Board of the Chicago Y.M.C.A. and understood trustees even better than he did professors. My wife had been President for three years of the University Settlement League and the Women's Society of the Hyde Park Baptist Church, and was also Acting President of the Young Fortnightly and President of it the year it combined with the Wednesday Club, and the first year of the new club thus formed, the Contemporary, so that she was at home with administrative problems. I looked upon the scene with pride as I saw my "team" as it were, engaging these Colorado administrators; they got on famously, having much to tell one another, and I held my peace.

We got back to the Island on September 10 after three-weeks' absence (we had done 3,454 miles), and spent the rest of the month there, getting back to Chicago just in time to start off lecturing again. We had not yet, it seemed, disposed of the translation.

Our first stand was my birthplace, Quincy, Illinois, which I now revisited for the first time since leaving it as a babe-in-arms fifty-three years before. I spoke thirty times in the autumn, mostly in Chicago and the suburbs, with excursions to Flint, Indianapolis, Bloomington and Peoria. The case for the translation was generally well received, and it was plain that progress in its behalf was being made. Certainly the popular interest in it was unabated.

Visiting Detroit early in October, Elfleda spoke on Saturday to the Y.W.C.A. and I on Sunday afternoon to the Y.M.C.A. In the evening we went to the Bethel Evangelical Church where I had been invited to make the evening address by the young minister. His name was Reinhold Niebuhr! It was interesting to meet these rising, stirring young men in different Christian bodies about the country.

The new year of 1925 brought no diminution in the demand for lectures; Beloit, Rockford, Freeport, Highland Park and Evansville occupied us in January. But in February, after a flying start in Mt. Carroll, Naperville, Van Wert and Fort Wayne, I entered upon a series that was certainly climactic. Miss Mary Ely, one of the Ph.D.'s of the department, was teaching the Bible at Vassar and she very kindly arranged a series of lectures for me on successive evenings at Wellesley, Smith and Vassar. If this would not dazzle a lecturer, nothing would.

On Monday I was lecturing at Buffalo, for my cousins Marie and Barbara Hill, who conducted a lecture bureau. My lecture was under the auspices of a large Bible class conducted by the accomplished sister of Elbert Hubbard. My cousins were Wellesley girls, and when I left they sternly advised me if I did not like Wellesley best never to show my face in Buffalo again! I stopped off at Rochester for a couple of addresses, and so on to Wellesley. Established in hospitable Tower Court with Mrs. Goodspeed, I read Wellesley history and felt at home at once, for the chief source for the earliest period turned out to be the letters written home to her people in Dayton, Ohio, by one of the first students at Wellesley, Elizabeth Stilwell, whom I had known in college as the accomplished wife of my professor of French and German, George F. McKibben. It was like seeing Mrs. McKibben again.

There was a small faculty dinner before the lecture and Elfleda as usual fell on her feet by discovering that Miss Kendrick who was to introduce me had been her teacher at Lasell Seminary in Auburndale, in Elfleda's girlhood. So we felt quite entrenched in Wellesley by the time we proceeded to Alumnae Hall and I faced that splendid audience. I had never seen so many raccoon coats; I had not supposed there were so many. It was the greatest audience of the week. As I write I have just met a Wellesley woman who actually remembers the occasion. She was there!

At Smith we felt at once that we were in the hands of students, not faculty. Chicago girls we knew well, the daughters of James M. and Clara Ingram Judson, met us at the train and took us to their "house" to tea. There we met the other house members. The audience was not as large as that at Wellesley but I remember it gratefully as one of the most responsive audiences I ever addressed. Nothing was lost upon them, not a word, not a nuance. You felt that you belonged to their world and spoke their language.

So on to Vassar where we had the Preacher's Room in the vast old college building with those extraordinarily high ceilings. The bedroom door looked high enough to make two doors of modern size. We dined with the students, in their great dining room. Familiar as I was with Benson J. Lossing's *Vassar College and Its Founder,* I could not recall the fine oval lecture hall in which I found myself about to speak. My hostess explained that it had originally been the Riding School, and the old engraving of it with the girls in their full-skirted riding habits circling around the tanbark came back to me, and I felt immediately at home. A student reception for Mrs. Goodspeed and myself followed the lecture, a fitting termination for this remarkable glimpse of American womanhood at college. Miss Ely, who was our very gracious hostess at Vassar, is now Mrs. Mary Ely Lyman, Morris K. Jesup professor of the English Bible in Union Theological Seminary, New York.

As we enjoyed the hospitality of Vassar, it came back to me that I had once heard my father tell an incident of his youth when he was staying with his brother Edgar at Poughkeepsie and completing his preparation for college; my uncle was very successful at coaching young men for college entrance exams a hundred years ago. Uncle Edgar was at that time pastor of the Baptist church in Poughkeepsie and one day Matthew Vassar, who was one of his parishioners, took him and my father out to see the farm where he was planning to build his college for women. How well he built may be inferred—perhaps—from the statement in the *Encyclopedia Britannica,* eleventh edition, volume 27, page 947, that "The college had in 1909 total productive funds of about $1,360,-000, yielding an income of about $600,000." This amazing item may be wanting from later, lesser editions, though I hope not. Certainly, those were the days.

A week of lectures at Lake Geneva and another at Chautauqua enlivened the summer and autumn brought the usual rush of public lectures. These were mostly local until the last of all, the most dramatic of the year, on December 14, before the Contemporary Club of Philadelphia. Every program of that organization is an event in Philadelphia and this one was an elaborate affair. It was preceded by a delightful dinner given for the speakers by the president of the club, Miss Violet Oakley, a beautiful woman and a distinguished painter whose murals of William Tyndale adorn the Capitol at Harrisburg. Miss Agnes Repplier, who had been our guest at Chicago, took Mrs. Goodspeed under her wing and an extraordinary turnout of distinguished Philadelphians assembled for the program.

It was opened by President Josiah H. Penniman of the University of Pennsylvania who had written a book on the English Bible. He spoke on the Bible as literature. I followed on behalf of the modern speech translations, the subject assigned me. The debate was opened by A. Edward Newton, well known as the adversary of new translations, who in his book, *The Greatest Book in the World,* had declared that he trembled for my reason. He relieved my apprehensions very much by drawing a folded paper from his breast pocket and beginning to read. But after a few minutes he returned it to his pocket, declaring that he could not go on with what he had written as when he wrote it he had not met me and talked with me. It was an extraordinary reversal on his part and really very handsome of the old fellow. Perhaps Mrs. Goodspeed had undermined him at dinner when she sat next to him. In the general discussion that followed my side found surprising support, notably from the leading rabbi, Dr. William Fineshriber. At the close, Mr. Newton and Miss Repplier took us out for supper and we parted the best of friends. Thereafter Mr. Newton would send us his famous Christmas greetings, usually a special reprint of some noted book of yore. Altogether, it was a happy outcome of the Philadelphia adventure.

We spent Christmas week motoring through Florida, then, as it seemed to us, at the very peak of its boom, very crowded and feverishly busy.

These journeys and far-flung lectures were now having their effect upon the department into which there was gathering an extraordinarily able and competent body of graduate students looking toward the Ph.D. degree. As I look back I am appalled to observe that during the thirteen years of my chairmanship we conferred no less than forty-nine doctorates, or almost one for each of the quarterly convocations of the University. These young men and women are now occupying high positions in the field of New Testament studies as leaders and organizers of research, and as deans, presidents and professors in leading seminaries and universities from coast to coast. The prestige of the department had never been so high; the Head of it was President of the University and was surprising everybody by the vigor and vision of his policies. They left a lasting mark on the University of Chicago. His sudden death in 1925, in the very midst of his achievement saddened the University again, as it had been so saddened almost twenty years before by the death of President Harper.

The sudden fame of the translation had also attracted students to the department, and our travels on its behalf from coast to coast further advertised its work. The men and women who came to us were well grounded in Greek and in biblical studies, and equipped with college and seminary preparation. They entered joyously into the atmosphere of research that we sought to cultivate and vigorously stimulated our inquiries. Dean Ernest C. Colwell has been good enough to say that the classroom in textual criticism, usually regarded as the driest form of research, was the scene of the most dramatic teaching he had ever witnessed, because one day I brought into class a carton of unlisted and unpublished manuscripts of the Greek New Testament and passed them around, calling upon each man or woman to take one and report next day a description of the manuscript, its date, contents, affinities and type of text. A few years later when we were busy at manuscript hunting, the news of our success from day to day possessed a positive sporting interest for the students in the department, which we did nothing to abate. In fact that was the way we felt about it ourselves. It was a goodly fellowship, which continues still as I watch their notable achievements in textual and lexical research with world-wide outreaches and involvements. Those numerous doctorates were not hastily bestowed; their possessors have made good. They are writing a fresh and brilliant chapter in sound New Testament research. Why, I could write a book on their achievements.

But this is not the place to recite the theories we hazarded, the class and campus labors we performed, and the books we wrote. Only our scholarly pursuits were not neglected or forgotten. In particular my departmental colleagues and my near neighbor Clayton R. Bowen of Meadville School were invaluable aids to me in mine. It was altogether a very happy relationship of students and professors, all of us keen on our own research and always ready to consult and advise.

In 1927 I wrote a book on the history of the New Testament canon embodying the results of long teaching in that field and analyzing the historical process, I thought, a little more minutely than had been done before. I also published a small book entitled *New Solutions of New Testament Problems,* embodying some of our departmental researches, which my old Berlin professor, von Harnack, tartly reviewed; he said they were not problems and mine were no solutions. The fact is I had displeased him keenly some years before by some comments on minor aspects of his work and he had not forgiven me. But of course such differences are simply part of the research game.

Such were the activities that absorbed us in 1926-27. The lecture demands declined considerably, except for a week of lectures at Lake Geneva again in July and August of 1926, and a course of instruction which took me to Ann Arbor for lectures every Monday through the autumn and early winter. I had some good visits there with Professor and Mrs. Henry A. Sanders about the splendid collection of New Testament manuscripts the Greek department was making, as a result of a fund raised among the Michigan alumni by Professor Francis A. Kelsey in his retirement. One of these seemed strangely familiar and on reaching home I looked over my facsimiles. There was one of a medieval gospel manuscript that seemed to me must be of a leaf of the new Michigan manuscript. I had seen the leaf in the hands of a young Levantine years before on shipboard. He was on his way to America to sell cigarettes for his firm in Greece or Egypt.

I borrowed the leaf and had it photographed but we could
not buy such things then at Chicago and I returned it to him.
Professor Saunders on seeing the photograph agreed that it
was a picture of his manuscript. Only in the years between,
some despicable owner, fearful of losing his treasure, had
written his own name, in modern Greek, in purple ink, completely around every page, on both sides! This is why these
treasures of antiquity must be gotten away from such
irresponsible possessors into the safekeeping of intelligent
libraries.

It was my custom to go up to Ann Arbor on the Michigan
Central train that left Chicago about 1:00 A.M. but was open
to us passengers by 10:30, so that we could get to sleep before
starting. We showed our tickets to the conductors ensconced
on the bridge above, and they took them up and let us get on.
One night about half past 12 (I was in Lower One), I heard
a man come noisily in exulting in the fact that after having
to put up with uppers for weeks he had at last got a lower, at
the same time hurling his two bags in upon me! Fortunately
not killed, I opened the curtains to confront him with my
Pullman pink slip, and his indignation and bitterness of soul
were sad to behold. The porter led him away broken in
spirit, to another bed.

The next week, finding the conductors awaiting us on the
bridge to take our tickets, I ventured to counsel them to cross
off my space after I passed them and they scornfully inquired
what I supposed they were there for. They soon changed their
tune after my report on the previous Sunday night and the
unfortunate affair of the two identical slips for the single
berth, and my narrow escape from what might be called death
by baggage-smashing.

A very happy incident amidst all this campaigning was the

Lincoln-Douglas celebration at Knox College. On October 6, 1928, Knox College, under the leadership of my dear friend President Albert Britt, celebrated the seventieth anniversary of that historic debate. The celebration was held on the college campus, the speakers' platform directly adjoining Old Main, through a window of which the speakers stepped onto the platform, just as they had done in 1858. With President Britt presiding, the leading biographers of Lincoln spoke one after another—William E. Barton, Carl Sandburg, Emanuel Hertz. Of course, I had no business in such company but I was there to echo my father's memories of the occasion which he had witnessed as a sixteen-year-old boy, perched with his fellow students on the roof of the one-story college dormitory behind the great audience of twenty thousand people.

It was fast company for me and I made up my mind that he would do best who made the most apt quotation from Lincoln's speech of that day. Going over it again that morning, I decided the best thing to quote would be the famous lines which he quoted from Henry Clay, about blowing out the moral lights around us and eradicating the light of reason and the love of liberty. The program began with a re-enactment of the debate, or a small part of it, with Frank McGlynn taking the part of Lincoln, and I was struck with the fact that the part he quoted was the one I had chosen for my own use. When Dr. Barton also quoted the same lines I was staggered in my purpose, but when every speaker that preceded me on the list did so, all of them uniting in blowing out the moral lights around us, I gave up. The great audience was already in total moral darkness before I was introduced, far beyond my poor power to add or to detract. I felt I could not hope to do anything about it, and with a superhuman effort I left that matchless quotation from Lincoln, Clay and Company out.

In that respect at least I believe I stood alone that afternoon. Still, people may have wondered, "Why did he say nothing about blowing out the moral lights around us? Doesn't he care?"

I began my brief remarks with an allusion to Judge Douglas as the founder of the first University of Chicago, for which he had given the site of ten acres back in 1856, in which my father and I had both studied, and which was the direct parent of the new University. This was a fortunate allusion for some complaints had just been handed the chairman, President Britt, that Judge Douglas was being belittled by the speakers and not getting his just deserts.

I remember once asking my father where Judge Douglas was buried, and he replied,

"Why, under his monument, of course!"

I had eaten my luncheon often enough on the granite steps of that magnificent monument, but I had always supposed it was a mere cenotaph and Douglas was buried in some cemetery. But Father assured me that he had been present at his burial early in June of 1861, as an officer of the student guard of honor. Father was graduated in the class of '62.

In the evening the Knox Dramatic Club played Drinkwater's *Abraham Lincoln* with Frank McGlynn in the title role. Dr. Barton sat directly behind us and in whispers identified the characters historically as the play progressed, to our great advantage. On my other side from Mrs. Goodspeed sat a venerable little lady who had played with the Lincoln children in her childhood and had even sat on the lap of Abraham Lincoln.

We had seen the Lincoln monument at Springfield in its wretched state, with what should have been the tomb chamber filled with show cases of posters and newspaper clippings, and felt a great relief when it was rebuilt under the direction of the State Architect, C. Herrick Hammond, my distant cousin, the chamber inscribed with Lincoln's greatest utterances and the corridors leading to and from it adorned with small replicas of all the famous Lincoln statues in the world. It is certainly now a most moving shrine and a place of pilgrimage not unworthy of the Great Emancipator.

It was after the publication of our translation of the Bible, in 1931, that the most singular incident in all this lecturing took place. I was speaking at Kenyon College, in Gambier, Ohio, on December 15, 1933, and pointing out to them how Mr. Henry L. Mencken had assailed my translation when it appeared in 1923, but had approved our Bible, on its appearance in 1931. I showed them the two newspaper issues with their widely different attitudes and asked them how it could be explained. I could only suggest, though I knew nothing about it, that probably Mr. Mencken had in the interval married some bright, knowledgeable college woman, who had lost no time in setting him right on the whole matter of the new translations. At this point in my remarks a fine-looking man in clerical dress stood up in the middle of the hall and said,

"I taught Sara Haardt Bible in Goucher College."

It was the Reverend C. Sturgis Ball, Professor of Ecclesiastical History in Bexley Hall, the divinity school of Kenyon College, who thus so crisply solved my problem.

FOURTEEN

Finding a Byzantine Art Gallery

IN 1927 it occurred to Mrs. Goodspeed that the Goodspeeds had not gone abroad for a very long time—since 1910—and it was high time they went again. I concurred in this in a general way, and she proceeded to plan a most fascinating summer. Our earlier trips abroad had been mere cloaks for some tedious and exacting job of work, finishing some close technical manuscript for the printers. What was now proposed was a pure piece of joyous sight-seeing. We would invite our friends George and Jane Pollock to go with us, bringing their young daughter Margaret Lee. With Tom's co-operation, we would motor to Quebec, travel Canadian Pacific, taking the Lincoln touring car. From Southampton we would motor about England and Scotland, then cross to France, touch on Spain, follow the Riviera to the Alps, thence into North Italy, back to Switzerland, through France to England and sail home. The Pollocks would leave us at Pau, as their time had to be short.

It all worked out splendidly. It occurred to me that if I was for the first time motoring Europe, I might see a lot of minor cities where in rare-book stores or antique shops there might possibly be an undiscovered manuscript or fragment of the Greek New Testament, that I might have the distinction of bringing to the attention of scholars. My class in Textual Criticism fully understood my high hopes, and sent me a farewell letter to the ship, expressing the derisive hope that I might find the lost last thirty leaves of the Codex Vaticanus! I did not succeed in this, but still I did not entirely fail them, as it turned out. So as opportunity permitted I browsed about at many a minor city and staggered its booksellers with demands for Greek manuscripts.

At Salisbury I almost found something, the very first thing! The bookstore man thought he had something of that kind but would have to hunt for it. When I returned next morning he had to admit it was gone. So on to London, then to Cambridge, Tintern and Caerleon, where they were doing some interesting Roman excavating; then Stratford and Oxford. At Oxford some old friends; Grenfell was gone; he had died the previous year. His cousin Sir Wilfrid Grenfell, the famous missionary to Labrador, told me that Bernard left all his worldly possessions to him. But Arthur Hunt called upon us; he had succeeded Grenfell as professor of papyrology at Oxford. We saw Sir William and Lady Craigie, lunched with him at Oriel, and went out with them to lunch at their house at Watlington. Then on to Brighton and Newhaven, and across to Dieppe, through the customs, and on to Rouen, Amiens and Beauvais, and so to Paris. But no manuscripts.

From Paris, so thoroughly shopped it wasn't worth while to look, on to Tours, and the châteaux of the Loire. Then Angouleme, Bordeaux, Biarritz. This was one of our chief objectives, for Mrs. Goodspeed had been commissioned to secure Stephen Leacock for a lecture at the Fortnightly, and we had sought him in Montreal, but they said he had gone to London; there we looked up his hotel but they said he had gone to Biarritz. Again in Biarritz we sought for him at his hotel but they said he had taken to the Atlantic Ocean, in short he was in swimming. We waited until he returned and after some mutual civilities asked him for the lecture and he agreed. We had achieved our first objective.

We were at the Palace, the hotel supposed to mark the place of the Empress Eugénie's retreat at Biarritz, and we asked Stephen and his small son over to tea just to show the little boy the hotel, about which he had some curiosity. At this tea, I may say, I alone of all present took that beverage, my wife drinking hot water, Stephen, Jr., taking ice cream, and Stephen a somewhat stronger British drink. He presented us with a new book, Siegfried's *America Comes of Age*, autographed by Stephen in his totally indecipherable manner. Of the lecture the following autumn, it was simply immense, with Stephen at his best. I remember one bold mannerism which only Stephen could put over. (Or had Artemus Ward done it too?) He had written his remarks and at the end of every page he would carelessly crush the paper in his hand and drop it on the floor. I could not help suspecting that he had a carbon of it safe at home. But it was perfectly in keeping with the substance, if we may so describe it, of his discourse.

Our mission to Biarritz accomplished, on by Irún into Spain, to Burgos and the Cathedral. And next day that wonderful ride down the King's Highway straight to Madrid. What a journey into the past! Here were the Spanish peasants shoveling the wheat into the air to let the wind drive the chaff away, just as they used to do in Palestine. I think I saw eleven such threshing floors on one hillside. People with a sort of cotton turban on their heads to block off the heat, and white cotton shirts and trousers—a strange half-oriental world.

Madrid was very attractive in summer and we liked the

Palace Hotel facing the Prado very much. But after one day in Madrid the terrific heat had us all down. So next morning we were off by Alcalá and Alhama for Saragossa. The day's views were magnificent and we felt that we were really seeing Spain—towns, plains, vast bleak mountains, curious villages with narrow Oriental streets, and antique ways of life and labor.

Next day, after luncheon in a huge darkened dining room up at Jaca, we were all immensely glad to enter the defiles of the Pyrenees and get through to France again where it was cool. We escaped from Spain by the Somport pass, by which Abd-er-Rahman's Moors pushed through into France in 732 to encounter Charles Martel at Tours, and be turned back. It was a glorious ride, below snowfields and soaring mountain masses, then through a lovely valley to Oloron and Pau where our rooms in the old Gassion faced what Lamartine called the finest land view in the world—the Pyrenees.

We had the good fortune to see the famous battlements of Carcassonne in bright moonlight which certainly gave them the last touch of magic and romance. Reaching Nîmes just in time for dinner, the concierge informed us with the air of one bringing surprising good news that there would be a show in the arena that evening and should he secure *posti* for us? We were doubtful, but after dinner we got more details and went. It was an American movie set in an English garden shown on a great screen set up on the floor of the old Roman amphitheater, said to be the best preserved in the world. The *posti* were reserved seats on the floor of the arena facing the screen. And it was strangely interesting to watch the foolish story in such a setting, with the full moon sailing above the lofty walls of the ancient building.

We felt for old sakes' sake like taking a little jaunt into

the Riviera, and ran over through Hyères to Nice where we had spent six weeks twenty years before, slaving over the Patristic Index. Monday we drove the Grande Corniche again as of yore, through Mentone to Monte Carlo, and the Petite Corniche back to Nice in time to hear *William Tell* sung at the Jetée in the evening—a typical Riviera day.

From Grenoble we drove up the mountain in an hour to the Grande Chartreuse, a most interesting spot, for though the buildings are not ancient they have a great deal to tell. Then down to Chambéry and by the Route des Alpes to Chamonix, and Geneva.

As we drove into Geneva we debated where we would stay. Elfleda recalled with much pleasure her stay at the Beaurivage when she had last been in Geneva with her parents and her sister, almost thirty years before. I resolved that she should fare no worse with me but the manager was most discouraging; he thought his rooms were full. I then told him of my good friend Tracy Drake of the Blackstone and the Drake in Chicago, and how highly he thought and spoke of Swiss hotelkeepers, "the best in the world." Thus mollified he showed us quarters facing the lake directly under the suite in which the Austrian Empress Elizabeth had last stayed. I asked him about her tragic death. She was stabbed by an assassin while waiting for the boat on the quay in front of the hotel and brought back there to die. He assured us that he had been present and she had expired in his arms.

At Geneva we were much interested in the great Reformation monument with its statues and symbols. Then on by Chillon and Territet and up to the Great St. Bernard Hospice and our highest pass, 8,111 feet.

We stopped on our southward way at Vercelli, to see the famous fourth-century manuscript of the Old Latin Gospels.

When we signed the guest book, Monsignor Paste, the librarian, showed us in it the signature of his holiness Pius XI, who had signed there as Cardinal Ratti before he became pope. So on by Milan and Pavia, to Venice, or at least to Mestre, where we locked the car up in a garage and took a motor boat out to the Danieli, on the Grand Canal!

At Venice my patience as a manuscript hunter gave way, and I expostulated with the antique dealer. I said to him, "We know that manuscripts are finding their way out of the Mt. Athos libraries, for Tisserant identified in the collection of Mr. Garrett in Baltimore a very unusual gospels manuscript with the text written in red and in the form of a cross, which he had previously seen in a convent library on Mt. Athos."

The dealer said that might all be, but at any rate they did not come out through Venice.

This reminiscence of Tisserant brings back to my mind a most gratifying and amusing contact with him, while he was Subprefect of the Vatican Library. I wanted to get photographs of the three important pages of the Muratorian fragment, a manuscript in the Ambrosian Library at Milan. But I could get no response from Milan to my appeals. I finally wrote Tisserant asking his help. He wrote a most amusing reply saying that he would be glad to comply but that while he would have replies in plenty we would get no photographs. He added, however, that a Paris publisher after long striving had secured a set and I might communicate with him. This I hastened to do and in due time received a fine set of the half-tone plates the publisher had made of the pages. Hardly had I thanked him for them, when I received from Tisserant a second set of the plates! He had written to the publisher at the same time that he wrote to me and the publisher had sent him a set too, and these Tisserant was most kindly forwarding to me. Previously, learning had had to depend for its accurate knowledge of these famous pages upon a hand facsimile laboriously made and published long ago by S. P. Tregelles.

At Venice we turned back from our farthest east, disappointed. It was getting pretty clear that there was nothing to be found. We felt that our long search for at least one more Greek manuscript of the New Testament was ending in defeat. We visited Salviati's and bought some most engaging Venetian glass. We also took a gondola out to Murano where they make it. When our shipment arrived, in Chicago, we discovered that they shipped fourteen pieces to the dozen to provide against possible breakage. But there was no breakage! Such a pleasant form of insurance.

We sped away from Venice to Padua, Vicenza and Verona, then on past the Lake of Garda to Brescia, Bergamo and Como, where we found our lodging for the night, after a glorious day's motoring across Lombardy. Next day to Chiasso and into Switzerland, and over the St. Gothard Pass, 6,935 feet, to Andermatt, then over the Furka Pass, 7,992 feet, decidedly awesome in spots especially when we got among the clouds and could see nothing above or below, but only the road ahead. We stopped at the Rhone Glacier and observed the rise of that river which flows right out of the foot of the glacier in a most gratifying manner. Next morning, on over the Grimsel Pass, 7,159 feet high, our third highest, to Interlaken, and the good old Victoria, facing the Jungfrau. There at luncheon we met Dr. John Timothy Stone, his daughter and her husband—quite a Chicago reunion. The Doctor's first question was, had we seen the Rhone Glacier, and we said we had, we had just slept on it. We did not linger at Interlaken but hurried on over the Brünig Pass, only 3,396 feet, to Lucerne, for a quiet Sunday.

It was sad to ride next day through war-torn France. But we sought out Ourches where Tom had spent his first winter in the war. We also visited Dole, where the Radiator Company's French plant was, and found some of Mr. Bond's loyal old French friends there. And so at length on September 8 to Paris.

I had, of course, by this time given up all hope of finding a Greek manuscript in Europe, or even a single leaf, *une seule pièce,* as I used to say pleadingly to the bookstore people. But Elfleda wanted to do some shopping, and it was raining, so purely from force of habit and without the slightest idea of success I resumed my quest.

It was the ninth of September, marked evermore with white, that I was picking my way among the showers along the Boulevard Haussmann looking for a rare-book store I could not find when a fine large antique shop caught my eye. There were some good tile in the window and I caught at a chance. With such tile, the man might have a manuscript; such things do happen; why not ask the old threadbare question once more? I went in, and asked the girl in the bureau if they had any manuscripts. Not Greek manuscripts; there would be no use in that, I knew.

She said Yes, a Persian one.

That should have been enough but I had ceased to reason and I brazenly asked to see it.

She took me up in the "lift" to the fourth floor where in a small room we found the safe which the girl opened. She could not find the Persian manuscript, however, and summoned the proprietor, M. Stora, who duly produced it. I took it mechanically and dully turned its beautifully miniatured pages.

"The *Shah Namah,* I suppose, isn't it?" I said to the dealer. Most such richly miniatured Persian pieces are of Firdausi's great national classic, the *Book of Kings.*

"I suppose so," he replied. He knew nothing about it either! But he began to think I knew my way about and became more expansive.

"I have a Greek manuscript," he murmured.

This roused me not a little.

"You have?" said I unguardedly. "That's what I'm looking for!"

He then drew from the safe a parcel wrapped in newspapers from which he extracted a dazzling object. It was a stout volume of moderate size magnificently bound in silver-gilt covers with gospel scenes in high relief; on the front a Crucifixion with the emblems of the Four Evangelists, on the back a Resurrection.

It was indeed a Greek manuscript and of the whole New Testament as ordinarily written in such manuscripts, that is, without the Revelation. Manuscripts of such scope are much less common than those of parts of the New Testament. But the amazing thing about it was that it seemed to have a painting illustrating the action of the text on almost every page. These were seldom full pages, being usually half pages or less in size. I had never seen such a manuscript or anything even remotely approaching it. And no wonder, for there was not another like it in the world! At some page openings three such gospel scenes would be visible at once, two on one page and one on the other. Breathlessly I asked its price.

"It is not for sale," M. Stora replied, adding that they had refused twenty thousand dollars for it.

This was most discouraging but I continued to explore the manuscript, though by this time any possibility of securing it had vanished from my mind. However, I decided to act the scene out, and finally in what now appears to me an inspired moment, I observed.

"I suppose there *is* a figure at which you would part with the manuscript?"

This found a chink in his armor. He summoned his brother and they conferred in the corner, casting an occasional calculating glance at me, as I fussed away at the codex, looking up this or that crucial reading. At length they spoke up and named a somewhat higher price. I gravely gave them my card with the address of my so opulent university and departed, with an option on the manuscript, but with not the slightest idea I should ever see it again. They promised to send some photographs of the manuscript, if they could find them, as I left. I remember I reflected somewhat bitterly as I walked downstairs—the "lift" had stopped for the lunch hour—that it was hard luck to have the only thing I had found in all Europe a thing so fearfully good that it was totally out of my reach, and I told Mrs. Goodspeed about it at luncheon as an experience, not a prospect.

But arrived in London a few days later, I thought there might be something more feasible there so I went around to Quaritch's and saw the redoubtable Mr. Dring who had been selling manuscripts for Quaritch for forty years. He was the typical bluff overbearing Briton, his métier being to put the customer in the wrong from the start and thus get the upper hand.

"Greek manuscripts?" said Mr. Dring indignantly. I seemed to have offended him by so unreasonable an inquiry. "You won't find any Greek manuscripts. If you did, anything you found would be worth a thousand pounds, and every miniature," he went on unguardedly, "would add two hundred pounds to its cost!" Seymour de Ricci used to say, rubbing his hands apologetically together, that Mr. Dring always made him think, "What have I said? What have I done?" That describes Mr. Dring precisely.

To a less domineering man I might have told something of what I had seen in Paris. But not to Mr. Dring. Heaven knows to what a pitch of fury it might have roused him. I merely made a note of his remark and sidled off. But it occurred to me: Perhaps that price in Paris was not as utterly unreasonable and arbitrary as I had thought. It had seemed merely like asking for all the money there was in the world. But perhaps not, perhaps there was a definite way of figuring these things: Count the miniatures! Why hadn't I done that, instead of looking up variant readings while the two brothers had been putting their heads together? I would write at once and ask how many miniatures the manuscript contained. For on Mr. Dring's scale, the Greek text was worth a thousand pounds and those magnificent covers of wrought silver-gilt were worth another. And I had certainly seen twenty miniatures and there must have been at least as many more. It began to dawn upon me as a possibility that the price might be actually low. I always learn something in a rare-book store.

Arrived in Chicago again I soon received the promised photographs—muddy, disappointing things, and yet they did tell us something; the handwriting was the main thing we had to go on for I had found there was no date given at the end of the codex. From the first news of it, my junior colleagues Dr. Harold Willoughby and Dr. Donald Riddle evinced the keenest interest in the manuscript. Each one soon came to see in his mind's eye a book he might be writing on its miniatures, or its text. Dr. Riddle soon found a facsimile of a Paris manuscript dated in 1262 that was written in a very similar hand and soon after Dr. Willoughby came into the office holding up a facsimile.

"How is this?" he triumphantly exclaimed. We pounced upon it.

"What is it?" we cried. "It's the hand of the manuscript. Where did you get it?"

It proved to be a page from the famous New Testament manuscript sent by Michael Palaeologus, emperor of the east, to Louis IX of France—St. Louis—in 1269, and now in the Bibliothéque Nationale. Our first impression that the hand in the two manuscripts was the same soon settled into a conviction, with the most important consequences. For it is generally recognized that Michael had that manuscript written to present to Louis and its hand and its miniatures may therefore be confidently assigned to the years just preceding 1269. No less certainly the miniatures of the new-found manuscript belong to that time.

We naturally began to compare the two manuscripts somewhat closely. Both contained the full Byzantine New Testament, that is, our own, minus the Revelation. The St. Louis manuscript contained fourteen miniatures; ours (as we began to call it!), its Paris owners reported, contained seventy-two. We found this number almost incredible. We could learn of no Greek New Testament with half that number although two or three gospels manuscripts were reported that exceeded it. The extraordinary thing here was the presence of miniatures in the Acts and the Epistles.

The difficulty in studying Greek Byzantine miniatures lies in their scattered and undated condition. One finds three or four in one manuscript, eight or ten there, a dozen or twenty yonder. The magnitude of our find we began to perceive lay in the fact that here was a whole gallery of Byzantine art which could be definitely dated and placed. It came from Constantinople and the time of Michael Palaeologus. It was therefore no mere curiosity but a serious document for the history of Byzantine art in its last renaissance, just before it gave up the ghost and found reincarnation in the first Italian painters. For when our manuscript was being written and painted, Cimabue was a youth and Giotto was born. We saw in it therefore the promise of a definite contribution to the history of Byzantine iconography and we realized that in no circumstances must it be permitted to disappear again from scholarly scrutiny. The peril of such a manuscript is division for its miniatures are so much more readily salable separately than as a whole. Perhaps its magnificent sixteenth-century covers have had a good deal to do with its preservation but it speaks well for its Paris owners that they had resisted any temptation to dismember it and sell it piecemeal, preferring to hold it nearly twenty years in the hope of selling it entire.

Now the fundamental weakness of American research in the humanities lies in our pitiable lack of materials. The necessity of them for research in the physical sciences is now recognized, while in the field of the humanities for some reason it halts and lags behind. Here was an opportunity to bring a matchless body of materials for the study of Byzantine iconography within the reach of American scholarship. Even without the miniatures the text alone would be a unique addition to our American research, for at that time there was but one complete Greek New Testament manuscript known to be in America, and it was in private hands and not accessible. The bringing of a Byzantine New Testament here would be no inconsiderable boon to American studies.

My colleagues had in the meantime become so deeply interested in the manuscript and its problems that it would have been a great disappointment to them to lose it. Each of them already saw in it the material for an ideal piece of research, the one on the text, the other on the miniatures, and with only a few photographs to work on they had achieved some very definite results in dating and placing the document. I perceived, in short, that they had done their part and I must now do mine. The fact is, I was beginning to lose sleep over the situation. I felt I had a duty to perform, but I did not see quite how to go about it.

In this crisis I remembered the friendly interest in the work of the department that Mrs. Rockefeller McCormick had expressed to me four years before, and the generous offer of assistance she had then made, and I sought an interview with her. I related the story of the finding of the manuscript and the progress of our study of it, and she instantly perceived its probable significance for Byzantine art. Without a moment's hesitation she said,

"I can see that this is a very distinguished thing. Would it meet your wishes if I authorized you—I do now authorize you —to buy the manuscript for me, and you and your department can have it for study and publication as long as you like."

I had hoped she might start a fund for the purchase of the manuscript but in a breath she assumed the whole affair, leaving me nothing to do but to enter in and possess the land. It was my third great moment in the pursuit of the manuscript.

Our first step was to close the bargain by cable, arranging to take delivery in London. Our next was to send our iconographer, Dr. Willoughby, as an expedition to get it (many a larger and costlier expedition has returned with less!) after verifying the representations made as to the miniatures. It was also most desirable that he should have an opportunity to examine other Byzantine masterpieces in London and Paris before setting to work upon his study of the manuscript's iconography. And as a matter of fact, it would cost no more to send him than to ship the manuscript, adequately insured, to Chicago. What was needed was a fund for such an expedition and this need we laid before that Friend of Humanity, Dean Shailer Mathews. He did not fail us and our iconographer, disguised as an "expedition" and carrying the largest check I had ever seen, was dispatched to London where we had agreed to take delivery.

And so it befell that on a Saturday morning in March, 1928, Dr. Willoughby entered the office of the Byzantine expert in the British Museum and asked him if he would join him at eleven o'clock at the American University Union to inspect a very unusual Byzantine manuscript. The expert kindly consented and at eleven the meeting took place. The manuscript was duly produced and the two men went over it for more than an hour. At the end of that time the British expert rose and took his departure, after privily charging the American not to fail to see the thing through.

His first cable to me reading "Manuscript amply fulfils expectations" brought me immense relief. Even then I did not know that the count of the miniatures, about which I had felt most concern, made them not seventy-two, but ninety, beside eight richly decorated pages of tables which might fairly have been counted. We can only suppose that M. Stora's assistants after counting miniatures up to seventy-two grew weary of the task and signed off at that figure, leaving about one third of them out. How differently Mr. Dring would have proceeded!

At any rate, the manuscript probably brought to our shores more Byzantine miniatures than there were in the whole country in 1928, the year of its arrival. We had in short broken into a Byzantine art gallery previously unknown, and from the very generation that witnessed the birth of Italian painting. Our expedition made haste to have all these miniatures photographically recorded, then depositing the manuscript at the kind suggestion of Sir Frederic Kenyon in the safety of the British Museum, he flew to Paris for a week in the Bibliothéque Nationale.

We were not by any means without anxiety even yet for the safety of the manuscript—and of course, Dr. Willoughby—and it was no small relief on the twentieth of April to see him emerge from the train, after the perils of Bloomsbury, Montmartre and Manhattan, safe upon the peaceful streets of Englewood. There followed a memorable hour when we gathered close about the manuscript and went over every miniature, exclaiming over the drawing of this one, the brightness of that, the richness of another, the novel treatment of another, the cradle of John, the table setting, the convincing representation of the lame and the maimed, the "continuous" treatment of some pictures and the successive character of others, the portraiture of Peter, who appears so often, and always with the same very individual face, and the distinguished individual pictures of him and James and Jude, perhaps the most perfect miniatures in the whole volume.

We rose from the rapid inspection of almost a hundred paintings feeling that we had passed through a whole gallery of Byzantine art and bathed our spirits in its beauty. For in spite of the ravages of time there was really beauty enough left to enjoy. And we could not help thinking that the emperor who had ordered the Paris manuscript with fourteen miniatures for Louis IX could have intended this one, so much more sumptuous and in its miniatures so incomparably richer, for no one but himself.

Mrs. Goodspeed who now saw the manuscript for the first time and entered fully into the experience, had a very excited group at her luncheon table that day, and joined the conspirators that afternoon as we handed the manuscript to its rightful owner, Mrs. McCormick, in the presence of a number of her friends, at 1000 Lake Shore Drive. It was deposited on a low stand in the drawing room and Mrs. McCormick told how it had come to her attention; I related the story of its discovery and Dr. Willoughby told how he brought it home. I thanked Mrs. McCormick for putting such a body of Byzantine art in our hands for research and she replied that she felt grateful to us for bringing it to her attention, and enabling her to secure it for America and Chicago.

Three days later we told our story and exhibited the manuscript at an open meeting at the University to an extraordinarily responsive audience of city and University people and at the close a representative Chicagoan—the Librarian of the Newberry Library—expressed the opinion that the bringing of the manuscript to Chicago marked the beginning of a new era in the cultural life of the city. In that meeting our effort was to show by a concrete and peculiarly happy illustration the importance of materials to any serious humanistic research. Only that winter I had heard an ambitious young man of science say in a public address that Greek and Latin departments dealt only with books and their contents. Yet books are mainly the tools of research, not its materials.

Mrs. McCormick had most graciously turned the manuscript over to our custody and we lost no time in having it all photostated and depositing it in a safe-deposit box at the bank. But as the commanding importance of its unique series of miniatures became more and more plain, we ventured to lay before Mrs. McCormick the great desirability of reproducing the entire series in full-color reproductions, and she generously undertook to provide the very considerable cost. It was this that enabled us in 1932 to produce what our generous colleagues in Harvard and Princeton, where such subjects are most cultivated, declared the most splendid edition of a miniatured manuscript ever made.

Dr. Willoughby had seized the earliest opportunity to pursue his Byzantine researches at Princeton where he was given every facility and assistance by Professor Charles R. Morey, Professor A. M. Friend, Jr., and the departmental staff, while Dr. Riddle toiled at the collation of the entire text. When I was on my visit to Princeton to speak before the New Jersey Institute of Archeology there, one member of the department, Professor Frank Jewett Mather, who could not attend my lecture, called on us at the Inn to look over the manuscript. He had gone through perhaps a third of the miniatures when he looked up and said,

"This must have been a perfectly beautiful thing!"

Going on over perhaps thirty miniatures more, he looked up again and said very earnestly,

"This *is* a perfectly beautiful thing!"

That was the impression it made upon an expert, and that was the way it affected everybody who set out to look it through. One's casual interest gradually becomes serious and then one is simply enthralled.

Dr. Willoughby came to me one day in the midst of his

research and told me he wanted to go on to make a collection of all the New Testament miniatures in Byzantine manuscripts and I encouraged him to do so. I had known so many University men who needed just such a stupendous project to lure them on—whether they ever attained it or not. But as I write, twenty-five years later, that great project of his is nearing completion, if it has not already reached it. Just one of the results of bringing materials within the reach of scholars.

In the course of our work on the manuscript we soon felt the need of a name for it, and I asked Mrs. McCormick if we might designate it as the Rockefeller McCormick New Testament, and she gave her consent. As Dr. Willoughby worked over it, he was struck with some resemblances to a miniatured gospels manuscript in Leningrad, the Four Gospels of Karahissar, which proved to be, as Professor Friend of Princeton put it, the twin brother of the Rockefeller McCormick manuscript. Aided by the American Council of Learned Societies through the generous interest of Professor William Albert Nitze, the head of the Romance department in the University of Chicago, Dr. Willoughby proceeded to Leningrad and made a thorough study of the manuscript. Meantime in our work on the Rockefeller McCormick, Dr. Ernest C. Colwell, who had recently joined the staff of our department, had come forward with some very useful and penetrating suggestions, and he now dealt with the Karahissar text while Dr. Willoughby handled the miniatures. Their edition in two large volumes uniform with the Rockefeller McCormick volumes appeared in 1936.

One of the difficult details of the Rockefeller McCormick codex was a colophon scrawled on its last flyleaf, invoking the curse of the three hundred and eighteen holy fathers who assembled in Nicaea upon anyone who should ever steal the book from the church or convent to which it was being given by Alexander the "boebota." This last word caused me some perplexity which was happily resolved by Dr. Colwell as representing "boeboda," that is, "voivode"! Of course he was quite right, and Alexander II, the well-known voivode of Walachia (1568-77), was probably the man who enclosed the book, or what was left of it, in its present sumptuous covers of silver gilt.

Some time later when I was down at Urbana lecturing at the University, Mrs. Goodspeed said to me quite casually, "Why don't you write a mystery story about that curse in the Rockefeller McCormick colophon?" And this I afterward did, as I have already explained, taking the title right out of her mouth—*The Curse in the Colophon.*

Dr. Willoughby had no difficulty in pointing out that a considerable number of miniatured pages had been lost from the Rockefeller McCormick, as well as the whole book of Psalms in Greek from the end, before I saw it in Stora's shop, and in my effort in our first volume to retrace the history of the manuscript I suggested that while some leaves were no doubt lost or stolen, some had perhaps been given away by a careless owner to some admiring guest. This charitable idea was scouted and ridiculed by the London *Times Book Review* as betraying my unacquaintance with manuscripts and their fortunes. But on the contrary it is here the *Book Review's* nonacquaintance which is the trouble. For on page 330 of that indispensable vade mecum of manuscript hunters, *Visits to Monasteries in the Levant,* by the Honorable Robert Curzon, afterward fourteenth Baron de la Zouche, he records how, when he once admired some features of a particular manuscript an abbot was showing him, the abbot took out his knife and cut out a handful of some forty leaves, which he presented to the astonished traveler! How strange that this wonderful book should be unknown in the city of its origin, the birthplace of its author, and to people there assuming to speak of manuscripts and their impulsive possessors. Curzon is the A B C of the subject and his manuscript trophies have long been in the British Museum.

One morning soon after the manuscript came into my hands for the department to work upon I met Mr. Martin A. Ryerson in Swift Hall and he expressed his interest in it. He was, of course, a connoisseur in painting, having formed a remarkable collection of Italian primitives. I was only too happy to show it to him, as I happened that day to have it in the office. I brought it in and he sat down in the Swift Common Room and went through it page by page. He presently asked me what we had had to pay for it. We were not telling the price of the manuscript but I saw no reason for concealing it from him and I said to him,

"You'll call me a fool, Mr. Ryerson, but we paid twenty-five thousand dollars for it."

"I don't call you a fool at all," said Mr. Ryerson. "When a thing like this comes on the market, you have to pay what they ask for it. You can't go somewhere else and buy one just like it." I was a good deal reinforced by Mr. Ryerson's judgment in which everybody who knew him had such confidence. Mr. Ryerson afterward helped us generously with our later manuscript finds.

Miss Elizabeth Day McCormick has told me that she once said to her cousin that of all her priceless collections the thing that she coveted was her Greek manuscript, and in the sale of Mrs. McCormick's treasures long after her death, Miss McCormick purchased it. I well remember at some Uni-

versity function meeting Miss Florence Lowden, now Mrs.
Phillip Miller, and learning from her that the afternoon
paper containing an inventory of Mrs. McCormick's principal
treasures, as listed by her executors for tax purposes, had reported a very moderate estimate on the manuscript. I at once
hastened to the executors and made a considerably larger
offer on the University's behalf. This the estate's representative refused, saying that they considered the sale value of the
manuscript much higher, and were sending the manuscript
to Dr. A. S. W. Rosenbach in Philadelphia for him to sell.
I was further told that he had already put a price of twice
what I was offering upon the manuscript. Indeed the executors later sent a representative to Philadelphia to further
enlighten Mr. Rosenbach on the manuscript's real value with
such success that he raised its price 40 per cent more. But of
course, as I had tried to show the executor, the manuscript
was just as valuable as ever, it was money that had gone up
in price, and the Philadelphia efforts failed. It was ten years
after Mrs. McCormick's death that Miss McCormick in 1942
bought the manuscript and gave it to the University collection. Dr. Colwell received it as it chanced on my birthday
just fifteen years after I had found it in Stora's shop in Paris.

We have often wondered who it was that had offered the
Stora brothers twenty thousand dollars for the manuscript
so many years—I think it was seventeen—before. An American, of course, since he offered dollars. But what American?
Mr. Walters? Mr. Morgan? I do not know, but it is said to
have been a trait of Mr. Morgan to enter a shop, see what
the dealer had to offer, name his own price and if it was
accepted take the article. If it was not, he would turn and
leave; there was no bargaining. Someday, someone who knows
—as of course the Stora brothers do—may tell. But I would

much rather know from whom the Storas bought the manuscript and what if anything he had to tell of where he got it.

At a great luncheon at the Casino years later when Miss McCormick gave her wonderfully illuminated Revelation manuscript to the University, Mrs. George Langhorne leaned over to me and mischievously remarked,

"It strikes me, Mr. Goodspeed, the McCormick family has been no bad thing for the New Testament department."

I could only reply, in the verbiage of the day,

"Are *you* telling *me*?"

Our magnificent edition, introduced by the perfect photographic reproductions of all the miniatured pages in full color, was completed in August, 1932, only just in time to be laid before Mrs. McCormick on her deathbed. But it will remain one of the monuments of the noble generosity of her spirit.

FIFTEEN

Manuscript Hunting

THE furor created by the finding of the Rockefeller Mc-Cormick New Testament with its wealth of miniatures drew attention to Chicago as a center of interest in Greek manuscript study. Up to that time we had been unable to learn of any New Testament manuscripts for sale anywhere, but from that time they began to turn up at the rate of one every sixty days.

The first one was indeed not Greek but Armenian, a gospels manuscript, on paper, and of the sixteenth century, which was advertised in a Luzac catalogue. We ordered it at once, and Dean Mathews generously provided the cost.

The second chapter of our search began in November, 1928, at Princeton, where we had been invited by our old friends Mr. and Mrs. Holmes Forsyth, and later asked to bring the manuscript and lecture on it to the local chapter of the Institute of Archeology. This proved a most delightful occasion all through, the Princeton department of art and archeology being very strong in precisely this field of Byzantine manuscript art, and giving us then as always generous support. One dinner in particular I shall always remember, having found myself seated between Mrs. Grover Cleveland and my hostess, Mrs. Alan Marquand, a very beautiful woman, whose husband was the creator of Princeton's famous department of art and archeology. The meeting of the New Jersey Institute of Archeology, which I was to address, was preceded by a magnificent dinner party, the largest I had ever attended, at the Ario Pardees', and I was introduced to this really appalling audience by Professor Morey, the head of the department. It was he who told me of a Greek Manuscript in the hands of a well-known New York scholar and traveler, whom I looked up in December and with whom I arranged to have the manuscript sent to Chicago.

It was written about A.D. 1300, and contained the four gospels with portraits of the evangelists heading their respective gospels, but it had been further enriched later on by the addition of three more, added to the book about 1700, when a monk named Chrysanthus had rescued the manuscript from the Turks and rebound and embellished it. These seven miniatures made this an expensive manuscript to buy but with the aid of Dean Mathews and Vice-President Frederick Woodward, and a group of public-spirited Chicago friends, Arthur T. Galt, Stanley Rickcords, C. Lindsay Ricketts, and my brother Charles, by May it was really ours—the first Greek manuscript acquisition in a generation.

Our next acquisition also was due to our Princeton friends. While we were there in November, Professor Edward Capps spoke of a Greek of his acquaintance who had some manuscripts to sell and offered to send me his address. But as six months had passed without any word from him we had given that lead up, when there arrived, no letter indeed, but a whole carton of Greek manuscripts. Of the six, two were New Testament: one, a dilapidated gospels, of about 1300, once the property of a certain Demetrius; the other, a beautifully written Praxapostolos, that is, a manuscript of the Acts

and the Epistles, a type of which there were but three examples then known to be in America.

This parcel was certainly worth waiting for but the letter
that followed the package was most disquieting. It seemed the
manuscripts were open to bids, and two or three rather
opulent eastern groups had already put in their bids. We
were in no position to bid as the Chrysanthus purchase had
not yet been fully covered and it was hardly possible to approach the University with so vague a proposition. Yet we
could not let the most distinguished manuscript that had
yet come within our reach slip by without an effort. Accordingly I hazarded a personal bid on the gospels and the Praxapostolos and returned the lot to Professor Capps.

On May 17 a letter arrived from him. A lifelong student
of Greek drama, Professor Capps imparts even to his business
letters something of that quality. Of our several bids, mine,
it appeared, had been the highest—and Hope ran high. But
the Greek, when apprised of it, declared a man in Canada
had offered him that much for the Praxapostolos alone, saying
he could double his money by selling it off a leaf at a time;
and Hope drooped. But Professor Capps had protested that
such vandalism would alienate all reputable collectors, and
the Greek would find no customers for further manuscripts.
(Hope revived.) The eloquence of Professor Capps moved
the impressionable Greek to repentance and remorse and
he willingly accepted the Chicago bid. (Hope triumphant!)
The next day the fatal parcel arrived. Professor Capps, whose
help in all this was beyond all praise, intimated that the
Greek would welcome an early remittance. Without disturb-
ing the University authorities this was arranged and I became—temporarily, I hoped—the owner of the manuscripts.

On June 15 I called upon Mr. Woodward and shared with

him my guilty secret. He readily gave me official absolution but had nothing more substantial to offer. Yet being the lawyer he was, he did give me a piece of advice, which was to see Mr. Llewellyn Raney, the librarian of the University. This advice was literally golden, for on going upstairs to Mr. Raney, he listened to my story, and at once undertook one third of the manuscripts' cost. Then he too gave me advice. He counseled me to visit Dean Mathews. But as the Dean had only three weeks before assumed more than one third of the Chrysanthus purchase, I had not thought of approaching him. Dean Mathews was in Colorado, however, and I thought Mr. Raney's advice should be good so I wired him, and his reply undertook all but a hundred dollars of the balance. The next morning with a light heart I went on my vacation.

The final hundred was soon after provided by Mr. David Stevens, and so the Demetrius Gospels and the Praxapostolos became ours, after one of the finest pieces of University cooperation I know of. And yet no less gratifying were the occurrences of Inauguration Day that autumn when the departments of the University sought to offer some visual exhibits of their work. This was easier for some scientific departments than for us poor humanities and theology people who deal so largely in ideas and methods. But my veteran colleague James Breasted came up with a fine exhibit for Egyptology, and our New Testament exhibit was near by, in the handsome Common Room of Swift Hall. Ours, of course, took the form of a series of glass cases showing our manuscript acquisitions for the year. In one case we showed the old manuscript Gregory had secured back in 1895. In another were the four manuscripts we had acquired in the first half of the current year, 1928. But in a third case we showed four more manuscripts which we had received from the Stora brothers in Paris, "on approval," as it were, which we craftily labeled "Awaiting Purchase." When Dr. Breasted saw this label, experienced showman though he was, he shook his head and remarked ruefully,

"Why didn't I think of that!"

These four manuscripts were gospels. One, on paper, was supposed to be of the fifteenth century. The others were parchment. Two were actually signed and dated by their scribes. The fourth was an impressive two-column codex, over twelve inches tall, with fine headings, and had once belonged to the church of Exoteicho near Trebizond. Thanks to Mr. Woodward and Mr. Raney we went into the exhibit on November 19 with more than a third of the money needed for them in sight. When Mr. and Mrs. Frederick T. Haskell saw them in the exhibit, Mr. Haskell asked to look at one of them more closely. It had a fine twelfth-century miniature at the beginning, and at the end the signature of the scribe, Nicolaus of Edessa (in Macedonia) with the date and place of writing—Edessa, A.D. 1133. Mr. Haskell handed back the manuscript with the announcement that he would buy it for the University. We immediately labeled the manuscript accordingly.

This gave us three fourths of the amount needed to secure all four and Dean Mathews, hearing of our progress later in the afternoon, voluntarily undertook to provide the rest. We were thus obliged to put upon the showcase a new label indicating that since the opening of the exhibit funds had been provided that ensured the purchase of the four manuscripts.

After the exhibit Mr. K. W. Clark and Mr. E. C. Colwell, fellows in the department and now internationally renowned figures in manuscript research, took up the paper manuscript and from its watermarks established its date as 1325-50. This made our total Greek manuscript acquisitions for the year eight manuscripts. But on December 2, Stora sent over an extraordinary, indeed a unique piece, which Mr. John Shapley and all of us felt must not get away. It was not a codex but a scroll, three and five-eighths inches wide and sixty-nine inches long, and inscribed to be read vertically. It contained the beginnings of three gospels, Mark, Luke, John, the Lord's Prayer, the Nicene Creed, and the whole of the 68th Psalm, 114 lines in all. A medieval roll containing gospel texts like this seems to be unheard of.

But the other great feature of the roll was that it contained seven miniatures, mostly in good condition. It was probably a charm or amulet to be worn by some rich and pious Byzantine. Mr. Ryerson and Mr. Galt had already undertaken much of the price and a little later Mrs. John W. Scott very graciously completed the necessary fund—fully half the total cost of the scroll. With this extraordinary, indeed unprecedented form of New Testament manuscript we took up the manuscript hunt for 1930, the whole department being united in what was becoming an exciting, even a thrilling quest.

One afternoon Dr. Willoughby telephoned me to ask what I would think of a ninth-century Greek lectionary of the gospels. I replied that there was not one in this country. He retorted that he had one at that moment in his room. I told him never, never to give it up, but what was the price? He said a thousand dollars.

It had come to him from the Greek treasurer, or perhaps cook, of the notorious Colosimo restaurant in Chicago, a place usually kept closed by the police, where it seemed it had long been kept in a trunk to be brought out when the gangsters wished to initiate a new member or swear to some new feud or vendetta, to make the oath upon.

I was dining out soon after at the home of generous friends on the north side, and my hostess teasingly observed,

"Well, Edgar, why haven't you been finding any more old manuscripts lately to show us?" With confusion of face I had to admit to her that since she mentioned it I happened to have one with me, in my brief case, and brought out the Gangster's Bible. For so the city journalists have named it and it became from the start our best-known acquisition. The anomaly of such a book showing up from such a source struck the newspapermen forcibly as something indescribably whimsical. What a place for such a book and what a new side for gangsterism which seems to have its sanctities, after all. A number of our generous friends soon made up the price asked and no manuscript we have found has ever equaled its notoriety.

Long, long ago, when in the Greek war for independence Argos was taken, this once splendidly miniatured lectionary, or book of church gospel readings, was torn to pieces and probably its miniatured pages carried off, leaving only its unminiatured ones which some pious Greek then collected and later had simply bound. This passed down the generations till it became the possession of our hero, if we may so describe him, and sank to the ignominious function I have described, until some dire need of funds drove its possessor to offer it for sale to just the right man. Who then can say what possible manuscript treasures may not still lie buried from sight in our very midst?

A Greek dentist in the Loop proved to have a manuscript of Matthew and Mark, which he was willing to part with, and we obtained. An elderly Armenian on the North Side invited Dr. Willoughby and me to supper at his house and showed us a good Armenian gospels with handsome portraits of the four evangelists, but he asked seventy-five thousand dollars for it. He had been hearing fantastic legends of what the Rockefeller McCormick had brought, for we had never publicly disclosed the price, as it was not one we had paid and was, strictly speaking, none of our business. But many years later, my successors bought the manuscript at a reasonable figure from the Armenian's sons.

A fine tenth-century Armenian uncial manuscript of forty leaves of Matthew and Mark was obtained from Professor Gregory's brother in Colorado. And only the other night, at Harold Lamb's house in Beverly Hills a half leaf of tenth-century Armenian uncial turned up tucked into another manuscript. I begged him to let me have a photostat made of it to send to Dr. Colwell then at Chicago to see whether it was not a bit of gospel text akin to what we had there already. He at once said, send the leaf itself to Dr. Colwell, and if it really is tenth-century gospel text, he would give it to the University's collection. This generous offer I gladly accepted. It proved to be gospel text and is now a part of the University's collection as the Harold Lamb manuscript.

Not long ago I had the pleasure of sending to the collection a quaint little Ethiopic manuscript of John which I had found in the catalogue of a Pennsylvania dealer in rare books and which very much resembled one in the Newberry Library, in Chicago, which I described for them many years ago. The fascinating thing about this one was the story that went with it that it had been brought from Abyssinia by Bayard Taylor, the famous American journalist, man of letters and world traveler just a hundred years before when he visited that country in 1851. This was a long time before the British government made their war on King Theodore and carried off the great treasure of Ethiopic manuscripts that is now in the British Museum, and used to engage so much of my London leisure.

Dr. Colwell has recently told how in 1930 he found the Red Armenian Gospels of Ganjasar in Stora's shop in Paris and nine years later secured it for the University. But none of these acquisitions surpasses in interest Miss McCormick's miniatured manuscript of the Revelation.

It was in the autumn of 1932 that on some social occasion the wife of a colleague told me that Miss McCormick had found a manuscript of the Apocrypha that she was planning to get my judgment on, and I accordingly brushed up on the matter in preparation for the interview. A little later Mrs. William Albert Nitze informed me that Miss McCormick had bought a miniatured Greek manuscript of the Apocalypse which she was going to show me. This was altogether different and I once more went about informing myself. I was accordingly not taken wholly by surprise when Miss McCormick asked us to luncheon at the Casino on December 11, 1932, and in the course of the meal—I remember Henry Field the archeologist was also present—asked me about miniatured manuscripts of the Revelation and whether I would be interested in one.

I hastened to express my keen interest and told Miss McCormick that Montague James, the great British manuscript expert, had declared that no miniatured Greek manuscript of the Apocalypse had ever been found.

"Well," she said, "I have one with sixty-nine miniatures," and after luncheon she showed it to us.

Miss McCormick had seen the manuscript late in March,

1932, in a shop window on the left bank of the Seine. She remembered having heard how thirty-three years before in a shop window in Orléans a Greek manuscript had been displayed for sale which contained the oldest Greek miniatures north of the Alps; it is now in the Bibliothéque Nationale. She went in and priced the manuscript, then returned to her hotel for the money and came back and bought it.

It was a paper manuscript in Modern Greek of the middle sixteenth century, but the range and vigor of the miniatures made it of the utmost interest to me, and it would be, I knew, to my colleagues. Mrs. Goodspeed hastened to invite Miss McCormick to come to dinner with us the next evening and bring the manuscript to show to my colleagues who would also dine with us. Then we could all go over to the meeting of the New Testament Club which was set for that night and the manuscript could be shown there. This was all duly arranged. Miss McCormick let us have the manuscript to study and we all plunged into it. At the dinner party it was especially interesting to see how from time to time one man or another would excuse himself and step into the living room to ask the manuscript some fresh question that had just occurred to him. For we would soon be expected to give our opinions of the manuscript at the general club meeting that would follow. But it would be expert testimony for Dr. Willoughby and Dr. Riddle were fresh from their monumental labors on the Rockefeller McCormick New Testament and Dr. Colwell was getting into his work on the miniatured Karahissar gospels which he and Dr. Willoughby were doing.

The interest at the club was naturally intense; the furor over the Rockefeller McCormick codex and the string of minor manuscripts since gathered in by the department had whetted the members' taste for such treasures and they had come to believe anything was possible. Henry Field and I had noticed the day before that some wicked dealer had erased or scratched out what had probably been an owner's name in the upper right-hand corner of the first page. We thought ultraviolet light would bring it out. But the extraordinary eyesight of Dr. Colwell made it unnecssary to await that test; he read it at once in spite of the dealer's efforts; it meant: "This also was with the other books of Parthenius of Larissa."

Miss McCormick was pleased with our interest and evident competence to deal with the manuscript and turned it over to us for research. And two weeks later Dr. Willoughby and Dr. Colwell read exciting papers about it before the sixty-eighth annual meeting of the Society of Biblical Literature and Exegesis in Chicago. They proceeded with their study of it and in 1940 published their results in two handsome volumes. And at a notable luncheon at the Casino later still, Miss McCormick as we have seen graciously presented the manuscript to the University collection. Miss McCormick's Apocalypse was splendidly published by the University Press in 1940 in two volumes by Drs. Colwell and Willoughby, which certainly marked an epoch in the iconography of the Book of Revelation.

The great thing about all these manuscripts is that they are not merely beautiful curiosities of long ago carefully preserved as a collection, but they are bought to be studied and explored and published and to train experts in such research. The extent to which they have achieved these ends is notable. I remember how, when Dr. Colwell and Dr. Clark were fellows in the department, I arranged one Christmas to have them go to Ann Arbor and make a full catalogue of the collection of New Testament Greek manuscripts Professor Kelsey had made there, Dr. William W. Bishop the Librarian

having agreed to their doing so. This task was but a step to
Dr. Clark's thesis, in which in 1937 he catalogued all such
manuscripts to be found in America, to the number of two
hundred and fifty-six. He has since done much to increase
this number, and has been identified with manuscript researches on a grand scale for the Library of Congress, researches that have taken him to Jerusalem and Sinai and now
promise to take him to Mt. Athos itself. Dr. Colwell, on
the other hand, has organized the re-examination of all the
variant readings of all known Greek manuscripts on a world-
wide scale, which promises a great advance on a wide front.
Dr. Willoughby on his side has carried his corpus of Greek
New Testament miniatures to practical completion and Dr.
Allen P. Wikgren has done great things with Greek ostraca
in which I used to dabble many years ago and with Armenian.
He is now the chairman of the department. These are but
examples of the truth that there is nothing our young American humanists cannot accomplish if only genuine research
materials are placed before them.

Shortly before my retirement in 1937, one of our alumni
called my attention to a manuscript of the Gospel of Mark
which had been in the possession of his people. At my request
they very kindly sent us the manuscript and we undertook
to pay their price for it. It was written in a hand not exactly
like any known hand, contained an extraordinarily primitive
form of text, very much like that of the great Vatican manuscript, and was adorned with sixteen spirited miniatures. The
fund to buy it was about half provided when I retired, but
was soon completed and the manuscript became the property
of the University. It is certainly one of the most interesting
and perplexing items in the whole collection, which has of
course grown steadily since I left Chicago, and now num-

bers no less than forty-three Greek manuscripts, beside twenty-one Syriac, Latin, Ethiopic and Armenian items.

Such has been the first period in the formation of our collection; with the progress of it since I left the University I am not very familiar. But the habit of manuscript collecting, with its excitements and its satisfactions, has I am sure established itself at Chicago and amply vindicated its serviceableness to a modern research University.

Why, even as I write these lines, Miss Ellen Shaffer of Dawson's in Los Angeles kindly sends me a Greek manuscript book to describe for them. It is the Four Gospels, beautifully written, in a hand which recognized experts like Mrs. Kirsopp Lake and Professor Wikgren assign to a date not later than A.D. 1050. Dean Colwell's tests confirm this conclusion. It was brought a few months ago from Istanbul by Mr. H. Kurdian of Wichita, Kansas, who has a personal collection of two hundred Armenian manuscripts. It is just such a manuscript as we hunted all over Europe for in 1927, and found it not. Of course I felt that it must go to Chicago; and I saw that it did. This raises the Chicago total of Greek items to forty-four.

SIXTEEN

The Seats of the Mighty

IT WAS in the summer of 1920 that President Judson intimated that he would like to have me take over the job of
Secretary to the President just being vacated by my old friend
David Allan Robertson who had been made Dean of the
Colleges. I was reluctant to turn aside into Administration,
especially in so important a post, for I knew that my favorite
habits of indecision and procrastination would have to be
laid aside. My own researches and publication projects would
also have to be indefinitely postponed. But the President's
close personal relations to my father and my cousins George
and Florence Goodspeed and his very fruitful suggestion that
had led to Father's history of the University made me reluctant to decline. So for four short years I served in the
President's office. I had what was then the finest office in the
University, admirable secretarial assistance, authority far
beyond my powers or wishes, football tickets and the dispens-
ing of them, fascinating new social contacts—an engrossing
life in fact, and as full of interest and surprise as can be
imagined. The President declared that he was not going to
have any more vice-presidents, but that administrative matters of importance would be settled by the President, the
Dean of the Colleges, and the Secretary to the President,

which naturally gave the post more importance than it had had before. But before the first week had passed he called me in to his office to point out a flaw in the weekly *News Letter* (which I had simply O.K'd), saying that one item in it had not been passed by the Board. I was, of course, much distressed, but accepted full responsibility for the mistake and assured him it would not happen again. This mollified him completely.

"Don't give it another thought," he hastened to say. "I don't care a button"—an expression of his for complete indifference. He never took me to task again about anything. At the end of the first month, I said to him,

"Mr. President, I want to say that I never learned so much in thirty days in my life." And this was quite true.

He was an extraordinarily smooth and efficient administrator and my four years in the office furthered my own development a great deal. There was, of course, a good deal of routine about my work. For one thing, the contacts of the newspaper reporters were with my office and while generally smooth and pleasant there were occasional clashes on what they had said or should say. I tried to have a sheet of whatever news the University had to offer, prepared perhaps twice a week for them, or oftener if something of importance came up. General public lectures, guests of the University, the arrangements for the four quarterly convocations, the editing of the quarterly University *Record*, were part of our routine.

The President said to me at the outset,

"Whenever you have something of importance to take up with me, come right in, no matter who may be with me." Our offices opened directly into each other so that this made some things very easy for me, though naturally I was careful in using this privilege. But while he remained President there was no locked door between our offices; in fact it could not be locked; the key was lost. Of course, our outer doors were provided with locks and keys, as was the big outside door of the whole suite.

The duties of the Secretary to the President were varied in the extreme. One of the first things that came to my desk was an invitation to a dinner of the Dutch consuls of the United States for the new ambassador. My first impulse was to decline, but then I thought, Oh well, if I'm going to do this job, I might as well do it, and I went. The consuls were a jovial crew and at every place were two bottles of Irish whiskey. It was really not my sort of party but in my neighbor at table, Henry Van Coenen Torchiana, the Dutch Consul General for the Pacific coast, I found a lifelong friend.

Another duty which the President passed over to me was participating one Sunday afternoon in a great Polish meeting at a down-town theater in honor of Copernicus. My part consisted in sitting all the afternoon on the stage on a chair without any back and making a few remarks on the President's behalf. I had previously given, I must confess, little thought to Copernicus though approving of him in a general way, but the hit of the afternoon was made by an indolent individual who merely read a long section from Alfred Noyes' poem on Copernicus.

Soon after coming into the office I noticed on the President's desk a huge pile of reports on the condition and needs of the University which some faculty commission was pouring in upon him. I said to him,

"Mr. President, wouldn't you like to have me take that material and summarize it for you?

His face brightened as he gathered up the whole armful.

"Take it right along," he said cheerfully, and I did. We

produced from it a much compressed booklet entitled *The University of Chicago in 1921.*

We sent five thousand copies of it out at once and it aroused much favorable comment for it contained pictures not before published of some great new buildings the University was about to build. Two evening papers, the *News* and the *Post,* each devoted a whole page the following Wednesday to these pictures, greatly enlarged, or blown up as they say. We were feeling modestly gratified by this piece of publicity when the President called me into his office. He handed me a letter from the representative of another evening paper, sternly rebuking the President for partiality in not sending his paper the booklet, and going to considerable lengths in denouncing him.

I said,

"Let me look into this for a moment. I don't think we left anybody out," and I withdrew to consult our clipping file.

Sure enough, here was a mean little item of a few lines in the complaining paper a week before. They had received it but thought it of no importance—until they saw what a find the other papers had considered it. I handed the scrapbook to the President. He glanced at the squalid little item and the date. Then he nodded, cheerfully.

"I supposed so," was all he said,

I did not see the letter he wrote to his critic, but he did send in to me the reply he got, and it was the most abject apology I have ever seen in my life. At any rate, the President ordered the printing of five thousand more copies.

My two years and a half with President Judson before his retirement, in 1923, were marked by numerous interesting occasions. In 1921 the University invited Marshal Foch to visit it and accept an honorary degree, and the arrangements for his arrival were all a civilian could imagine. With the Marshal of the University, Algernon Coleman, I was to meet the great man at the Mitchell Tower door and escort him into Hutchinson Hall where the procession was to form, but like the great strategist he was, he came twenty minutes early. Fortunately, I lived only two minutes from the Mitchell Tower, and warned by the booming of the cannon in the welcoming salute, I was there on time. My civilities were, I fear, lost upon Marshal Foch, but Algernon being a professor of French was fully equal to the occasion. Everything about the affair was promptness itself. Everybody was early, and the celebrities that gathered in Hutchinson to form the procession had a long social before we could reasonably start them into Mandel Hall. In the midst of it word reached me that the leading physician of the city with his daughter had arrived and there were no places for them. I had invited them but they had not replied. The middle sections of the main floor were devoted entirely to our college veterans of the war and I could only have two chairs put in front of them for our invited but unexpected guests. The Governor, on the other hand, whom we had planned to seat with his family in a box, preferred to march in the procession, and we had to make a place for him on the platform.

At length, at the precise moment we set the procession in motion and at exactly eleven o'clock it entered Mandel Hall. There was an invocation by Bishop Kelly, Marshal Foch was presented for the degree, it was conferred, we sang the Alma Mater, and marched out, all in exactly twelve minutes. Algernon and I called the President's attention to the precision of our arrangements. He was delighted, falling for once into the vernacular.

"Boys," said the President, "you done well!"

Algy and I were satisfied.

Another great French visitor who came to the June convocation for an honorary degree was Mme. Curie. She had to arrive after the exercises were under way and it was my privilege to meet her at the University Avenue door of Mandel, escort her and her party through Mandel and the Cloister to the stage door of the outdoor platform, and show her to her place beside the President. She was escorted to the front to receive her degree by two very attractive young women instructors in chemistry, both Ph.D.'s of the University. I saw more of her party, which included one of her daughters, as I took them to their box.

But of all these French guests the most appealing was the French Ambassador, Jusserand, who came from Washington to give the convocation address in 1922. I met him and his American wife at Englewood, and as the train pulled out for down town, from every vestibule door hung grinning porters and waiters waving them farewell. If there ever was an ambassador of good will it was Jusserand. I found him and Mme. Jusserand being photographed by a newsman, a policeman standing close beside them. He later explained to me that he was glad to be photographed with some distinguished people, he wanted to send the picture back home in the east, or was it in Britain? Certainly the Ambassador had elevated democracy into a fine art. We tried to get him to accept his travel expenses at least, for his services, and had great difficulty, he complaining that we were paying him five dollars too much. I had bought his tickets from Englewood to Washington, while he had bought his from Washington to Chicago (meaning down town). He finally submitted, remarking (and his autograph letter is before me), "I had actually paid $85 on the same train from Washington to Chicago. . . . It must obviously be that the distance is not the same from Chicago to Washington." We let it go at that.

One affair at the Quadrangle Club I well remember. It was the farewell dinner given for Robert Millikan when in 1921 he left the University for Pasadena and the California Institute of Technology. President Judson was toastmaster and the address on behalf of the faculty was made by James Weber Linn. He said that the physics department reminded him of the tonic of his youth, Beef, Iron and Wine. Mr. Michelson was of course the Wine of the combination, and his old friend Henry Gale would forgive him if he designated him as its Beef. But the Iron of the department was unquestionably Mr. Millikan. This was received with roars of laughter and great applause.

It was not until next morning that I got the full force of this felicitous metaphor. Up to that time Mr. Millikan was chiefly associated in the popular mind with his researches into the ion, and it was to that Mr. Linn referred. I mentioned this to others who had been at the dinner and had shared in the amusement and they said, No, that connection had not occurred to them. I am satisfied that to this day many of those present have never seen the joke, in all its overtones. This is one of the dangers of after-dinner speaking and goes far to justify the practice of many such speakers of charting their more intricate jokes after getting them off, proceeding, "But, seriously"—and so on.

In the spring of 1921—it was April 26 to be exact—the President had to be away for a while and left important duties to me. He explained to me, confidentially, that Mr. Max Epstein, a generous friend of the University, had hopes of bringing Dr. Albert Einstein to the University for a series of lectures in Mandel Hall. Dr. Einstein was just then making his first public appearance in this country in a short series of lectures at Princeton. The President instructed me to have everything in readiness for the lectures in case Mr. Epstein who was handling the whole affair should telephone me that he had completed his arrangement with Dr. Einstein. Then the moment I heard from Mr. Epstein, I was to go ahead issuing the invitations and announcing the series. A day or so later I had word from Mr. Epstein to go ahead and did so.

There was a very nice reception for the Einsteins at the Epsteins' house in Kenwood on Monday evening. When I mentioned to Dr. Einstein that I had studied in Berlin, he at once asked with whom. Harnack, I replied.

"Ach, Harnack!" he rejoined. "Er is auch von dieser Welt!"

It was true Harnack had so advanced in favor with the Kaiser that he had almost achieved the stature of a courtier and Einstein felt this rather keenly.

I had to consider whom to ask to introduce Dr. Einstein, in the President's absence, and thought it wise to call upon the Dean of the Ogden Graduate School of Science, Professor Salisbury. He agreed and we happened to cross the quadrangle to the lecture together. I expressed my fears of not having room enough for the crowd and said I had had to seat the platform to accommodate the faculty, but he said he did not anticipate any large attendance or great interest. Yet the place was simply packed, of course.

Salisbury's introduction was not up to his usual competent style. As nearly as I can remember it, he said,

"Ladies and gentlemen, we are indebted to Mr. and Mrs. Einstein, I mean Epstein, for bringing Dr. Epstein, I mean Einstein, to the University today.

"Some men of science who gain wide public recognition

do it by the value of their results, others by the notoriety they have achieved. Our speaker today belongs to the latter class. I now introduce Dr. Albert Einstein."

This incredible introduction being fortunately in English was probably not intelligible to Dr. and Mrs. Einstein, at least we hoped not! The audience is probably wondering yet what could have led Salisbury to utter it. But I think he was as always only trying to be sincere and fair. He represented the Ogden Graduate School and its personnel, its scientific rating was second to none, and like many scientific men of that time Salisbury was not prepared to say that Einstein's results were sound and valid. He could not in his position be just meaninglessly polite. He was speaking for the best scientific thought of the country. It was at least possible, as he saw it, that Einstein was not the serious and competent thinker that the modern world has since recognized him to be. That is the explanation of his amazing introduction. In general, Dr. Einstein was received with great enthusiasm by his Mandel audience, and a dinner was given that evening in the Quadrangle Club in honor of Dr. and Mrs. Einstein.

Let it not be supposed that Salisbury, an experienced writer, was careless in the use of words. Once in connection with some slight article of mine that he had seen and approved, he said to me that he always told his students, "It is not enough to write so that you can be understood, you must write in such a way that you cannot be misunderstood!" And I quote this strange, and the reader may think better-forgotten, introduction of his, only because it was so manifestly conscientiously done. Salisbury felt that his intellectual integrity demanded it.

After Dr. Einstein's last lecture his car was surrounded by

students asking for his autograph, and he patiently wrote his name until the last one was satisfied, before he and Mrs. Einstein drove away.

How impulsive yet sound Salisbury was is shown by an experience I had with him one day in the office. We had had a somewhat heated conversation over the telephone on some small official matter and I put down the telephone with a groan. I got up and started out of the office but was delayed by some question in the secretaries' room. As I reached the outer door it flew open and Salisbury rushed in.

"Mr. Goodspeed, I came over to apologize to you. I should not have said what I did over the telephone just now."

"Mr. Salisbury," said I, "I was just going over to your office to say the same thing to you."

We shook hands, better friends than ever from that day.

Among the French heroes who visited Chicago after the war was Clemenceau, the famous Tiger premier. He addressed a great audience in the Auditorium in 1922, being introduced by General Charles G. Dawes. He stood behind a small table on which stood the loud-speaker, or amplifier, so necessary in that huge hall. But the speaker's interest and eloquence soon got the better of him, and to get nearer his audience he edged around the corner of the table and away from the microphone, becoming immediately inaudible to half his audience which at once stopped his remarks by breaking into loud and continued applause. He did not seem to understand that he must return to the microphone and the audience continued its deafening clapping, trying to drive him back, until General Dawes got up and gently lifting the little table put it once more in front of Clemenceau, when the applause immediately ceased. A few minutes later the Tiger once more edged around the corner of the table, the applause again began, and again the General stepped forward and moved the table around in front of the speaker. Three times this extraordinary comedy, with two of the greatest figures of the day taking part in it, was enacted, to the great delight and relief of the audience which really wanted to hear what Clemenceau had to say. With a lesser man, some mere lecturer, they might have given up the attempt, but they simply would not give up the chance to hear Clemenceau.

Through her dear friend Mrs. Carl Bullock, Mrs. Goodspeed had become active in the Field Committee of the national Y.W.C.A., and when in 1919 it was proposed to introduce the work of that organization into Chicago, she accepted the chairmanship of the campaign committee to raise three hundred thousand dollars to establish the Y.W.C.A. in Chicago.

Meantime, she and some of her friends like Mrs. Bullock became interested in improving their oratory and formed a small private class in public speaking under Professor Bertram Nelson of the University. This short course was of much assistance to my wife who got a great deal out of it. The training came importantly into play in this new chairmanship where she had to preside day after day over a sort of inspirational luncheon of the campaign workers, at a down-town hotel. She was active in seeking some of the larger initial gifts so necessary to such campaigns. I remember well with what anxiety she pursued this difficult and testing preliminary work.

One day when she had gone with some concern to her daily luncheon meeting down town, sad because the initial pledges were slow in coming in, the mail arrived and I noticed a letter from the home of Mrs. G. F. Swift, one of the city's leading givers. I did not ordinarily open my wife's mail but it occurred to me that this letter might contain something that would help her in her luncheon remarks, and it did. I reached her at the luncheon, called her to the telephone, and told her that Mrs. Swift was giving ten thousand dollars to the campaign. This was naturally most welcome news, and did much to make that luncheon and the whole campaign, as it proved, a complete success.

My father, as an old campaigner, was much interested in Elfleda's Y.W.C.A. campaign and told his friend Julius Rosenwald about it, adding that Elfleda was hoping to have an opportunity of presenting her cause to him sometime at his office. But Mr. Rosenwald very kindly said No, he would call upon her. He explained that he took his grandchildren to school out at the University Elementary School every morning and went right by our house, so he would stop there on his way back some morning—as he very graciously did.

Mrs. Goodspeed's interest in the Association continued and in 1921 she was again active in its behalf. One of the Chicago bodies such campaigns strive hardest to reach is the Association of Commerce, and its huge weekly luncheon, with twelve hundred members in attendance, every moment of which is so coveted. One of the leading men whom Elfleda had interested in her campaign was Mr. David R. Forgan of the First National Bank who was kind enough that year to get her six minutes at their weekly luncheon, to present her cause. With some trepidation she undertook the task and performed it, sitting down in just six minutes. Mr. Forgan was jubilant. He wrote on his program,

"You did it. I knew you could do it. There isn't a man in hicago that could have done it!"

These generous words she always preserved, calling them her diploma in public speaking. Of course, both campaigns met with complete success and had far-reaching results in the subsequent years.

She also did so well in inspirational talks that she went about among the cities around Chicago speaking for the Y.W.C.A. An address of hers first given at a Mothers and Daughters banquet out on the South Side she was called upon to repeat in other churches, and I was quite accustomed to seeing her off and welcoming her back, or when possible going to hear her. For in those years she was definitely the speaker of the family: my province was my study and my classroom. Her Mothers and Daughters address Dr. W. C. Covert invited her to give one Sunday evening in the First Presbyterian Church and my father and my brother Charles accompanied us to that occasion. After her address, Dr. Covert espying Father sitting with his sons in the back part of the congregation, said,

"I will ask Dr. Goodspeed, the father-in-law of Mrs. Goodspeed and the friend of Abraham Lincoln, to dismiss us with the benediction."

It was very lovely of Dr. Covert, to whom we were all greatly attached from our summers' contacts with him up in the north woods, and I have always remembered it gratefully, though to describe Father as the friend of Abraham Lincoln seemed pitching it a little strong, for his only contact with Mr. Lincoln was hearing him debate with Judge Douglas at Knox College in 1858 when Father was sixteen, from which date Father was certainly a friend of Abraham Lincoln, though not an intimate friend.

Mrs. Goodspeed also became active in the Young Fortnightly, to which she was introduced I believe by Mrs. Carl Bullock. One year—it was 1925—the much-loved President, Mrs. Gunn, was ill virtually the whole year, so that Elfleda as Vice-President occupied the chair. The next year she was President and the plans were consummated for uniting with the Wednesday Club to form the Contemporary Club, of which Elfleda became the first President, the following year. She also became active in the Fortnightly having charge one year of the program committee. I remember once when we were driving to the North Shore she pleaded with me for a lecturer for the Fortnightly's program which she thought I, as I was in the President's office at the University, ought to be able to suggest. Finally in desperation I said, "Well, the other night at the Mayflower meeting I had a fine talk with Admiral Wat Cluverius and he talked like a man who could lecture, though of course they're not exactly the same thing."

She followed this lead and the Admiral more than fulfilled our hopes. He was descended from a famous Dutch geographer whose family had afterward petitioned the Pope to let them assume the Latinized form of the name he had made famous. He was on the *Maine* when she blew up and had afterward married Admiral Sampson's daughter. Oh, the Admiral was certainly the answer to a program-chairman's prayer, and went on to a successful season of lecturing in the Chicago area.

In 1921 Elfleda's gifted young cousin Clara Olney interrupted her college course at Denison to spend the spring and autumn quarters at the University of Chicago, and to our great joy stayed with us from March to December, spending the summer at the Island with us. She crowned these achievements by flying back from Chicago to Ohio in a two-seater airplane on the invitation of my aeronautical cousin Parker Van Zandt, who has recently been in Washington as Mr. Finletter's first assistant. We were a good deal relieved to learn of their safe arrival! But Chicago had made a deep impression upon Clara for she left as the fiancée of Herrick Goodwillie, just returned with honors from the First World War, whom she married when through with college a year or two later.

When Sir Humphrey Milford was at the head of the Oxford University Press, he visited the University and Mr. Bean, the Manager of the University of Chicago Press, gave a dinner for him. I immediately opened the conversation by begging Sir Humphrey, as the greatest publisher in the world of the King James version, to correct the misprint "at" to "out" in the expression "strain at a gnat," in Matthew 23:24.

"Is that a misprint?" he graciously inquired.

"Oh, yes," said I confidently, "Isn't it, Sir William?" for Sir William Craigie, of Oxford Dictionary fame, was sitting beside him.

"Of course it's a misprint," said Sir William, heartily, "Everybody knows that!"

Even this sterling testimony did not move Sir Humphrey to comply, nor has any other publisher of King James, even John Stirling or Sutherland Bates, ventured to take this obvious step, though no end of other King James misprints have been corrected.

I had the hardihood to suggest to Sir Humphrey that he should restore the great preface, "The Translators to the Reader," to its rightful place at the beginning of the book, and he replied, "Well, I believe I did order that put back in a recent lectern Bible we published."

I might have told him how little use there was in that, for the rector could hardly be expected to read from it to his congregation while one can hardly imagine the parishioners repairing to the church during the week and seeking the book out to read it. And yet its restoration to its rightful

place in home copies would save the book from half the misunderstandings that now pursue it. Its omission by the American commercial publishers of King James one can understand, even if one cannot forgive it, but that Oxford should
withhold it one cannot explain. Cambridge has, I am happy
to say, recently published it in a very convenient complete
octavo Bible.

It had been in the winter of 1917 that Mrs. Goodspeed's
mother, Mrs. Joseph Bond, was approached by her old
friends Professor Burton and Dean Mathews about erecting
the Divinity School chapel in memory of Mr. Bond. He had
been a trustee of the Baptist Theological Union, the Board
that controlled and maintained the School. They called upon
her at our house on Woodlawn Avenue where she was visiting us. It was first proposed that the chapel should not be
a separate building but should be a specially designed room
within the new Divinity building. This plan did not greatly
appeal to Mrs. Bond. Nor was she interested in a Bond
Chapel. But when it was suggested that the chapel be a de-
tached and independent structure and be named the Joseph
Bond Chapel, she agreed to provide the necessary funds.

But the administration was in no hurry to proceed with
the building and when some years had passed, Mrs. Bond
began to think the University had lost interest in the project
and from California where she was spending the winter with
her younger daughter, Mrs. Joseph F. Rhodes, Jr., in Pasadena, she wired President Judson suggesting that perhaps
the University would prefer to put the money into Divinity
scholarships. This wire caused the President some perplexity
and he conferred with Professor Burton as to just how it
should be answered. They wanted the money put into the
chapel but were not yet ready to proceed to build.

I shall never forget an evening in Mandel Hall when after a concert the President and Dr. Burton came to our box and laid the problem before Mrs. Goodspeed. They showed her the telegram. She did not hesitate an instant but immediately told them in a sentence just what to reply. She knew her mother well, of course, and understood her whole attitude in the matter. President Judson looked at Dr. Burton and quietly nodded his approval.

"That is just the thing to say," he observed. "That is the message we will send Mrs. Bond." And they did, and she was entirely satisfied.

A beautiful design for the chapel was duly prepared and shown to Mrs. Bond who was much pleased with it, as we all were. Mr. Ryerson allowed us to publish it in the booklet on the condition and needs of the University that I prepared for the President in 1921. The building of the chapel was not, however, begun in his administration. When Dr. Burton became President he asked me to call on Mr. Hodgdon, the local representative of the architects, Coolidge and Hodgdon, to see if the building could not be substantially reduced in cost. He had sent me on a similar errand about the Theology building the chapel was to adjoin and we had reduced its cost at a number of points, although all these reductions were later given up by reason of additional funds given to restore them. As to the chapel, however, Mr. Hodgdon would not yield an inch. I tried one economy after another on him but he found a defense against my reasoning on every one. Finally he said, very earnestly,

"Mr. Goodspeed, that chapel is designed exactly the way it ought to be built in every particular and I don't want it altered. It is planned just exactly right and I want it built that way, even if it isn't built till after I am dead!"

He did eventually give up the balcony over the antechapel, which I thought a decided improvement. But I carried this discouraging report back to the President, and we gave up trying to shake the architects.

The cornerstone was laid on April 30, 1925, in President Burton's administration, but he was too ill to be present and Mrs. Bond was escorted by Vice-President James H. Tufts when she laid the stone. It was dedicated on October 21, 1926, under the administration of President Max Mason. At her request I shared the dedication service with Dean Mathews and President Mason and made the brief speech of presentation on her behalf. But Mrs. Bond was present, seated in the front row, and as President Mason left the chancel, in his courtly manner he offered her his arm, and she walked up the aisle between the President and her old friend Dean Mathews, I think a proud and happy woman. It was a beautiful, gracious gesture on the part of the President.

Mrs. Bond later gave generously to the erection of the cloister connecting the chapel with Swift Hall, and later still provided the beautiful chancel window, which was designed and executed by Charles J. Connick of Boston. Mr. Connick became our very dear friend and on his later visits to Chicago and to Los Angeles was usually our house guest. The great east window, erected in 1951, is in memory of Mrs. Goodspeed, and the twelve aisle windows since installed will complete a memorial of her, doubly appropriate in view of her extraordinary devotion to her father whom she so idolized. These windows are all from the Connick studios so as to be entirely harmonious.

This completion of the decoration of the Joseph Bond Chapel came just one hundred years after the birth of Joseph

Bond, and fifty years after his death. The Chapel has served the University well for twenty-five years, accommodating the daily chapel service of the Divinity School at noon four days a week. It is also being used by the Episcopalians for a Sunday morning service, and by the Lutherans at another hour. Many public lectures are given in it, and it is in frequent use for University weddings and funerals which do not require the enormous seating capacity of the Rockefeller Chapel. Indeed, on Monday, August 2, 1926, some weeks before its dedication, Elfleda and I had the pleasure of attending the first wedding in the new chapel, which was that of Clair Dux and Charles H. Swift, a brilliant and interesting occasion.

In 1926 Elfleda went on the board of the Visiting Nurse Association of Chicago and became very active in its work. She was expert with her needle and did a great deal of needle point at one time; in fact, she did the chair seats for our dining-room set, which are still in use. At the V.N.A. she learned that there was much need for simple dresses for little girls. She got an acceptable pattern and for some years her fancy work was making these dainty little dresses, in all sorts of material. I wish I knew just how many she had made when she stopped; it was between three and four hundred. On two occasions she was asked to accept the presidency of the Chicago V.N.A., but she declined.

No one was more alive to progress in travel than Elfleda and we were soon drifting along with the rest of the mobile population from a Ford, for use up in the north woods, to a Buick, then a Lincoln, and then for a few brief months we basked in a Cadillac limousine. That was, of course, in 1925 when, in spite of what everyone says, it was good to be alive.

It called down the greatest compliment any car of ours ever incurred, and from a real expert, the second Mrs. Marshall Field.

Mrs. Field had come back to Chicago for the funeral of an old friend, and had gone to the old Field mansion on Prairie Avenue. She had kept it occupied and open, but had herself been living in Washington, D. C. Mrs. Janet Ayer Fairbank, the novelist, and a great friend of the University's hospitals, had seized the opportunity to show them to Mrs. Field, and a small luncheon had been arranged at the Field residence, in which to my great surprise I found myself included, as one presumably familiar with the history of the University. The fourth member of the party was Professor William Albert Nitze. It was, of course, a fascinating experience for an old Chicagoan like myself not only to meet Mrs. Field but to see Mr. Field's house, just as it had been at the time of his death almost twenty years before. He was a very handsome man and all the portrait painters wanted to paint his portrait, and most of them, British and American, did so. Every great room had over the mantlepiece a fine picture of him. They would have made a distinguished portrait gallery all by themselves.

As soon as luncheon was over we went out for the drive to the University. All Mrs. Field asked was not to be taken to the Field Museum; she had evidently had enough of that. I timidly suggested to Mrs. Fairbank that we should take my car. She gave it an appraising glance and nodded. We all got in. As Mrs. Field settled herself comfortably, she said,

"Well! I'd just like to know whose shebang this is! Most comfortable car I was ever in in my life!"

I was pointed out as the guilty man. She shook her head.

"I can't understand these modern professors," she admitted

sadly. Of course, it was all the balloon tires; they had just come out and she had probably not encountered them before, though she had a whole fleet of automobiles in Washington. But I could hardly wait to get home to tell Mrs. Goodspeed the latest compliment for her new car, and from Mrs. Field.

In 1926 Bishop Anderson brought Bishop Winnington Ingram out to the University, to have tea with us and then speak in Mandel Hall. He was Bishop of London and preached in such an informal popular way that he was said to write his sermons while riding on the tops of the London buses. I remember how pleased he was to find the tea strong. A few years later the Archbishop of York came to the University for a series of lectures at one of which I had the honor of introducing him. I also had the pleasure of introducing President Glenn Frank of Wisconsin for his lecture in Orchestra Hall.

It was toward the end of April, 1928, that Burnett Hillman Streeter of Queen's College, Oxford, visited the University and lectured there. Canon Streeter (he was Canon of Hereford Cathedral) stayed with us and we enjoyed his visit exceedingly. He had recently published his very able book on the Four Gospels and was, I suppose, at the time the foremost New Testament scholar in Britain. Three years later he became Provost of Queen's College. Those were the days when limericks were the rage, and when about to sail, he sent this one to Mrs. Goodspeed:

> As from the Mauretania, 2 May, 1928.
> I ne'er thought that I should so far go
> As to reach the fair town of Chicago
>   I lack words to employ
>   To utter my joy
> But—on superlatives there's an embargo.

Critics of creative literature will perhaps say that this is not in the top flight in its field, thinking of such masterpieces as "A Young Lady of Niger" or "A Young Woman Named Bright"; to which we reply,

"Yes, yes, but who wrote them?"

In the department we were, of course, all constantly absorbed in research and the give and take of scholarly controversy. I remember once my old friend Kirsopp Lake, at Harvard, was annoyed at being caught up on some small technical point by one of my "young men," as our junior colleagues were playfully called. Lake protested that he and I when young had never indulged in such liberties with our seniors. Of course, I wrote him a mollifying note, explaining that I was sorry but I did not see what I could do about it. I had signed the letter when I had a sudden flash of memory, and added a postscript to remind Lake of an exploit of his youth when he was engaged in a controversy with another scholar who was a bishop, and Lake had ended his item with these words: "In criticism, as in chess, bishops move obliquely." Certainly my young men had said nothing brighter than that!

What a figure in the literary Chicago of those days was Harriet Monroe! I recall her courage in rescuing for me the presidency of the Midland Authors by bringing the retiring president to time when he was about to adjourn the annual meeting without having the election of officers. He was one of these absent-minded poets, but though also a poet she was not absent-minded. Her early fame was, of course, due to her "Columbian Ode" for the dedication of the World's Columbian Exposition of 1893. But my most vivid impression of Harriet is of the night we were both doing our first broadcasting at some down-town studio. She seemed awfully white and her broadcast evidently wearied her. I asked if we might drive her home and she welcomed the idea. She said she had been knocked down by a car on her way to the studio and had not fully recovered from it! We got her home to her near-by apartment as gently as Tom and Elfleda and I could manage it but learned later that she had broken some bones and went the next morning to the hospital. Yet she had gone through with her broadcast with stoical composure. Almost anybody else would have canceled the broadcast and gone home to bed, but she was a trouper.

Later in our Chicago residence Elfleda became actively associated with the Mayflower Society and with the Colonial Dames, the latter by reason of her maternal ancestor Thomas Olney having been Roger Williams' principal ally in the establishment of Providence, Rhode Island. The Dames appointed her to write their illustrated lecture on the history of Illinois, and for this we motored over the state with its chief historical sites in view. It was a most interesting journey and we picked up some good illustrative material. Traveled friends added to this from their researches and the officers of the Newberry Library very kindly took down and had photographed for her the Library's Healy portrait of Abraham Lincoln. When Elfleda had finished her task we had a little interview with Mr. and Mrs. John V. Farwell, when Elfleda read him the lecture to get his criticism, since he knew Illinois history so well. His only correction was that Grant was a native of Ohio, not of Illinois, which we had overlooked. This lecture Elfleda gave on numerous occasions to the accompaniment of the slides.

It was for the Colonial Dames that she arranged with a young Chicago sculptor named Bernard Frazier to make a bronze tablet of Old Fort Dearborn, to be erected on the front of the London Guaranty Trust Building, on Wacker Drive, facing the River. The afternoon it was unveiled traffic on Michigan Boulevard was halted for two minutes by the Mayor's order, and Colonel A. A. Sprague, the Commissioner of Public Works, made the address on behalf of the city.

In 1932 Lord William and Lady Florence Cecil were again in America—he was now Bishop of Exeter, Myles Coverdale's old see—and they spent a few days with us. One evening we invited President Hutchins and the Divinity faculty to meet them. It happened to be Election Day and all our guests felt much interest in the contest between President Hoover and Mr. Roosevelt. There was no television but the radio was much in evidence and cast a pall of gloom over most of the company, though not our English guests who seemed not displeased at the outcome.

It was on this second visit that I was able to show Lord William over the new University Chapel (we could not call it Rockefeller as long as Mr. Rockefeller lived). He was very much interested. I remember he stopped at one point and said to me very earnestly,

"This is the finest building I've seen in this country!"

In 1933 President Hutchins very graciously invited me to accept the Ernest D. Burton distinguished service professorship, which I was especially happy to do in view of my long connection with Dr. Burton, as his student, his colleague and his secretary. Really the appointment can never mean so much to any other holder of it.

The coming of Professor Alfred North Whitehead of Harvard to the University to lecture in October, 1933, was almost as divisive as Einstein's visit had been twelve years before. We sat in the very front row in Mandel Hall next to the Paul Shoreys. Professor Whitehead concluded with a well-known sentence from a Greek philosopher to the effect that philosophy begins in mystery and also ends in mystery. Before the applause ceased, Shorey, greatly excited, turned to me,

"It's a trick, don't you see it is? It's a trick!" he declared hotly. I had never seen Shorey excited before, and was amazed. Mrs. Goodspeed and I nevertheless hastened up to meet Professor Whitehead after lecture, and she invited him to have luncheon with us the following Tuesday. He seemed to hesitate, and I put in my oar.

"Professor Whitehead," said I, "it may help you to decide about Mrs. Goodspeed's invitation if I inform you that the past summer, my first waking moments have been hearing Mrs. Goodspeed call to me from her bed, 'Are you wide enough awake yet to listen to these passages I've been marking in Whitehead?'"

We all laughed heartily, and he consented. We had Dr. and Mrs. Charles H. Heimsath of Evanston to meet him, and it was a memorable hour. Mrs. Heimsath, as Mrs. Goodspeed knew, was making her Ph.D. thesis at Yale on the philosophy of Alfred North Whitehead.

In those great years at Chicago when we were so surrounded by wit and genius, Dr. and Mrs. Soares arranged a dinner at the South Shore Country Club for Dr. Breasted on his return from one of his visits to Egypt. It was soon after the Tutenkhamen discoveries in the interpretation of which Dr. Breasted had participated. Dr. Soares explained to the guests that he had with great difficulty secured the attendance of a number of ancient Egyptians who would speak through various guests, he did not know which ones. He first introduced Ramses II, and sat down. We all looked at one another to see through which of us the old potentate would express himself and at length, with one arm uplifted to shield his face as though rousing from a long sleep, Ernest Wilkins staggered to his feet. In the person of this old monarch he told two or three exquisite old Egyptian stories, which he has since published in his essays entitled *Above Pompeii*. The child wife of Tutenkhamen was then called for by the chairman, and after a suitable hesitation Elfleda rose and spoke in the person of the princess. She had studied up the girl's background to good purpose. The parts of the tomb robbers and the architect of the tomb were then taken by two distinguished Chicagoans, Marquis Eaton and Lorado Taft—altogether a very star list of performers in which my wife found herself! Finally Dr. Breasted himself spoke and told some very good stories of modern Egypt. It was a remarkable evening in conception and in execution and I took a just pride in my wife's share in it.

In 1936 Elfleda planned an interesting motor trip through New England on which Charles accompanied us. We did some of the principal places—Boston and Cambridge—it was the week of the Harvard Tercentenary, and the great storm. We saw Yale and West Point, Princeton, Philadelphia and Washington, then as we went on southward a sign indicated Gunston Hall, a few miles away on the banks of the Potomac. Mr. Louis Hertle, who had restored it so successfully, had invited us to call (he was an old Chicagoan), and we went over. He was most hospitable and showed us everything— the room where George Mason wrote the Bill of Rights (he built the house in 1758), the box hedges eighteen feet high laid out by Washington—and kept us for a delightful luncheon. Then on to Richmond and Williamsburg, and then back through Ohio, where we revisited what were for Charles and me old college scenes. It was a wonderful September outing.

At his death, a few years later, Mr. Hertle bequeathed Gunston Hall to the State of Virginia, and designated the Society of Colonial Dames as trustee and administrator.

When I was lecturing at Benton Harbor on the books of the New Testament in my last years at Chicago, a Negro minister came up to me after my remarks and asked me why I did not embody the lectures in a book. I answered that I had long since done so in my *Story of the New Testament*. No, he said, he had the *Story* but much of what I was saying in these lectures in the way of evidence and illustration did not appear in the *Story* at all. A little reflection showed me that he was quite right and I proceeded at once to write a book which should illustrate and support the positions I had simply outlined in the *Story* twenty years before. So true it is that we learn from our listeners.

My relations with my faculty colleagues at Chicago were cordial in the extreme. Of their courtesy and consideration there were countless instances. I remember the kindness of Professor Stieglitz, Chairman of Chemistry, who meeting me on the street one day in 1923 gave me such cordial and generous congratulations on my New Testament translation. My colleagues elected me to all sorts of posts. As president of the Orchestral Association, I remember, I had the privilege of escorting Dr. Frederick Stock to the stage door of Mandel Hall for the Tuesday afternoon orchestral concert. As president of the Renaissance Society I prevailed upon our old friend and neighbor Lorado Taft to tell the University public about his great "Fountain of Time" at the head of the Midway, and introduced him to do it. I clambered up onto the sculpture for the introduction and then he clambered up and spoke in his easy popular vein to the delight of hundreds of people who clustered about the great piece. Thousands actually came but only a third of them could get near enough to hear. I remember he stayed afterward to answer all the questions they wanted to ask, especially the one as to which figures represented his three daughters, one of whom is now the wife of Paul Douglas, a distinguished member of the United States Senate.

Then in 1928 they made me president of the Quadrangle Club, the famous faculty club at Chicago, founded by my old professor of Assyrian, Robert F. Harper. We had a busy year at the Club; I got William Gillette, the original Sherlock Holmes, out for a luncheon speech which packed the clubhouse. He told me of his taking his play built on the *Adventures* to England to read it to Sir Arthur Conan Doyle for his approval. I asked him if the author had any objections to the play, and he said,

"Oh no, he said he was glad to have the old fellow heard from again."

Mr. Gillette had one marvelous story of playing Sherlock Holmes and I suppose Secret Service also, in London at the "Adelphy" as he very properly pronounced it. The young people of the royal family had come to hear him, occupying a box close above the stage. A few nights later they came again, with the elder members of the family, and Mr. Gillette could hear now and then from the royal box a deep-throated protest, in what was meant for a whisper,

"Don't tell me! Don't tell me!"

It was his royal highness Edward VII trying to keep his children from spoiling the show for him. If anything could add to the excitement of playing such plays, surely such comments would do it. Certainly it entertained Mr. Gillette enormously.

Our club season closed with a faculty reception for the new President and Mrs. Hutchins. One man who had passed along the receiving line paused, a little dazed, to ask which was President Hutchins. When I told Mr. Hutchins of this incident, he said,

"Oh well, we might as well have the photographers back and start all over again!"

In other respects, however, the reception was a success. Oh yes, it was a busy year at the club. Yet the faculty good nature was not yet exhausted. Why, I even remember one spirited outburst of mine in the Senate meeting one afternoon which they actually received with applause. Imagine that! The Senate in those days still consisted only of men of professorial rank and a less likely crowd to give way to hand clapping I have never seen. It was the only time I had ever heard them indulge in it. So happy and cordial were all my faculty relations through the well-nigh forty years of my faculty connection.

I was chairman (really vice-chairman, President Mason was nominally chairman) of the committee on sculpture and inscriptions for the new chapel and found it a most interesting task. The architect, Bertram Goodhue, was very much given to enriching his great designs with sculptured figures, and for this chapel he had projected no less than fourteen free-standing figures and fifty-three demifigures. There were also frequent text inscriptions which it became our duty to select. The great range of fourteen figures that crown the front gable, like the French kings in French cathedrals, we made to represent the March of Religion through the centuries, from Abraham and Moses, with Christ in the gable, on to Francis, Luther and Calvin.

The figures from Abraham to John the Baptist form, as Walter Sargent, who had preceded me as vice-chairman, said, in the fine phrase of Eusebius, a "Praeparatio Evangelica," the preparation for the Gospel, and the others from Peter and Paul to Calvin, a "Demonstratio Evangelica," the demonstration of the Gospel.

Then to relieve this somber mass of male figures, prophetic and patristic, we introduced at the spring of the arch of the great south window the exquisite figures of St. Monica and St. Cecilia which lend a touch of inexpressible grace to the entire front. We had especial satisfaction when we came to the demifigures flanking the east, or tower door, in the interior, in choosing figures representing Music and Architecture in the service of religion. John Manly at once suggested Bach for Music, and I proposed Goodhue himself for Architecture. The committee agreed and Goodhue's great friend Lee Lawrie carved what is really a portrait statue of the great architect holding in his hands the model of the chapel, with his other great academic chapel, West Point, behind him. But I need not go over the amazing wealth of symbolic sculpture in this noble church, for the University very graciously asked me to write the book on the chapel, to be finished the day it was opened, and this I most gratefully did. And nothing I did at Chicago or was asked to do, touched me more deeply than this service.

I had the satisfaction of suggesting the student personalities whose portrait figures flank the northwest campus door, and I had the extraordinary pleasure of preaching in this noble edifice, an experience never to be forgotten. As one who had attended the University's first chapel service in 1892, I was asked to address the Commemorative Chapel service in the great chapel, on October 4, 1933. The University invited me to give the convocation address at the March convocation of 1934, which I was happy to do. I have told elsewhere how the faculty committee in charge of the William Vaughan Moody lectureship invited me to lecture on that foundation, and at a time when I very much needed such recognition, as I had the newspapers of most of the country at my heels. Such was the generous consideration of the University faculty in my latter days at Chicago.

There were countless individual manifestations of consideration along the way by one and another, sometimes in quite other fields than mine. Edwin B. Frost, the Director of the Yerkes Observatory, and in his later years the blind astronomer, while still in the flush of health once said to me that I must speak at his funeral. I lived to do so, at the service for our beloved Dr. Frost in the great new chapel. But I could name man after man who had suggested to me a book to write, or a papyrus to decipher, a problem to solve, a source of funds for manuscripts or for publishing some departmental research. This book has recorded numbers of them. It was a great and goodly fellowship at Chicago and I was proud to have shared in it. I only hope I was half as generous as my colleagues were.

When Mr. Rosenwald offered to aid in erecting an undergraduate residence hall for men, and the spacious building on the Midway was built in 1931, I was asked to act as chairman of a committee to suggest to the Trustees names for the two courts and the various entries. I suggested to the committee that we should go back to early Chicago and the Old University and name them Ogden and Douglas, for William

B. Ogden, the first mayor of Chicago and a great benefactor of the University, and Stephen A. Douglas, the founder of the Old University. But the professors on the committee were not old Chicagoans like myself and these names did not appeal to them. I then suggested that as President Harper had a memorial in the Library, the courts be named Judson and Burton for the second and third presidents of the University and to this they willingly agreed. I was, of course, especially glad to have had a hand in thus commemorating on the quadrangles two men with whom I had worked so closely and happily.

I don't know why the task of preparing the text of the Reynolds Club tablet was entrusted to Ernest Wilkins and me but I shall never forget the morning when we sat down in the office to prepare the legend. Of course, we knew Joseph Reynolds' story from Father's sketch of his career. But it was positively antiphonal, the way Ernest would utter a phrase, and I another, and he would cap it with a third and I with a fourth—

"Master of transportation—"

"By river and by rail—"

It was all so perfectly spontaneous. When last in Chicago I observed that it had been removed from the Club and placed on the cloister wall outside for all to read.

As I look back over my Chicago years I really do not see what more my colleagues could have done for me. While I was in no sense conspicuous among them I can think of none of my contemporaries whom they appointed to more honors and responsibilities. What further office or dignity could they have bestowed upon me? I have tried to make a list of the ones to whom I was especially indebted but it is simply too long to print and would mean little unless in each case

I told what the man had done for me. Some of the most successful books I have written were suggested to me by Chicago colleagues—Burton, Woodward, Soares, Case, Laing, Bean. Professor Nitze very kindly and successfully presented our department's needs for publication now and again to the American Council of Learned Societies, a most gracious act on his part.

They were altogether the most co-operative, understanding and generous lot one could imagine, both socially and professionally. A few years after our departure to California, the University authorities asked me to return and address the sponsors of its new campaign, and long after summoned me to return again with Mrs. Goodspeed, to celebrate the anniversary of my translation with a series of half a dozen evening addresses. I could certainly ask no more. Why, the University has even gone so far as to name its growing collection of New Testament manuscripts for me.

Ten years after I had retired and left Chicago for Los Angeles, my generous Chicago colleagues had a sketch of my uneventful life, together with a list of all the articles and books I had ever published, prepared and printed at the University of Chicago Press—a courtesy seldom extended to us superannuated professors. A more sensitive man might have recognized in this a signal that his work was done, and it was time for him to stop, but I was not bright enough to take the gentle hint. I did not see the point until too late.

SEVENTEEN

Western Islands

VISITING California in the winter of 1938 for some lecturing at the suggestion of Dr. James W. Fifield, Jr., we went over Bel-Air, and from a house terrace on Bellagio Road saw the distant prospect of Santa Catalina Island, forty-five or fifty miles away, in the blue Pacific. This stirred in us a desire to live with such a view and while that particular house escaped us (Mr. Conrad Hilton bought it), Elfleda came west again a few weeks later and found a near-by lot with the same view, where we immediately built a long one-story house overlooking the golf course and the ocean, and such a stretch of vega that Elfleda was reminded of the Vega of Toledo and named the house Vega Vista. In it we spent ten extraordinarily happy years.

Soon after we had built and occupied our house in Bel-Air, looking out across the golf course toward the University, Bennett Cerf came west in 1940 to be married, and came to see me to talk about the Modern Library and the inclusion of *The Short Bible* in it. Of course, I showed him the house and the remark he made about it was simply classic:

"This is the most amusing house I have ever seen!" We agreed to let it go at that.

I was reminded of a remark Howard Shaw had made when

our Woodlawn Avenue house was new. One Sunday afternoon he appeared, always a Gothic figure of a man, tall,
ascetic-looking and distinguished, but even more so in a
frock coat and carrying a tall hat. I suppose it was his practice
to call on his new houses as it were, to see for himself how
they came out when the people were really in them. We received him in the music room, and he looked about him
critically at the furniture and the wallpaper. All he said was,

"This is not nearly as dismal as they usually are!"

We found this remark, though carefully guarded, quite
reassuring.

Dr. Fifield had commended us to President Sproul and
the University of California at Los Angeles to such purpose
that the hospitable institution invited me to give a course
in the history department in the winter session on the
"Founding of the Christian Church." In response to this
very pleasant University connection Elfleda, while we were
still building, entertained the department and other friends
in our Beverly Hills hotel with a lecture on "The Battle of
Lake Champlain" by our old friend William R. Folsom of
Chicago, who had a summer place on Lake Champlain and
had witnessed the very recent raising of one of the ships sunk
in that battle. The department is very socially minded and
responded most generously, and we felt quite a part of the
University. After all I had worked on California's papyri and
helped publish them some forty years before! Our reception
in Los Angeles and at the University was most cordial and
gave us great pleasure for the ten years that followed. Of
course, we had also many old friends in Pasadena where
Elfleda's sister, Mrs. Joseph F. Rhodes, Jr., and her husband
had lived for many years and their four sons had grown up
and two of them, Foster and Robert, had married most hap-

pily. Early in our California residence the two younger boys, Kenneth and David, also married just as happily, and all these young people added most delightfully to our social circle. My nephews were all four of them Stanford men, and two of them, Foster and Kenneth, had gone on to graduate work in the Harvard School of Business Administration and the Harvard Law School respectively. Their young people growing up were a source of endless interest and enjoyment.

My cousin Harper Goodspeed had long since distinguished himself in a long career as a botanist at the University of California at Berkeley, and his young people Stephen and Ellen gave us much satisfaction. When Steve and his gifted wife Grace came down to Santa Barbara College they carried the family academic tradition into the fourth generation, and in their amiable little boy Roger I found myself possessed of a fourth cousin. Speaking at the college two or three years later, I had the rare pleasure of being very happily introduced by my third cousin.

My modest duties of lecturing at U.C.L.A. two hours a week through one semester were made much of by my next-door neighbor, Count Frederick Thorne Rider, who took it upon himself to introduce me to the local faculty in a great luncheon for President Sproul and sixty-five professors in Kerckhoff Hall. He had just returned from his church duties in Rome where he had been acting a month a year as one of the lay secretaries to his Holiness the Pope. He had also given a new building to the University of Perugia and thus so gratified the Italian government that it had conferred the title of "Count" upon him. I found satisfaction in addressing him as Count, but he demurred.

"I am only an ordinary man," he protested.

"By no means," said I. "As a count, you are the real article, but as an ordinary man, Count, you are an impostor!"

I recited the incident of this luncheon given by a great Catholic layman for a Protestant instructor in biblical history to some colleagues on a later occasion when they were declaring the hostility between Catholic and Protestant communions, where academic appointments were involved.

My niece Paula (Mrs. Foster Rhodes) once taxed the Count with the coincidence of his gift to Perugia and his building the first house on Perugia Way, asking which was cause and which effect. He declared it was pure coincidence. But that will never satisfy the future historian, with his bent for tracing subtle connections of cause and effect. He will never be able to decide whether the Count helped the University of Perugia because his home was on Perugia Way, or built his house on Perugia Way because he had erected a kind of International House for Perugia. Still, it will be something for him to ratiocinate about.

We found, however, that in Los Angeles one met Catholic friends on every hand and found them warmly religious and generously thoughtful people. There was no sense of religious separation from them. Dr. Cantwell, the genial archbishop, we met soon after our arrival, at President Sproul's hospitable board, where we also met Mr. and Mrs. Alfred Noyes.

At a friendly dinner party in Bel-Air we soon met Lloyd Douglas and Mrs. Douglas and began a friendship which lasted as long as they lived. Dr. Douglas did not hesitate to send carbons of the chapters of *The Robe,* for example, about to his intimate friends for their enjoyment as he wrote them. I know my wife read the book in this form as it was being written. He followed these carbons with the proofs of the book when they were ready. Midway of the writing of the book, I remember a dinner party at which in response to a general demand to know how the story was going to turn out, Lloyd stood up in front of the fireplace and told the rest of the story, even more interestingly than he could write it. There was about him none of the self-conscious offishness one associates with some authors.

When I reached seventy, President Sproul wrote me regretting that he could no longer appoint me for winter instruction, but he crowned the University's generosity by conferring on me an honorary degree at the Charter Day exercises in 1943. The other guest of the occasion was Archibald MacLeish, the poet, whose father, a successful Chicago merchant, had been one of my father's deacons in his first charge in Chicago in 1866 and had remained Father's lifelong friend.

I now thought the University had done its full duty by me but when Dr. Clarence Dykstra came out from Madison to become Provost, he decreed that while I was too old to teach in the regular school year I might still be employed for a course in the summer session and so I returned to the history department for summers until I was eighty when even California's patience gave way. But they will never know what all this generous reception, social and academic, meant to an old man, and especially to Mrs. Goodspeed, who was some nine years my junior. So in the city and in the University, and especially from the Sprouls and the Dykstras, we received a most generous welcome. Dr. Dykstra even insisted upon attending my first summer lecture. The first people to call upon us in our new house, I remember, were Judge and Mrs. Russ Avery who became our very loyal friends. The Judge was the founder of the University Club of Los Angeles which in 1952 celebrated its fiftieth anniversary. All this was especially valued because in leaving Chicago we were leaving behind the friends and scenes of a lifetime, and yet a new life no less absorbing and delightful was now opened to us in our new home. The west is proverbially hospitable but I cannot believe many immigrants to it experience quite the warmth and cordiality of welcome that came to us in 1939 and after.

Our experiences with the ministers and among the churches was just as heart-warming. In fact, I have sometimes felt that there was a combined effort on the part of three leading ministers of the Los Angeles area to transform me into a metropolitan pulpit orator. Dr. Fagerburg at the First Baptist Church not only opened his pulpit to me on various occasions but when he launched his radio program of three broadcasts a week, gave me the Tuesday night broadcast for two years in succession, a series of seventy-two evenings. I at least enjoyed these broadcasts very much but on one occasion, when I had not heard my introduction, on reaching home I was surprised by the information that the announcer had declared that our music director would now take us on a journey through the hymn book assisted by a quartette! My listeners must have wondered what had happened to the quartette. Had I been warned I might at least have called the Four Evangelists or the Four Major Prophets or the Four Horsemen to my aid to cover my retreat.

In Pasadena Dr. John F. Scott brought me before his people for more than one series of Lenten lectures at All Saints. And Dr. Robert Freeman overtaken by an illness put me into his Presbyterian pulpit for five Sundays one April. Through Palm Sunday and Easter the congregations naturally filled the church. But the fifth Sunday was just after Easter and a rainy day, and the service was broadcast so the Presbyterians cannily remained at home. The leading man of the church was later heard to say at a luncheon at which Mrs. Goodspeed was unfortunately present that it was the smallest congregation in the entire history of the church. I hope no one has since beaten my record.

As for Dr. Fifield, when he once was planning to take Mrs. Fifield to the Holy Land, he invited me to occupy his pulpit in the First Congregational Church in Los Angeles, perhaps the largest church in the denomination, for one Sunday while his brother who now occupies Henry Ward Beecher's pulpit in Brooklyn took the other two. This meant preaching twice Sunday morning, at nine-thirty and again at eleven, but I felt that for one Sunday I could do it and complied. The nine o'clock congregation was fair but the eleven o'clock filled the great sanctuary with eighteen hundred people. The next evening I was expressing to Mrs. Goodspeed my relief that the ordeal was over when the telephone rang. It was Dr. Fifield's secretary saying that his brother was ill, and would I take the next two Sundays also? Otherwise, Dr. Fifield felt he would have to return and take them himself. Of course I complied. And after it was all over and the Fifields had returned home, Dr. Fifield was showing me some letters about my sermons including with some reluctance an anonymous one, complaining bitterly of some kind things I had said about the medical profession.

"Do let me have that one," I said. "I want to answer it."

"But how can you?" said Dr. Fifield. "It's anonymous."

"Oh, I know who wrote it," said I. "I know his handwriting. He's written me before, and signed his name."

We were thus happily able in our efficiency to answer the

modest fellow and I asked that he be put on the church mailing list. He builded better than he knew.

One of the great moments in the life of a modern public speaker, in California at least, is to find himself in the gray dawn of an Easter morning facing a visible audience of thirty thousand people with nobody knows how many more picking up the service in the East and Middle West where people are already up and about at that hour. Friends of mine who were motoring in Florida told me of hearing my brief remarks one Easter as they were bowling along in their car. On later Easters (with other speakers!) the attendance rose to forty-nine thousand. Indeed, it sometimes seems as though public speakers had never really had a fair chance before, doesn't it?

At the University Religious Conference in which Tom Evans and Miss Adaline Guenther united Catholic, Protestant, Mormon and Jew in a goodly fellowship, one met Rabbi Edgar Magnin, Bishop McGucken, Bishop W. Bertrand Stevens, Dr. Glenn Moore, Dean Vern Knudsen, and many other religious leaders of the city, lay and clerical. And as for friendly personal hospitality, it simply knew no bounds. I must not even begin to record it.

As we were coming out of church one December morning, and getting into the car Tom said,

"The Japs have attacked Pearl Harbor!"

And so it was! Incredible news, but the radio went right on with it. We were going from church to lunch with the Sydney Temples at Canoga Park and all the way we heard more and more of the bad news. The mood at luncheon can be imagined. Especially that of Bishop and Mrs. Stevens who arrived without benefit of radio and learned the news first from all of us speaking in concert. Then after luncheon speeches by all and sundry—First Impressions. None of us, I think, then really foresaw the length and breadth of what had begun.

In Honolulu, they tell you that when the word went over the island that the Japs had bombed Pearl Harbor, everyone said, "Well, just wait till *our* planes go up! They'll fix 'em!"

But not one went up. They waited . . . and waited . . . utterly incredulous, unable to believe their eyes. One gets a new slant on it, over there.

In Los Angeles we soon found ourselves involved in the hospitality of the P.E.N. Club under the leadership of Lionel Stevenson and Joel Keith, and there we found a stimulating group of authors such as Harold Lamb, Rupert Hughes, Margaret Lee Runbeck, Margaret Leighton, Lewis Browne, Fern Rives, Joel Keith, Richard Armour, Mr. and Mrs. Norreys Jephson O'Conor and many more. The whole club even dined with us one evening. What a page in the guest book! The Lloyd Douglases and their daughters were our neighbors in Bel-Air. Hamlin Garland and Mrs. Garland we had known in Chicago.

The educational side of Los Angeles and Southern California was also most hospitable. Not only the University of California at Los Angeles but Chancellor Rufus von Klein-Smid of Southern California and the numerous colleges of the area, Pomona, Scripps, Pepperdine, Chapman and Redlands in particular—made us generously welcome. For as the mountains are round about Jerusalem, the colleges are round about Los Angeles.

Scripps, the delightful women's college at Claremont, asked me to teach in a freshman humanities course along with Professors Barrett and Westbrook, a service I much enjoyed. On my first journey out to Claremont in that connection I saw in a junk yard by the roadside what looked like a Spanish or Mexican oil jar, and on the way home that afternoon I stopped and bought it. Happily enough that Saturday our old friends the David Robinsons of Johns Hopkins were dining with us and after dinner I said to Professor Robinson,

"David, is it true that you have a collection of Greek and Roman amphoras of which you have published ten volumes of catalogue?"

"Yes, and I have enough more to make five more volumes," he replied, "if I had time to write them up."

"Well," said I brazenly, "come and see mine!" and from the terrace doorway he surveyed it.

"Oh yes," he said, comfortingly. "Yes. It's all right. I hope you didn't pay a hundred dollars for it. It's not Greek," he broke the bad news to me, "it's Roman, end of the first century, the latter part." He then approached it and confirmed his judgment. The reporters were around on Monday, and the genial press, evidently confusing it with the Portland Vase in the British Museum, finally boosted its value to eight thousand dollars. David said it was worth between five and ten dollars and as I had paid the junkman one dollar for it I was content. The wild fancies of the papers I fear made the dealer who had so joyously sold it to me unhappy, though I tried in vain to get the story corrected. But how the vase had found its way into a junk yard on Garvey Avenue can only be imagined. Indeed my niece Mrs. Kenneth Rhodes has, with the aid of her historical imagination, reconstructed its origin and wanderings.

In the Bel-Air Garden Club Mrs. Goodspeed in 1939 found congenial spirits interested in keeping up the neighborhood

and even improving it. In 1942 she was made chairman of a
standing committee concerned with getting unsightly trash
cans and rubbish generally off the curbs and parkways, but
no substantial progress had before been made in this direction. She gathered a representative group of women of the
club and of other Bel-Air residents and in 1942 obtained a
hearing for them before the Board of Supervisors, which on
consideration gave the residents permission to keep such
things within their lot lines on the pickup days, in return for
an additional payment for each residence in Bel-Air. This
was a great forward step but it was clear to her that this
should not be a garden club responsibility, but should enlist
all the residents in its support and so she assembled a group
of representative men and women in our living room and in
that year they organized the Bel-Air Improvement Association, to look after this and a number of other neighborhood
interests. As the Bel-Air Association it is now a flourishing
and indispensable institution with a full-time manager and
the support of all the Bel-Air public, and is being imitated
in other parts of the city. This was very characteristic of her
mental vision and her social interest.

She aided in the organization of the Visiting Nurse Association in Los Angeles; she had long been active on its board
in Chicago. And when the First Congregational Church had
its Victory Dinner after paying off its prodigious mortgage—
half a million dollars—under Dr. Fifield's leadership, she
was one of the after-dinner speakers.

While these years of retirement were filled with much
lecturing before clubs, churches and colleges in the Southern
California area, I found time for a fair amount of writing. In
early days at the University my cousin George and I used to
chaff each other a good deal about our writing, though of

course he was far ahead of me and wrote with great speed and skill. He was writing so many book reviews that I once charged him with doing a review a week, and he retorted that I was doing an article a month, and we then agreed that a competent University man should turn out a review a week, or an article a month, or a book a year. This has sometimes been quoted as though we meant all three at once, but not so. At any rate, in my retirement I almost managed the third of these ideals, acting upon impulses from various quarters. In particular, Mrs. Goodspeed once suggested to me writing a life of Paul which I soon after proceeded to do. And later still she suggested a life of Christ which I regret I did not take up at once so that it might have come out in her lifetime.

An invitation from my old friend Selby Vernon McCasland to deliver the Richard lectures at the University of Virginia gave me an opportunity to work up the habits of book publication and sale that prevailed in the world of the first century and had much to do with the rapid rise of the New Testament and Christian literature. My publisher picturesquely entitled this book *Christianity Goes to Press,* to the great indignation of its reviewers. A telegram from an enterprising agent in New York summoned me to write *How to Read the Bible,* but hardly had I sent in an outline and a few chapters when the publisher who wanted it died, and his successor sent back the sample pages. The young agent then found another publisher for it and it appeared at Philadelphia, and later with the Oxford University Press. The gentleman who had so hastily sent the outline back now complained to my agent that she had run off with their idea, but I comforted her with the news that there had been seven books of that name in the past twenty-five years, and he said no more.

The debates in the Revision Committee stirred me to write some of my own ideas and experiences as *Problems of New Testament Translation.*

My near neighbor Mr. W. L. Honnold, distinguished mining engineer, long in South Africa, and assistant of Mr. Hoover in his Belgian Relief enterprise in the First World War, was interested in my labors and expressed a wish to read the manuscript of *How to Read the Bible.* He was unable to get about, and mostly in bed he read the manuscript, offering a few penciled annotations. He expressed confidence that the book would have a much larger circulation than I had anticipated and his judgment proved sounder than mine. I inscribed the book to him. Upon its appearance its publisher, Winston, took us on a great autographing tour—Philadelphia, New York, Detroit, Chicago. It has since been reprinted by the Oxford Press, London. Later I was very much pleased to have Harold Lamb, my neighbor and dear friend and one of the busiest of men, offer to read my *Paul* in manuscript, and in doing so he made some very pertinent and needful suggestions. But this is a service one cannot fairly ask of one's friends. I was happy to dedicate that book to him.

At hospitable dinner tables in the city or the University we met very interesting people. At President and Mrs. Sproul's, meeting Alfred Noyes and Mrs. Noyes, I learned of her possession of two of the most valuable miniatured manuscripts in the world, the Luttrell Psalter and the Bedford Hours and Psalter. I think they have since been bought by the British Museum as they contained portrait materials of national interest.

And one day Margueritte Bro came to call upon us, bringing Mrs. Walgreen and Mrs. Carrie Jacobs Bond, who was our good friend for the rest of her life, and showed us much kindly hospitality.

And think of catching up with Galli-Curci in Westwood. We met her at a University concert, and I taxed her with the Chicago story that she had said to the reporters there,

"I have washed my hands thirty times today, but I love your city!"

She did not deny it but asked us to dinner in her very Italian house. The left of my hostess was the best I could do, for Lloyd Douglas was on her right. Later she and her husband Mr. Homer Samuels dined with us, delightfully. The Charles Rann Kennedys too were in Westwood and came to luncheon with the Percy Boyntons who were old friends of theirs. But I always thought of her as Edith Wynne Matthison, with her wonderful beauty and that beautiful rich voice.

Dropping in at the Provost's residence to join Mrs. Dykstra's party for the Charter Day ceremonies in 1949, I had the pleasure of meeting Viscount Alexander of Tunis who was to deliver the address, and learned to my surprise that Dr. Dykstra had been showing my translation to him the preceding evening. The Viscount, who was then Governor General of Canada, pleased me very much by saying,

"It's so readable!"

which is all I ask for it. I ventured to send him a tall copy afterward and received a most gracious letter of acknowledgment in his own hand, signed, "Alexander of Tunis."

One evening at the P.E.N. Club a Captain Williams, an English author, was guest of honor. I took merely a perfunctory interest in Captain Williams, until some remark at dinner revealed that he was Valentine Williams, the mystery writer whom I had so much enjoyed. I almost broke up the occasion by getting up and walking around to his place, to shake hands with him all over again.

"Captain Williams," said I, "I did not recognize you. I have read all your books, ending with your autobiography."

We persuaded the Captain and Mrs. Williams (Alice Crawford) to come to dinner with us, with President and Mrs. Sproul, and found them most interesting guests. She had been an actress, and was amused to remember that once at Windsor she had acted before four kings. He had been a war correspondent, I think for Reuter's, until he was blown up by a shell. As he described it, he went up a war correspondent and came down a writer of mystery stories.

Elfleda and I were pleased to be called on one day by our Bel-Air neighbor, Emil Ludwig. He brought with him the proofs of his book on *The Mediterranean* on some point in which he professed to wish to consult me, jocularly remarking that he was a journalist, not a scholar. But we found so many things to talk about that he never quite came to the point. He did, however, present us with an autographed copy of his book on the Germans in its English version. I later returned his call but was almost devoured by an enormous and most menacing watchdog who prowled his grounds and was relieved to have Ludwig brought to the door to introduce me to the animal in its native German.

This recalls my meeting with Lewis Browne. I wanted to use a sentence of his in something I was writing so I looked again at the book containing it to see who held the copyright. I found the author himself did so I looked Lewis up in *Who's Who* in order to write to him. When behold! his address was The Uplifters' Ranch, Santa Monica, a few miles over the hills from our own house. So I simply called him on the telephone, and we became good friends. Lewis later asked me for permission to use my translation of the Apocrypha for a volume of selections he was making, saying he did not want to use "that old fogy translation"—meaning I am afraid King James!

When Dr. Harper traveling east in the old five-thirty to New York that September day in 1890 prophesied to me the University of Chicago Press, we little dreamed what it was going to mean to me in future years. But in the University Press from my student days, I may say, I saw possibilities. In fact, as early as the autumn of 1893 as Steigmeyer's song put it, Theodore Soares and I saw that it was where we must publish our joint pamphlet entitled *The Student's Handbook* which we had written and financed for distribution among incoming students at the opening of the second year, on behalf of the University Y.M.C.A. Some of my colleagues could not do business with the Press and took their publishing elsewhere but I found the Press a strong ally. They had done several small things for me during my student and early faculty days, the *Story of the New Testament,* for example, but it was, of course, the translation that fastened us together with hoops of steel. This was largely due to Mr. Laing who had asked me to write the translation, and to Mr. Bean, who was really the publishing man at the Press and who gave me every possible co-operation. They were both my lifelong friends. But when the Press on its fiftieth anniversary published its catalogue, I was simply appalled at the number of titles it charged me with. We have had our differences, of course, but on the whole it has been a happy and fruitful relationship and to this day the Press annually reports to me on a dozen lively titles going back all the way to 1916. And as one of President Harper's old students I feel sure that his mild and universal eye dwells pleased upon our work of translating the Bible for the Press he founded.

It was at Chicago, at the very outset of the celebration of the twenty-fifth celebration of the translation, that Mrs. Goodspeed was stricken with the illness that ended ten months later in her death. She endured its limitations, all the more trying to one of her indomitable energy, with wonderful patience and good cheer. Indeed, we felt that she was improving and thought of the months as a long but happy convalescence. But with her departure I came suddenly to realize that all the joy in this world is the creation of these wonderful women, our wives and mothers. I could only throw myself into writing the book on the life of Christ she had so much wanted me to write and then devote its material fruits to her memorial. Three months later my brother, whose generous interest had been a shield to me ever since I was born, also passed away, still remembering me with characteristic lifelong generosity in his will!

To one who has shared vigorously in the fight for periodic retranslation of the Bible, and sometimes against great odds as it seemed, it is cheering to see that battle now nobly won. As I write, the Revised Standard Version has just made its appearance. Our Catholic friends are hard at work on their Old Testament, aided by the Pope's counsel to take account not only of the Latin Vulgate but of the "original tongues," the Hebrew and Greek, as well, and determined of their own motion to modernize the Bible diction. The Jewish Publication Society of America has undertaken a new translation of the Old Testament and also of the Apocrypha, into modern English. Above all, the Protestant bodies of Great Britain, Anglicans, Presbyterians and Independents, have united in a great committee to make not a revision but a new translation, of the whole Bible including the Apocrypha, and into modern English. This is, of course, the best plan of all.

This is what should be done every fifty years. Archbishop Soderblom once told me that in Sweden the Bible is revised every fifteen years. Never has there been such interest in the improvement of the English Bible. And we translators and revisers of other days, like the aged Simeon, will be of good cheer as we breathe our Nunc Dimittis.

The reader may well exclaim,

"But you have received and enjoyed an extraordinary amount of patience, forbearance, encouragement, assistance, regard and affection!"

I have indeed. And in the presence of it, I cannot doubt the patience, forbearance, mercy and love of God Himself. What else can it all mean?

INDEX

Set in Linotype Baskerville
Format by Edwin H. Kaplin
Manufactured by The Haddon Craftsmen, Inc.
Published by HARPER & BROTHERS, *New York*